INTERFACES

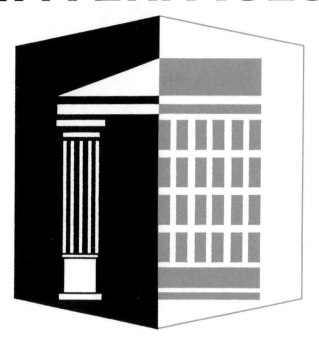

INTERFACES

Relationships Between Library Technical and Public Services

SHEILA S. INTNER

1993
LIBRARIES UNLIMITED, INC.
Englewood, Colorado

LIBRARIES UNLIMITED, INC.
P.O. Box 6633
Englewood, CO 80155-6633

Library of Congress Cataloging-in-Publication Data

Intner, Sheila S.
  Interfaces : relationships between library technical and public
services / Sheila S. Intner.
  xvii, 231 p. 17x25 cm.
  Includes index.
  ISBN 1-56308-059-1
  1. Processing (Libraries) 2. Processing (Libraries)--United
States. 3. Libraries and readers. I. Title.
Z688.5.I577 1993
025.02--dc20   92-47063
                                                        CIP

Contents

Part 1
FAIREST OF THEM ALL?
A Long, Hard Look at Technical Services

Part 2
PROBLEMS AT THE MAIN INTERFACE
The Catalog

Part 3
ROCKY ROAD
Relationships Between Technical
and Public Services

Part 4
FUTURE SHOCK
Policies for the New Millennium

Foreword

Readers who have taken formal course work in cataloging and have gone on to establish themselves in other areas of librarianship may have a tendency to look back on their cataloging classes as requirements that had to be met for graduation purposes. For many students they constituted a difficult and often unrewarding experience. I shared that point of view until I began to read Sheila Intner's articles. Suddenly I found someone who has the ability to breathe life into what had been, for me at least, a thoroughly uninteresting subject—a necessary part of librarianship that had to be addressed from time to time and avoided whenever possible. Sheila Intner has proven beyond a shadow of a doubt that writing about cataloging can be lively, entertaining, and instructive.

A few years ago, when Sheila had little spare time to devote to a new writing project, *Technicalities* just happened to be looking for someone to write a regular column. We were seeking fresh ideas and opinions to share with our readers, and Sheila's friendly, informative approach to library professional writing was just what was needed. She began producing six columns a year and attracted an immediate following. *Technicalities* soon started receiving requests for subscriptions from librarians who wanted to make certain that they didn't miss a single issue. It is also interesting to note that Sheila's columns have been equally appealing to library school instructors, who regularly request permission to reproduce columns for their classes.

For those of you who did miss some of her columns or who would simply like to see them all collected in one volume, Sheila has brought her *Technicalities* essays together in this book. They are excellent examples of sound reasoning, solid judgment, and good sense. They will serve as a source of motivation and inspiration for years to come.

Brian Alley, Editor
Technicalities

Preface

Interfaces has been several years in the making. They have been especially interesting years in the field of library and information science; looking back, I have a better understanding of what the wise Chinese meant by their well-known curse, "May you live in interesting times." The word that best characterizes the years since 1985, when I first proposed a column called "Interfaces" to *Technicalities* editor Brian Alley, is *change*, and there have been enough changes during the period to provide plenty of grist for any columnist's mill.

The purpose of the column is and always has been to explore the problems, issues, and ideas that originate and develop in the twilight zone where library public services and technical services meet. Authors of articles in the professional literature and papers given at important conferences may proclaim that the traditional divisions between frontline and backroom services no longer obtain. However, I suspect their assessments are premature, and there still are many vital organizations in which the phenomenon can be observed even as a new millennium approaches. And in those forward-looking libraries where the divisions don't show on organizational charts, librarians have different perspectives and different goals, depending on what they see.

Writing a column for a monthly journal has its good points and bad points. One has recurring opportunities to say whatever one thinks to a wide audience of interested people. On the other hand, one faces recurring deadlines that seem to pop up at inconvenient times. I once asked A. J. Anderson, whose "How Do You Manage?" column in *Library Journal* is a personal favorite, how he managed to meet his deadlines without any fuss and bother. He replied, to my amazement, that he kept a notebook of ideas and incidents and, when the muse moved him, wrote three, four, or five columns all at once. I admire A. J.'s style, but I can't emulate it. I seem to require a rapidly approaching deadline to intensify my concentration to the point where I must sit down and write.

Writing the "Interfaces" column has prodded me to think about ideas and issues from various perspectives. Much of the time I knew what I wanted to say and, once seated in front of the computer, my fingers couldn't keep up as my mind raced, formulating sentences to explain my thoughts. Occasionally I knew what I wanted to write about but wasn't sure exactly what I had to say on the subject. Then, I discovered that writing everything I knew about the subject forced me to take the stand I had vaguely in mind or to change my initial stand. In either case, slogging through all the arguments, turning an idea around and around to see all of its facets, and taking each point in turn before forming an opinion has been the great fun of writing "Interfaces."

In writing the thirty-nine columns for this book, each column has become a chapter, and each has been thoroughly updated. Four general areas of inquiry are covered: defining technical services, examining the catalog, identifying common ground between technical and public services, and speculating about the future.

Thirty-eight of the columns have been published in *Technicalities* as of this writing, although some of the titles have changed and all have been heavily edited. One has yet to appear in *Technicalities*, although it certainly will before long. I take responsibility for the views and ideas represented in this book; they do not represent the views of the managements of either Westport Publishing or Libraries Unlimited. Readers are welcome to point out discrepancies and errors, for which I apologize.

I hope that people interested in efficient and effective bibliographic services — librarians of all persuasions, library faculty, and students — will find *Interfaces* useful, either because it helped explain something clearly, or argued a particular viewpoint effectively, or raised questions that merit careful thought. Excelsior!

Acknowledgments

This book would have been impossible without the help of three magnificent Lindas. Linda Watkins, the Simmons College library science librarian, conducted helpful searches and never flinched at my requests for obscure sources, even when I made them at the last moment for a column that was due to go out in the afternoon mail. Linda Willey, now administrative assistant to the dean of the Graduate School of Library Science at Simmons College, was the administrative assistant to the faculty during nearly all of the years in which I wrote the columns on which this book is based. Linda never failed to *cheerfully* translate and word process my scribbles from sheets of yellow paper onto floppy disks or prepare disks and printouts, when I had them, for mailing or make one more trip to the postal center when I was late with a column. Linda Messmer, my chief contact at the Media Publications Division of Westport Publishers, liked the idea of compiling the columns and cooperated with me and the good people at Libraries Unlimited to make it happen.

I also owe a debt of gratitude to three editors: Brian Alley of *Technicalities* and David Loertscher of Libraries Unlimited, the *de jure* editors, and Mathew Intner, my husband and *de facto* editor. Brian and David read every word in every chapter and fixed my prose whenever it faltered. Mat performed his "Can I understand this even if I'm not a librarian?" test on nearly all the material so I could feel confident about reaching a wide spectrum of readers regardless of their expertise or experience.

No continuing effort of this kind comes into being without the ongoing encouragement of the author's institutional leadership. Thus a large measure of my appreciation goes to Robert M. Hayes, dean (now *emeritus*) of the Graduate School of Library and Information Science at UCLA, where I began "Interfaces" and wrote the first four columns early in 1986, and to Robert D. Stueart, dean of the Graduate School of Library and Information Science at Simmons College, who, as wise leader and friend, has facilitated its writing since I came to Simmons College in September 1986. I dedicate this book to them.

PART 1

FAIREST OF THEM ALL?
A Long, Hard Look at Technical Services

1

The Technical Services Mystique

Some libraries call their technical service units "support" services. Others use the traditionally popular name of "technical" services. Still others, including the Library of Congress, call them "processing" services. What's in a name? Are these all synonyms for the same old thing? Or do subtle but significant differences in the nomenclature produce problems at the interfaces between public and non-public departments and their personnel? (Yes, that was a deliberate sidestep.) How come very few places call their technical service units "bibliographic" services? What difference would it make if they did?

How does all this relate to the functioning of technical and nontechnical services? To library services in general? How does it relate to helping people succeed in finding what they want and need when they come to the library?

SUPPORT SERVICES

What is the mystique of support services? Briefly, it is negative—a downer. It embodies playing second fiddle which, while respectable and even decent, upright, and necessary, is essentially dull, pedestrian, and lowly. No matter how well support librarians provide the underpinning, they are still underneath, subordinate, and servile. Their posture is bent, straining, like Atlas supporting the world. They do not look beyond the horizon to an as-yet-unseen future. They take direction from above. They plod. They persevere. They trot beneath their burdens like dumb beasts.

To what are they subordinate? What are they supporting? Library services, of course. And who furnishes library services to the public? Public service people. They select. Support librarians acquire. They plan. Support librarians catalog. They advise. Support librarians inventory. They program. Support librarians file. They serve the public. Support librarians serve the files, the materials, the shelf arrangement—all inanimate things. It is no wonder that support librarians begin to perceive themselves as prosaic and routine.

It is hard to feel glamorous when the biggest thrill of the day is completing a periodical volume to send off to the bindery or erasing an entry that doesn't conform to the library's authority records. Does a support librarian feel the excitement of the chase in tracking an intriguing question to its lair and pinning down an answer? Dear me, that is hardly appropriate to the species.

3

PROCESSING SERVICES

Processing services is another technical services synonym. It lacks the quality of servility or subordination associated with support services, but it also seems to lack imagination, fire, or color. Its mystique is mechanistic, repetitive, and colorless. Processing. The word implies being bound to a treadmill that grinds on relentlessly.

The Library of Congress employs the term *processing services* for its technical service operations. It is an apt name for use by the greatest library bureaucracy on earth. In that enormous place, the parts of the puzzle were once forever separated—descriptive cataloging from subject cataloging, both of these from classification and shelflisting, acquisitions, serials control, preservation, and all of the other services associated with our field. Currently a great experiment in whole-book cataloging is bringing the first three of these elements together, but the rest remain remote from one another.

Processing services are in tune with the bureaucracy. The term implies great size and specialization with a concomitant loss of unity and control. In processing, one can lose all identity. Interest in the larger picture is subordinated to complete absorption in one's own job. One imagines an enormous bibliographic assembly line in which each employee performs the same little task over and over while the unfinished entries move slowly and inexorably down the line.

In addition to overall hugeness, the term *processing services* implies superspecialization. Perhaps it was once a mark of significance to reach such a size that specialization became necessary, as in business and industry, large universities, and government. But the loss of unity in library technical services can make for disjointed output at the same time it allows for efficient operations. Vigilance must always be exercised to insure that the left hand really knows what the right hand is doing when such an order of magnitude is reached that processing services are necessary.

TECHNICAL SERVICES

Here is the term with which we are most familiar—good, old *technical services*. What does it imply? What is its mystique? Like processing it is faintly mechanical, but that is not its primary thrust. To librarians technical services is abstract, abstruse, hard to understand, maybe even impossible to fathom. After all, it is technical, which implies that only an initiate—a technician—may participate in its mysteries.

There are some interesting parallels between the image of technical services in the library world and that of engineering in the scientific world. Both are perceived somewhat negatively—they involve technical, as contrasted with scientific, work. Both are thought of as applying theories that belong to the parent disciplines. In both instances the technician is subordinate to the scientist, applying ideas unlikely to have been created by the technician alone. In this scenario information scientists are the purists, the theorists, and the creators, while technical servants are the implementers, the interpreters, and the reactors. It is the interpretive function that technical servants hold nearest and dearest to their hearts. It is their act of creation.

Because the interpretation of theory is the rainbow's end of technical services, technical servants squeeze everything they can from it. Technical servants are fearfully happy as they debate, endlessly, the interpretation of a theory. They plunge into their frightening jungle of rules and requirements with fanatic glee. They revel in their ability to interpret and apply the laws of librarianship, reserving this function for themselves. No nontechnical service staff member should ever try to usurp this function. It is the very breath of technical service librarians' lives, their reason for being.

Since they believe they are the priests of the profession, they also assume their applications are holy—the order files, the shelflists, the catalogs, the serials files. If they could, technical service librarians might put a small force field around each of these products to prevent encroachment by public service staff members or—even worse!—the lay public. But of course this is not to be; the products of their labors are doomed to be pawed over by both kinds of users. Their products are forever exposed to unfair criticism, particularly from staff users. Can you recall the face of a reference librarian reporting the discovery of an error in the public catalog? Fortunately, technical service librarians are able to keep some of their treasures locked away in their own departments, far from the eyes of barbarous ingrates who have no idea how long and hard technical service librarians labor to create the best, most consistent, reliable, elegantly-designed, information-packed, error-free tools for their use. Instead of being properly awed, as are the lay users, staff users take technical service efforts for granted, thinking the job isn't so difficult and that anyone could do it as well. Such impudence could only arise from enormous ignorance.

But as technical services is not the top of the pyramid, organizationally speaking, decisions about its activities, staffing, and budgets are beyond its control. Sometimes these decisions are made by Philistines who have no idea how gravely they wound technical service staff with their cuts and their productivity schedules. They do not count the suffering in terms of errors, lowered standards, or accumulating backlogs. Only when a crisis occurs are they likely to appreciate how deeply technical services is crippled by lack of funds, staff, and supplies. How can Excalibur be produced without highly trained smiths working in fully equipped smithies using only the finest of steel—if not metals of a higher order?

BIBLIOGRAPHIC SERVICES

The last of the labels is *bibliographic services*. What is its mystique? It describes what technical service librarians do in terms that are inextricably linked with the rest of the profession—bibliographical terms. Bibliographic services is intellectual. It is formal. It is sober. It fairly reeks of scholarship and scholarly endeavor. Bibliographic services is the best of the lot.

If technical service librarians want to cast their lot with tradition, bibliographic services is the way to go. The historical picture of the scholar-librarian, used nowadays to justify the appointment of nonlibrarians to high positions in libraries, is reflected in the term *bibliographic services*. Perhaps it is stretching things a bit to equate technical service librarians with lonely searchers after truth—ascetic, virtuous, indomitable in the face of all obstacles—but it sure beats the alternatives. Technical service librarians do tend to be virtuous and indomitable, don't they? They track down the most elusive data for their authority files and spend long hours verifying each fact, no matter how many sources must be consulted or how difficult the sources are to obtain. No matter what the pressure of production may be, they parse every classification number and every shelf mark until they are sure each conforms to their standards. They fight every effort to cut corners and accept "quick and dirty" cataloging.

Bibliographic service librarians are not slovenly. They leap on uncapitalized letters, missing spaces, improper use of commas, periods, and colons. In libraries that haven't been automated, they lobby for electric erasers so catalog cards can be corrected neatly, updated, or otherwise enhanced. They seek perfection, nothing less. They are proudest when they finally find themselves atop the pinnacle of internal consistency and integrity in their catalogs. No matter that no one else notices. No matter that no one else is there to share the prize. Scholars search for the sake of truth. So do bibliographic service librarians. How unlike the technicians, who need someone to use their tools in order to be fulfilled. Bibliographic librarians need only their own recognition, their own satisfaction.

PROBLEMS AT THE INTERFACE

Once again I ask, What's in a name? Why should it create problems at the interface between public and nonpublic services to call the latter "support," "processing," "technical," or "bibliographic" services? Or, for that matter, to call them "preparation" services or any other kind of services?

If any of the mystiques described contain just a grain of truth, then problems at the interface occur, at least in part, because of the perception each group has of the other. When I was in library school, I thought that the public service people had all the glamour and romance. They served the public. They found out what people needed and delivered it up to them. They understood and forged the connections between ordinary humans and the vast resources of humanity ensconced in library collections. They were the true professionals.

When I began to work in a library, even though it was a public library with a very large group of professional reference librarians and a tiny handful of mostly nonprofessional technical service librarians, I heard the reference people say, to my amazement, that they thought the technical service department had all the money. The library budget was squandered on building catalogs that no one really understood except as locators of titles purchased. Catalogers couldn't even answer the simple question, "Can I have this book?" except indirectly: "Maybe you can, if it is on the shelf!" The reference folks said that technical service librarians ran all the professional associations. The technical services people had all the breaks. The technical services people didn't have to stand on their feet all day and work hard. I could continue, but I won't. My point is that in place of mutual pride, respect, and cooperation I found confrontation and contention.

For one group to win, the other had to lose. Each group nursed its grudges while slugging it out. Each group used every weapon at its disposal. Nomenclature became one of those weapons.

In my former library the term *Reference Services* was discarded and *Information Services* was adopted to identify reference with the Information Age. In other libraries *Circulation* was discarded and *Access Services* adopted to identify stamping out books with fancy technology and the Age of Access. (Personally, I prefer *Document Delivery Services*, as is explained in chapter 25.) But instead of gussying up old *Technical Services* into *Bibliographic Services* for the psychological boost it might give the staff, more than one library decided, after much consideration, to stick with the terms *Technical, Support,* or *Processing Services.*

THE POWER OF NAMES

The mystiques associated with names people call one another manifest ideas and perceptions that hold the power to affect their relative positions and relationships. Departments do not always name themselves. Often they were named in the past by people who used language differently than it is used today. Perhaps some librarians have never thought much about the names they use. Are the public service people called reference librarians? Are they bibliographers? Are they reader's advisors? Are there some of each in a potpourri of public services?

In a library I visited nearly a decade ago, the public service department had recently changed its name to Information Services. The reference desk was called the Information Center. It hummed with newly installed electronic devices. The nonpublic services department was called Support Services. It suffered from budget cuts, space cuts, lack of direction, and devastating morale problems. I suggested the department change its name to something more elegant to induce a sense of self-worth. I suggested Bibliographic Services. The suggestion was ignored, and the department still staggers under the burden of supporting its Information Services department. Too bad.

Mutual support and respect between public and nonpublic services (or technical and nontechnical services) are necessary to keep the interfaces trouble-free. Nonpublic types need feedback from those who work with the public to recognize and address issues affecting clients' success with bibliographic products. Nontechnical types need the products of technical service operations to function. The gap must be bridged so the needs of the public are conveyed to the staff responsible for technical operations and the effectiveness of bibliographic tools can be maximized.

Then there are computers. The introduction of computers into a library requires rethinking the hallowed division between public and technical services because contact with the public is not synonymous with contact with the computer. No longer is there a neat criterion for categorizing personnel and services. Computerized services presume that everyone with an interest in bibliographic files is in the same boat.

Years ago Michael Gorman suggested that a "compleat" librarian should have feet planted firmly in both camps, employing personal expertise to advantage in both types of service. Preparing an entry takes certain kinds of knowledge. Using an entry takes similar knowledge. This is easy to see if one thinks of foreign languages or special subject expertise. Clearly, non-English speakers might have problems using English-language entries. A nonmusician might have difficulty classifying musical scores. She or he also might have difficulty browsing a collection of musical scores. The logic of music is foreign to someone without knowledge of the language. Many libraries duplicate special knowledge by having separate staff members with the same areas of expertise serve as special subject catalogers and reference librarians.

It is less clear but equally true that familiarity with the way catalogs are constructed helps one get the most out of searching them. The more complex a catalog becomes, the more important such knowledge becomes. Gorman's method—removing the division between the front desk and the back room—is a very good way of handling the knowledge problem, but it is taking a long time to become the norm. In the meanwhile one way to eliminate the confrontational posture is to do everything that can be done to develop a common interest and commitment to one another's success. One way to accomplish this is by using appropriate nomenclature.

To be understood by the rest of the library and information science profession, the nomenclature must cut across boundaries. The term *Bibliographic Services* does it. Even public service librarians offer bibliographic services to the public. They often are engaged in compiling bibliographies, using bibliographies, and selecting from bibliographies. Some of them are known as bibliographers. If the catalogs and files produced by nonpublic librarians were termed bibliographic, too, then their creators could be included in the set of persons who furnish library service to others. One could go further and use the term *Bibliographic Information Services*. This name captures both the bibliographic and the information aspects of the library services that technical service departments provide.

The idea that technical service librarians are information providers cannot be taken too lightly. I sometimes wonder whether or not the technical service people I know really think of themselves as information providers. Too often, I fear, they think of themselves as supporters of information services or as processors of information but not as purveyors — not even to the librarians whose public services they support. That is the greatest failing of the names for technical services currently in use.

In addition to perceiving themselves as providers of bibliographic information, technical service librarians should broaden their perspective regarding the public. Every so often I read an article in which the myth of the reclusive cataloger is laid (once again) to rest. That image must be stamped out forevermore. The best way to accomplish the task is to come out of the back rooms and basement lairs, out from behind the unmarked doors or the doors marked "Staff Only," and work at bibliographic information services in full view of the public. (When I see a door in a library marked "Staff Only," I always wonder whether it is a bathroom or a technical service department. Thus far my unscientific survey totes up about 50 percent for each option.) Not only do technical service librarians have expertise that might be employed to provide direct public benefits, but technical service tasks should be performed with the lay user in mind. Technical service librarians should be acquainted with their library's various lay users, their bibliographic needs, and the problems they encounter using the catalogs. Most technical service librarians speak blithely about users without ever defining exactly who those users are or how they may be affected by decisions made in the cataloging department.

If they aren't seen or served directly, it is easy as pie to forget that users exist. No one orders technical service librarians to do user surveys. The librarians themselves must initiate the effort. Few users complain about the catalog. They don't know that the entry they didn't find really is there. Users complain because titles they find in the catalog aren't on the shelves — a problem that librarians can point out is inevitable when materials circulate. Users don't complain because the shelves lack cross-references that might lead to related materials that, because of differences in format or approach, are located elsewhere. For example, our classifications presume that people browsing in literature about computer software aren't interested in computer hardware. Finally, our reluctance to clutter up our catalogs with great numbers of cross-references doesn't make it easy for people with up-to-date vocabularies to find materials filed in a subject catalog under early- or mid-century-bound terms.

Having specialists in bibliographic information services on hand could help these users and others. But technical service librarians are rarely on hand. They are out of sight and out of mind when it comes to serving the public directly. Thus, policies of using the archaic language in LCSH, limiting the number of subject headings or cross-references, avoiding directional signs at the shelf, and so forth continue to limit access rather than promote it. For the most part, users are unaware that their needs are being subverted by technical service librarians' concentration on nonpublic concerns.

Heaven help technical service librarians if they are found out before they can shift their focus from support, processing, or technical services to bibliographic information services. Heaven help them if they fail to shift their focus—and soon. What they are doing now soon will be replaced by expert systems mounted on a few computer terminals. In time, there may be no justification for employing graduate professional librarians in nonpublic services. All of us should think about what's in a name—for technical services.

Order and Disorder:
Learning from Chaos Theory

There is a wonderful book by James Gleick entitled *Chaos: Making a New Science* (Penguin Books, 1987, ISBN 0-1400-9250-1). The book explores the development of a set of mathematical theories that describes phenomena in fields as diverse as physics, economics, biology, cartography, and meteorology in terms any educated layperson can understand.

I believe chaos theory may help us understand why things happen the way they do in the field of library/information science, and I urge every reader of this book to go to the nearest library, get a copy of Gleick's book, sit down and read it immediately, and think about it for a good long time.

Chaos. The very word inspires shivers of terror. Chaos is what existed before the division of the universe into day and night, into earth, water, and sky. Why should we want anything that dreadful to explain libraries?

Frankly, I yearn to find a theoretical structure that helps explain how libraries work. The theories we have do very little to help us predict what kinds of library systems and services will succeed or which will provide optimal service given our circumstances. One could easily claim that the weather bureau is more successful in forecasting the weather, and everyone knows their track record. So allow me to share some speculations about this new body of theory that I believe might offer insights into the weather as well as behavior in our field.

WHAT IS CHAOS THEORY?

Chaos is disorder. In Gleick's words, "For as long as the world has had physicists inquiring into the laws of nature, it has suffered a special ignorance about disorder in the atmosphere, in the turbulent sea, in the fluctuations of wildlife populations, in the oscillations of the heart and the brain. The irregular side of nature, the discontinuous and erratic side—these have been ... monstrosities" (p. 3). Chaos theory is the result of recent efforts by individual scientists—mathematicians, biologists, physicists, chemists, all sorts of scientists—to describe and find explanations for the monstrosities and to use the knowledge to predict future behavior.

10

Gleick says that, since chaos theory is "a science of the global nature of systems" (p. 5), it cuts across the lines of different scientific disciplines. The science of chaos seeks to describe, analyze, and understand phenomena of human proportions. Unlike Establishment science it is focused on the fuzzy, disorderly way things actually happen in the real world, not on the laboratory phenomena of perfect entities in perfect settings. Chaos theorists might look into the flow patterns of running rapids; they might investigate weather patterns, seismic activity, or examples of biological diversity; or they might explore how the cream will behave when it is poured into a cup of coffee.

Chaos theory does more than describe chaotic phenomena. It also tries to explain them. One important element in the explanations has to do with the idea of scale. Another has to do with bifurcation, or branching. For the best visual demonstration of both elements, construct a Koch curve (*curve* is used here in its mathematical definition of an unbroken line) according to the following instructions and imagine how the pattern would look if the "1" in the instructions was 1 inch, 1 mile, and 1 light-year.

> Begin with a triangle with sides of length 1. At the middle of each side, add a new triangle one-third the size; and so on. The length of the boundary is 3 x 4/3 x 4/3 x 4/3 ... infinity. Yet the area remains less than the area of a circle drawn around the original triangle. Thus an infinitely long line surrounds a finite area. (p. 99)

As you draw the curve, you can see the branching effect, the triangle becoming a six-pointed star, then becoming a more complex figure that begins to resemble a true snowflake after a few transformations. And as you think of the curve's original side being 1 inch or 1 mile or 1 light-year, you can imagine the scaling effect, much as one might imagine a shoreline would look to a person standing on the shore or flying in a hot air balloon a mile or so up in the air or standing on the moon. In fact, after a dozen transformations the Koch curve begins to resemble an actual shoreline.

Chaos is a study of dynamic systems — systems in motion. The speed of the motion may have far-reaching effects on the system's behavior. At slow speeds or low temperatures, for example, the behavior of a system being examined for chaotic features may appear quite regular. As the speed or temperature is increased, the regular behavior may continue for a time and then suddenly go berserk. The chaos theorist will examine the data for the chaotic behavior and try to discover a new kind of pattern that repeats itself as the variable (i.e., the speed or the temperature) continues its progress. The behavior may return to regularity, persist in irregularity, or alternate between the two. Order in disorder — that's chaos.

A group of chaos scientists at the University of California, Santa Cruz, addressed chaotic implications of "information theory," developing relationships between the chaos mathematics they were studying and findings about the communication of information bits reported in the 1940s by Bell Labs researcher Claude Shannon. (You may know, although I didn't, that Shannon's work led to the use of redundancy to insure the accuracy of transmitted information bits, which is where we got things like eight-bit bytes and check digits.) I hasten to tell you, as Gleick does, that Shannon and the Santa Cruz group defined "information" as an electronically transmitted entity — one or zero, on or off, yes or no — not as we define it to mean texts or their meaning. Chaos, Santa Cruz's

Robert Shaw concluded, was the *creation of information*, i.e., new bits one would not have expected to be delivered. Santa Cruz scientist Norman Packard said, "Intuitively there seems a clear sense in which these ultimately complicated systems are generating information. Billions of years ago there were just blobs of protoplasm; now billions of years later here we are. So information has been created and stored in our structure. In the development of one person's mind from childhood, information is clearly not just accumulated but also generated — created from connections that were not there before" (p. 261-62). It seems to me that this is "information" to which we librarians can relate.

It may be that the science of chaos began to flourish when it did because one of its primary tools, the computer, had reached an essential point in its development where it could be employed to analyze systems in global terms. In any case, chaos theory came into its own in the 1970s and 1980s concurrent with the spread of microcomputing.

LIBRARIES AND THE SIGNIFICANCE OF SIZE

Chaos theory relies to a degree on intuitive knowledge, for example, the way we know intuitively that the figures defined by the Koch curve resemble a snowflake or a shoreline or the way we perceive an image when the relationship between the observer and the area being observed changes. Suppose we apply this kind of thinking to libraries, especially to the differences between small, medium-sized, and large libraries. Might chaos theory help us recognize and describe important patterns of difference?

One thing that immediately leaped to mind was organizational structures. As libraries grow from one-person operations to huge entities like the Library of Congress, they tend to move from unitary organizations without any divisions to simply divided organizations with a few areas of specialty to enormously complex organizations with many divisions within divisions. Are there recognizable break-points where one can predict that a particular organizational structure will not work well? What are the implications for staff efficiency when new divisions are established? Are more complex organizations less efficient? Do they create more "noise"? Do they tend toward greater disorder? Or is the effect just the opposite?

Similarly, collection arrangements tend to grow from one set of shelves on which all materials are interfiled (which is the way my village library's tiny collection is shelved) to a few shelving sections for a few major types of materials to multiple divisions and sections differentiating all sorts of things, including audiences (children's, young adult, adult, older adult, undergraduate, graduate), media (monographs, periodicals, audiovisuals), treatments (popular versus scholarly, fiction versus nonfiction), age (current, retrospective), type of loan (circulating, reserve, reference), and so forth. When does dividing a collection enhance its accessibility and when does it detract? Are there ways to evaluate the accessibility of materials shelved at varying levels of complexity?

As a cataloging teacher, I began to think about the proliferation of divisions and subdivisions within classification schedules, from the forty-four-page original Dewey Decimal classification to its present four volumes with thousands of pages and, beyond, to the LC schedules comprising more than forty volumes. Are small libraries that adopt the LC classification putting themselves into a mismatch of scale akin to a person trying to see the shape a Koch curve with a side one light-year long or to a person on the moon trying to see the shape of a Koch curve with a side one inch long?

Besides classification schedules the growing complex of cataloging rules came to mind, along with the criticism of unnecessary rule proliferation that always has been leveled at cataloging codes. Is there a pattern to rule proliferation? Is it possible to discern principles (read: recognizable patterns) in the morass of interpretations and exceptions treated in the special chapters of AACR (i.e., chapters 2-12) as opposed to the first, general chapter? Do we need to see these things from a different perspective of scale in order to discern their true significance? The thought is captivating.

DICHOTOMIES AND BIFURCATIONS IN LIBRARIANSHIP

As with classification schedules and cataloging rules, librarianship is full of dichotomies and bifurcations—elements on which chaos theory thrives. One of the hallowed dichotomies is fiction versus nonfiction. Another is technical versus public services. Others are open versus closed shelves, circulating versus reference materials, classification by topic versus form, type of library versus function-oriented divisions in the American Library Association, approval plan versus title-by-title selection, current versus retrospective, and monograph versus periodical. One of my favorite dichotomies is the finding list versus the collocating functions of the catalog (thank you, Charles Cutter); another pet of mine is subject versus descriptive cataloging.

Wherever we look we find dichotomous ideas. Are we creating library paradoxes—infinitely long curves in teeny-weeny closed spaces? What does this mean for the creation of librarians' information—namely, the purposeful collecting, organizing, and use enhancements of the materials under our stewardship?

WHERE CAN WE GO FROM HERE?

A lot of questions were posed here (as were a few possibilities for applying chaos theory to issues of librarianship) but none of them were answered. If I were doing a dissertation today, I would try to find answers to one of the questions, applying the principles of chaos theory in a rigorous manner to data collected by observing library operations. That is where librarians might go from here. I hope we are so intrigued by the potential of this powerful theory to explain library phenomena that some of us will try to apply it in practice. After all, it is a short hop from describing and explaining a phenomenon to understanding it and another short hop from there to learning how to predict its behavior. Once a phenomenon is described, explained, understood, and made predictable, can complete control of it be far behind?

Last of all, I worry about Shaw's remark that chaos is the generation of information. Are librarians the high priests of chaos? Do they preside over an inexorable movement of intellectual production toward ultimate disorder? Perhaps the thrill of discovery may one day elicit an answer to this question.

Meanwhile, it seems worth the effort to examine how chaos theory might apply to our problems and help explain our paradoxes and what it might help us learn about our field. Perhaps the features of librarianship will become clearer, which would be worth a great deal.

Get Outta Here and ...
Get Me Some Money, Too!

There is an old song made famous by jazz singer Peggy Lee that goes, "You had plenty money, back in '22/You let other women make a fool of you/Why don't you do right like some other men do?/Get outta here and ... get me some money, too."[1]

The sentiment might seem out of place in a book about library issues. But, sexual stereotypes aside, it is exactly what I'd like to sing to every library director who goes after special funds for developing collections (a.k.a. buying new materials) but fails to make equally heroic plans for how those materials will be made accessible to and usable by the library's clients.

If I were the head of acquisitions, bibliographic services, and shelf processing, I would want to scream, "Get outta here and ... get me some money, too!"

THE LET 'EM EAT CAKE SYNDROME

Why is adequate processing (i.e., preparing and adding bibliographic data for new items into the network database, shelflist, and local catalog as well as readying them for the shelf and shelving them) not an accepted cost of acquiring materials factored into every proposal for new materials? Why is it that grants for new collections sometimes explicitly exclude, rather than merely ignore, the cost of processing? It is clearly irrational to expect that cataloging and processing departments with staffing and budgets already pared to the bone will be able to integrate additional windfalls into their routine work flows.

Do these grant-minded directors ever think much about the added cost for reference services when adequate bibliographic processing is neglected or ignored? Do they ever worry that specially purchased titles might spend a long time in a queue awaiting proper integration into the collections? Or, if specially purchased titles are given high priority in processing, other titles purchased in the ordinary course of events will wait in backlog because there aren't enough staff members, terminals, and hours in the day to process everything coming through?

The idea that buying materials is enough to provide client service is what I call the "let 'em eat cake" syndrome. Does it really matter to library clients if they don't get what they want because it hasn't been purchased (starving because there is no bread) or because they can't find it (starving because they can't afford cake)? One experiment I'd like to try is to see whether spending a given amount of money to buy materials but not catalog and process them provides as much service, measured in terms of material use both in-house and through client loans, as spending half the amount for materials but adding the most sophisticated bibliographic access support possible to the purchases.

COLLECTION OBJECTIVES:
Why Are We Buying?

Clearly, library grant writers need to be apprised of the problems their successes engender. Before a grant for new materials is written, its objectives should be scrutinized carefully: Are the materials being acquired for future researchers — people who will use the materials whenever they are finally made available? Then the grant writers may rest easy, knowing that it will not matter much if there are no funds for processing now, since *someday* processing will take place and the materials will then be used. But if the materials are intended for immediate use to support some new degree program or a previously underserved subgroup in the library's constituency, then quick processing is essential. Without attention to the processing, only half the job can be accomplished.

"But," the grant writers might say, "we are doing our jobs by developing the collections. Let the catalogers and binders and processors do theirs. They should do their part by figuring out how to catalog and bind and process the collections we develop. We should not have to think about their jobs, too. Why do we need them if they cannot contribute their share toward fulfilling the library's overall goals and objectives?"

And they are correct. No one else in the library should have to do the job of the catalogers, binders, and processors. Is there another problem here? Is it that the catalogers' job is perceived as beginning with the appearance of materials to be cataloged?

SORTING OUT THE STRANDS

In the bureaucratic, hierarchical organizational structures we have built for libraries of any size, it is entirely plausible for catalogers to assume that their job begins when trucks roll through their doors bearing uncataloged books. Indeed, I've seen technical service "departments" where the acquisition, cataloging, and serials control staffs were located on different floors or in different wings. With my own eyes, I've seen acquisition departments that did pre-order searching for bibliographic data in OCLC, making printouts of whatever they found but not passing the printouts along to the cataloging department, where a second, identical precataloging search was conducted. It doesn't take too much effort to imagine that if collection development is assigned entirely to the public service staff of a library, no information about impending purchases will be sent to technical services staff — or even trickle down to them before waves of incoming receipts hit the loading dock.

When purchasing is routine and tends to wax and wane in the same fashion year in and year out, the need to find out how collection development and acquisition operations are going is unnecessary. The typical response to a sudden, overwhelming surge of new acquisitions is the creation of a backlog for some of the new materials. The possibility that, in some institutions, the backlog becomes the final resting place for whatever unlucky materials are assigned to it is something I hate even to contemplate, but horror stories from colleagues confirm that it happens. A colleague once told me that at her university an audiovisual collection of about one thousand items that had been accumulating in backlog for almost twenty years was weeded in its entirety because decision-makers determined the cost of cataloging such old materials was a waste of resources.

I read somewhere that for every dollar spent on materials, a dollar is spent processing them. That is a considerable sum if we assume that the average nonfiction hardbound book purchased by an academic institution is likely to run $25 to $75 or more, depending on its subject, treatment, and size. Even considering the large number of current fiction purchases made by public libraries (remember those multiple copies of best-sellers?), the cost is unlikely to be less than $15 and might be as much as $40 per item without raising any eyebrows. (To digress a moment, one can't help thinking that popular video recordings, traditionally considered expensive nonbook media, tend to average $20 to $50 — right in the same ballpark as books.)

Where is a matching fund for processing to handle special purchases of any significant size going to come from?

GET ME SOME MONEY, TOO!

Here are four suggestions for solving the problem of how to obtain the processing funds to handle purchases funded by special project grants or allocations.

1.   Write them into the collection development grant proposals.

2.   Write separate grant proposals for matching processing funds or seek donors who will underwrite bibliographic and physical access services.

3.   Allocate the operating budget for processing differently in years when a grant for special purchases is expected.

4.   Allocate capital sums for special processing projects to match the special collection development purchases.

Write Them into Collection Development Grant Proposals

This is the easiest and best solution, since it avoids having to write a separate grant proposal for processing and it enables the grant-seeker to describe in more detail exactly how the proposed new collections will create, augment, enhance, support, or otherwise contribute to the library's programs, satisfying the objectives of the granting authority. More importantly, it also serves to raise the consciousness of the granting authority to the fact that it takes more than a bunch of books, films, recordings, software, or other materials to make a collection.

Creating a collection also takes access, bibliographic and physical, to the materials that make up the body of the collection.

Write a Separate Grant Proposal for Processing

Sometimes a collection development grant explicitly forbids asking for anything but money to buy new materials. In such cases a separate grant proposal for processing funds should be submitted under the terms of a different grant but, if possible, should be linked with the collection development grant. It might take a little research, e.g., a call to the granting agency or a careful reading of its objectives and grant lists, to obtain the information necessary to locate and prepare the processing grant. When there is no alternative, a separate grant might be submitted to an altogether different granting authority; you may include in explanatory remarks that the funds relate to a special project being funded by another grantor. If, in researching the funding sources for processing, you come across a granting authority that permits requests for collections, too, you have the option of submitting a second proposal for more materials as well as the proposal for processing funds. The library might end up getting them all.

Allocate Extra Funds from the Operating Budget

If top administrators are doing their jobs right, they are aware that receipt of a collection development grant means a surge of extra activity for the acquisition, cataloging, and processing departments, and they plan to allot additional funds from the operating budget to account for it. After all, isn't that the administrator's job? Acquisition librarians can be expected to assume that their job begins when they receive requests for purchases, just as catalogers can be expected to assume that theirs begins when uncataloged materials come through their doors. Why should acquisition or catalog department librarians worry about funds for reference services or other departments? That's the job of whoever coordinates the whole library budget and allocates funds among its component departments, isn't it? It sounds like the top administrator's job to me.

Where should those funds come from? Frankly, it doesn't matter much as long as the entire load doesn't fall like a ton of bricks on the departments that must do the ordering, cataloging, and processing for this special group of materials they had no hand in requesting. Funds might come partly from regular purchasing funds; they might come partly from planned across-the-board salary increases or from planned additions to either the public service or administrative staffs. If additions to staff were planned, the personnel could be hired with the understanding that they would be assigned first to complete the special processing tasks and then be shifted to other duties.

If the collection development grant doesn't come through, the extra monies can be subtracted from the technical service departments and returned to their original lines.

Use Capital Funds for Processing

I fail to see why buying a computer qualifies as a capital expenditure but building the database the computer contains does not. Sloan and Zurcher (*Dictionary of Economics*, 5th ed., Barnes & Noble, 1970, p. 178) give the following definition of a capital or fixed asset: "An asset of such a nature that is used directly or indirectly to produce goods or services and is not for sale in the regular course of business. Examples are land, buildings, and machinery." The issue here is not whether the catalog of a library represents a capital asset but whether capital funds can be expended for cataloging and processing services. That is the decision of the people who control the capital funds—who, in many libraries, might not be the librarians.

Perhaps because librarians deal in free products and services, people begin believing that everything related to them, including the materials and the catalog, are free, too. Instead, we should educate ourselves and those who direct library policies about the value of various library components. We might even assign real values to them. Then we might think of the catalog as the piece of basic equipment it really is—the central piece in our array of intellectual equipment.

CONCLUSION

Since library administrators may not readily anticipate the need for exceptional allocations for the technical service activities associated with grant applications for materials, it behooves technical service librarians to make greater efforts to control their fates. Aside from the suggestions in the previous section, technical service librarians can become better apprised of what is happening in their libraries' collection development units or, to go still closer to the source, in the municipalities, universities, schools, or corporations of which their libraries are part. Take a collection developer to lunch. Read the annual report. Examine the policy speeches of the president, board chair, or mayor. Work out a "disaster plan" to accommodate a sudden increase in work load and decide where shortcuts might be taken. If your bureaucracy isn't too onerous, communicate with those above and below you to find out if they are aware of these issues, how they view them, and how they might deal with them. Don't give up and bemoan your fate. Get outta here, and ... get me some money, too!

NOTES

[1]Peggy Lee, "Why Don't You Do Right?" 1942. Sung with Benny Goodman's Orchestra.

Circulation,
the Third Service

Quick! Name the technical services. I'll bet you said acquisitions and cataloging and then paused a moment to think about what else could be subsumed by the rubric "technical services." Preservation and serials control might come to mind, especially if you are a member of the Association for Library Collections and Technical Services (ALCTS), the division of the American Library Association that caters to technical services. That division has six sections, four of which correspond to the four functions just named. The other two focus on reproduction of library materials and collection development. There! All done, right?

For some librarians this definition of technical services already exceeds the bounds of propriety. They would attribute only acquisitions and cataloging to technical services and frown on extending the definition beyond the traditional activities of ordering, receiving, and paying for new materials and assigning unique identifications, subject descriptors and call numbers to them.

Why are these kinds of services technical? Why do they require the services of a technical services librarian? What makes them require special training—professional training—to perform? Why shouldn't we extend the definition of acquisitions to include collection development and management services for all kinds of materials, whether monographic or serial? And why not extend the definition of cataloging to include all other processing, such as reproduction and preservation?

Are we missing an important function/service in naming the technical services? What about the service most likely to be paired with acquisitions and cataloging in an integrated automated system—circulation? Is circulation the third technical service? What is it that makes any of these services technical?

THE MEANING OF TECHNIQUE

I submit that it is the requirement of bibliographic knowledge and competence in designing, creating data for, and managing bibliographic systems that makes technical services technical. It is the prerequisite of bibliographic knowledge that necessitates the skills of professional librarians in conducting and supervising the technical services, depending, of course, on the level of bibliographic expertise needed to perform particular tasks. The following paragraphs offer arguments why ordinary office managers aren't prepared to do the work of technical services.

Acquisition of materials, whatever their physical manifestations or publication patterns, first requires ascertaining that a particular item exists and is not already part of an institution's collections. Determining that a title exists means searching bibliographic databases in print, online, or in other formats, recognizing that what one finds is, indeed, the correct item, and monitoring this item in a constantly changing file containing millions of other items. Serials are particularly difficult to search and monitor because their existence extends over time and may include changes in titles, sponsoring bodies, publishers, places of publication, frequency of issue, style of dating, etc. Unlike monographic items, which tend to be received, processed, and forgotten, serials require constant care, including careful inventorying, periodic binding, and indexing.

Cataloging in its most specific sense involves the generation of bibliographic data, subject indexing, classification, and storage of all this information in a fashion that permits quick, easy, and logical retrieval after long periods of time have passed. Clearly, cataloging demands the most intimate knowledge of bibliographic theory and organizational principles.

Processing and its extensions—binding, preserving, and reproducing materials—are important because they maintain the integrity of a fully organized collection, not merely individual items. These tasks demand a special sort of knowledge, including recognition of the bibliographic importance of certain editions, translations, or related works and the value of those works to the collections. Aside from the knowledge of the physics and chemistry of paper, film, and other information-bearing materials, preservationists and reproductionists make use of the same kind of special professional knowledge that the original developers of the collection used in determining what to add in the first place. Among other things, this means bibliographic knowledge. Added to this is the responsibility for maintaining bibliographic control of the materials being preserved or reproduced.

If the technique required by technical services is not merely routine office organization but bibliographic organization and control, isn't it reasonable to claim that all functions based on the same special knowledge and proficiencies are technical, too?

THE MEANING OF PUBLIC

Since technical services are usually twinned with public services, the same inquiry should be made about them. Too obvious? Perhaps. But it does no harm and the contrast might shed light on the discussion.

Public services are so named, I believe, because they involve direct service to members of the lay public for which the collection was established. Quick! Name the public services. I'll bet you said reference and circulation. Maybe you added bibliographic instruction and interlibrary loan. Maybe you also added serials control and government documents, which sometimes are administered by reference department staff members. In fact, collection development for monographic materials—not just serials—is as likely to be administered as a public service as it is a technical service. A number of reference departments routinely receive and catalog government documents, order reference materials, and manage binding and other preservation activities for all library materials—an extension of the binding and preservation of serials.

Do public services require bibliographic knowledge and competence? Certainly. Reference involves searching the library's catalog—every library's primary reference tool—as well as other kinds of indexes and bibliographies. It also involves creating individualized indexes or bibliographies to answer queries. Circulation requires performing inventory control tasks in which the inventory is identified by its bibliographic data. But these aren't the things that make these services public. It is answering people's questions that makes reference a public service and it is putting library materials into the hands of borrowers that makes circulation a public service. The public aspect of circulation services is not maintaining inventory control over holdings, just as the creation of bibliographies is not the public aspect of reference services.

AND THE DIFFERENCE BETWEEN THEM IS ...

Facing the public in the normal execution of one's professional tasks is the essential difference between public and technical service librarians, in my opinion. And although it is somewhat less satisfying as a clear line of demarcation, another rule of thumb might be that, for bibliographic storage and retrieval systems, the "storage" part, which involves no contact with the public, is the technical part, while the "retrieval" part, which often involves retrieving data for a member of the public, is the public part.

One thing is clear: all librarians use specialized bibliographic knowledge in the performance of their professional work. Perhaps that is what makes them professional. Some of the tasks that everyone accepts as technical, such as acquisition of materials and cataloging, may be done at times by public service librarians; and one of the tasks that almost everyone accepts as public, i.e., circulation, quite often is done by technical service librarians, usually when it involves the use of a computer-based bibliographic system for inventory control. If this is true, then what is the best way to distinguish between public and technical services? And, to repeat the question, where does circulation *really* belong? Is it technical services' third service, after acquisitions and cataloging?

TAUBER, TECHNICAL SERVICES, AND CIRCULATION

As far back as the 1950s (and perhaps even earlier), Maurice Tauber identified the technical aspects of both reference and circulation services, publishing his theory along with detailed descriptions of acquisition and cataloging tasks in the landmark work *Technical Services in Libraries* (Columbia University Press, 1954). Since then other teachers have followed suit, including Maurice Freedman and Sheila Intner, who followed Tauber at Columbia University and whose courses and writing on technical services issues and technical services automation included circulation services with the rest. Nor are they alone. The definition of an integrated automated system for technical services includes modules for acquisitions, cataloging, and circulation control. Experience with computer-based systems shows that only linkage between the cataloging and circulation files can answer the question most frequently asked by the public: "Can I have ...?"

Some, though not all, recent books about technical services follow suit. *Library Technical Services* (Irene Godden, ed., Academic Press, 1986, 1992), *Technical Services in the Medium-Sized Library* (Sheila S. Intner and Josephine Fang, Shoe String Press, 1990) and *Technical Services Today and Tomorrow* (Michael Gorman, ed., Libraries Unlimited, 1991) include long chapters on circulation services, while *Technical Services in Libraries: Systems and Applications* (Thomas W. Leonhardt, ed., JAI Press, 1992) does not.

Why have writers and educators followed Maurice Tauber in accepting circulation as a technical service worthy of notice by information professionals? I believe it is because circulation control is not just stamping or scanning books being borrowed by the public. It involves both the storage and retrieval of bibliographic data. Similarly, reference service involves more than answering questions for the public. It involves acquiring and organizing reference information for public use without the presence of a mediator—much like the library catalog. The availability and wide dissemination of user-friendly, self-service CD-ROM databases for all sorts of subject areas have led public service librarians to speculate on the possibility that their jobs might become obsolete in the future.

DIFFERENCES AND SIMILARITIES

There really are two aspects to reference and circulation services. The technical aspects of reference and circulation include designing, creating data for, and managing the ongoing maintenance and use of indexes, bibliographies, and the inventory control system. The public aspects of reference and circulation involve answering questions and stamping and handing borrowed books to the public. Are there comparable public aspects to the technical services? I think there are, although some libraries have policies that prohibit interaction between technical service librarians and the public, always interposing a public service librarian to convey the message from the technical service librarian to the information seeker.

Obviously, the service best rendered to the public by technical service librarians is interpretation of the files they create in their technical roles: the order file, the serials record, the shelflist, and the catalog(s). We could go a step further and suggest that technical service librarians can serve their public service colleagues by interpreting those files as well as by lending organizational expertise as consultants when reference librarians plan local indexes and bibliographies.

BUT IS IT PROFESSIONAL?

A great many articles and books claim that cataloging and acquisitions no longer require the services of professionally trained librarians. Cataloging has been de-professionalized, according to DeGennaro, Hafter, and others. Acquisitions has always been perceived as an order-plus-accounting function with little need for the librarian's special knowledge. Circulation is thought of as the least professional function, requiring only a steady hand for holding bar codes over or under scanners or planting a date stamp squarely on its appointed spot. Control over the inventory is a matter of printing and mailing overdue notices—no great intellectual demands there, either. So why bother with this whole discussion?

The answer is that the individual tasks performed in executing technical service work do not always require special knowledge of bibliographic systems. Those tasks can be done (and always could be done) by anyone who can read, operate simple machinery, and follow directions. But the systems that execute each of the functions of acquisition, organization, and control—whether for books, serials, government documents, or nonbook media—must be designed, monitored, and evaluated—in other words, they must be managed—by professionally-trained specialists. Decisions and policies that govern the systems must be made by people who understand the implications of those decisions and who have the ability to weigh the alternatives in terms of public benefit or institutional cost. Until the successful completion of a computerized substitute, the generation of data for technical services systems must be done or, at least, supervised by specialists.

CONCLUSION

In weighing the arguments, I can't help but conclude that we divide library tasks badly by making direct contact with the public the crucial element. Instead, all professionally-trained librarians should be involved in the design and management of information systems as well as the generation of data for them. All librarians might be expected to mediate between user-hostile tools and the public; all might be expected to make recommendations and give advice to members of the public for satisfying specific information needs. All have the requisite knowledge for supervising the various tasks associated with implementing policies and procedures. Professional capabilities are not required to do the tasks, any more than physicians are needed to empty bedpans or attorneys are required to serve subpoenas.

Circulation is as technical as any other bibliographic function. It can be thought of, logically and logistically, as the third technical service. Local library computing logically makes it the third service after acquiring and organizing materials. Computer-based data that serve multiple functions make it logistically practical to include circulation with acquisitions and cataloging. Is local library computing "technical" or "public" in your library? Is the definition based on efficiency of operations or on tradition? It may be time for a change.

PART 2

PROBLEMS AT THE MAIN INTERFACE
The Catalog

Cataloging Myths Debunked

Every now and then we need to look our myths in the face and see which ones cause us to nod sagaciously and say, "There is a grain of truth in that," and which ones cause us to shrink back in horror, gasping, "For heaven's sake, can't we ever erase that piece of stupidity?"

During a midwinter conference of the American Library Association a few years ago, I heard some of the myths about catalogers and cataloging that anger me the most repeated by people who should know better. I'd like to mount a campaign to debunk them, even though I know success in these endeavors is elusive. (After all, Americans still respond positively to the myth about George Washington and the cherry tree, even though we have long been aware that evidence doesn't support it.)

MYTH 1: CATALOGERS HAVE NO PEOPLE SKILLS

One of the worst myths is that catalogers are shy and retiring people who cannot interact effectively with other people. It belongs with the image of librarians as single, old, bespectacled, bun-wearing females. Go ask one hundred ordinary people on the street about librarians and you might be surprised to hear — still — about mean old maids wearing glasses and buns who go around the library hushing everyone. Even worse, however, is the probability that if you went up to one hundred ordinary librarians — say, in the busiest aisle of an ALA conference exhibit area — and asked them about catalogers' interpersonal skills, they would — still — mumble replies about timid souls lacking people skills.

If you are a cataloger, for pity's sake give vent to your aggressions, push ahead in the cafeteria lines, and keep a list of snappy retorts to requests for more work without extra pay or added responsibilities without more pay, more authority, and extra staff thrown in for good measure. And don't you dare agree to take your turn at the reference desk unless a reference librarian takes a turn at the cataloging terminal.

MYTH 2: CATALOGING IS BADLY TAUGHT
IN LIBRARY SCHOOL

Certainly the catalogers at that ALA conference who were attending a session on recruiting and educating catalogers were anything but shy and retiring. I would have used the adjectives strident and angry to describe them. I was among them, to be sure. I was annoyed by the myth expressed by members of the speakers' panel and the audience that cataloging is poorly taught in library schools. I think I teach it quite well and I number quite a few excellent cataloging teachers among my close friends. I defy anyone to treat the subject better than we do.

Most cataloging professors are forced by the educational systems in which they operate to teach descriptive cataloging, subject cataloging, classification, and MARC content designation in a single term. I challenge everyone in the world of library education to try to teach a complete novice everything there is to know about AACR2-revised in five weeks (which is the amount of time I devote to description and access — and it is more than I should, since it means each of the other topics gets less than that in a fourteen-week semester). It can be even harder to teach standard methods to students who already work as paraprofessional catalogers in small libraries and believe that the nonstandard "rules" they follow are correct. These students have to unlearn what they know before they can make room for an objective learning experience. It is very hard for them, since they spend much more time at work doing things the other way. But at least currently employed nonprofessionals do not have to learn a whole new language, full of strange and terrible acronyms that whirl around in their heads like dervishes, failing to broadcast their individual significance until the poor students are well past the initial required course.

We cataloging professors try, and usually succeed, in balancing theory and practical skills, but a corollary myth is that we *only* teach theory or that we *only* teach rules. There ought to be library encounters patterned after marriage encounters in which the participants are forbidden to say "You *always* ..." or "You *never*...."

MYTH 3: "REAL" CATALOGERS TEACH
CATALOGING BETTER THAN PROFESSORS

Another myth about cataloging courses, perpetrated mostly by practitioners, is that they could do a better job than the ivy-covered professors if they only had the time. Some of us full-time cataloging faculty who face anywhere from fifty to more than two hundred beginning cataloging students every year might point out that there are library schools where beginning cataloging *is* taught by practitioners who moonlight as educators. Any blame for poor teaching in these programs should be laid at the door of these sometime-educators and the administrators who believe that courses as important as beginning cataloging do not need to be taught by full-time faculty.

Many adjunct faculty are fine teachers. I can vouch for that because I was taught cataloging by one and I have served as an adjunct myself more than once. But adjuncts are not committed to teaching as a career, nor are they accountable to the same degree as full-time faculty, nor are they directly involved with curriculum development, faculty-led program development, or service to the rest of the university community. They can't be faulted if they don't teach their hearts out (although some do) after working all day and arriving for class only to be greeted by the graveyard shift maintenance crew, which raises a ruckus in the halls with floor polishers and heavy equipment until classes are over. Adjuncts usually find the offices dark and all the administrative facilities locked up for the night, so they have to prepare their teaching materials elsewhere. They may share an office with all of the other adjuncts and have no private place in which to counsel students. They simply do not have the roots, links, and time in the library school to do what full-time faculty are expected to do as a bare minimum. Part of the bare minimum expected of full-time faculty is the obligation to conduct research. Part-time faculty are not hired or retained on the basis of their research or publications, while it is a time-honored practice among university professors that they must publish or perish. The research done by cataloging faculty, especially when it is significant and well-executed, triggers widespread reaction in the field, building on the findings of these studies. This leadership function—an integral part of the job description of full-time faculty—sometimes goes unrecognized by the practitioners who benefit from it.

MYTH 4: STUDENTS HATE CATALOGING

Another myth that really annoys me is that students hate cataloging, some even before they take it. Mine don't. If yours do, then you should look to improving your teaching methods and style, assignments, curriculum, etc. After each semester a number of students tell me they liked cataloging. Many admit that they were frightened of it because it is touted as difficult (I won't argue with that) and a great deal of work (that is true, too). There are, however, other courses with equally intimidating reputations (beginning reference, for example). Students who come to graduate school expecting to breeze through with minimal effort are dilettantes who should be drummed out of the corps before we get stuck with them as colleagues.

Many of my students, taught by their practitioner-bosses to do copy cataloging, tell me they never knew cataloging was so intellectually demanding and that it could be so much fun—like doing puzzles. (I hear this even from students who don't do copy cataloging in their jobs. Perhaps a generation brought up on *Trivial Pursuit* is perfectly prepared to become the new crop of original catalogers.) The way paraprofessionals are taught to work obviously bears no relation to the process of cataloging. They seem to be given a mess of unrelated and uncoordinated rules to apply by rote. They learn little or nothing about the principles that underlie the rules or the development process by which the rules are formulated and amended, about the investigative work that cataloging requires, about access and user behavior, and about library cataloging policies and how they affect access. In short, copy catalogers seem to get none of the good stuff—the intellectually challenging theory and its relation to practice.

MYTH 5: LEARNING CATALOGING MEANS MEMORIZING THE RULES

It is a myth that all it takes to learn cataloging is memorizing gobs of rules. A corollary to this myth is that cataloging teachers only have to assign the rules to be memorized and give tests at the end of the semester to insure that the assignments were done. Nothing could be further from the truth. The rules and tools of cataloging are dynamic—they change all the time. If students just memorize the rules at any given moment, what will they do when they get out into the world and find the questions have changed and the answers they learned are obsolete? To function in the real world, they need to learn how to solve problems and what ideas drive the rules and are embodied in the tools they use so they can make decisions and handle real-life cataloging.

MYTH 6: NEW CATALOGERS DON'T NEED ON-THE-JOB TRAINING

Another big myth that isn't limited to catalogers is that a graduate professional librarian shouldn't need extensive on-the-job training. This goes hand in hand with a similar myth about turnkey computer systems, e.g., you just turn it on and use it. As any owner of a turnkey system can tell you, it takes months of incredibly hard work consuming many staff hours to use a turnkey system. It also takes months of hard work to train a graduate professional librarian to do the particular job for which she or he was hired, provided, of course, that the job is truly a professional one. The only way to avoid a training period is to hire someone who is already employed at the institution, who knows all of the local practices and idiosyncracies, and who is doing the job now without the benefit of the title.

I suspect that institutions who hire new professionals as catalogers expecting not to train them think they are saving money. To be sure, they are hiring the least expensive professional—the person without any experience—a person whose professional confidence is not yet established and who probably will not negotiate effectively for a higher salary. The directors and middle managers in these places are naive or stupid if they think they can just walk off and have this newly hired person do a good job all alone. One former student told me that after being hired as an entry-level cataloger she was given a nice tour of the library, including being shown where the OCLC terminal and the card catalog were, and then was told to get to work, which included supervising several support staff. These libraries will get what they pay for. As soon as their new catalogers get their bearings and accumulate some experience, they will leave.

MYTH 7: BEGINNING CATALOGING TEACHES YOU EVERYTHING YOU EVER NEEDED TO KNOW ABOUT CATALOGING

I hear practitioners say that they don't feel it is their job to teach someone with a professional degree how to use OCLC or catalog a rare book, a government document, or a video. It is definitely a myth that library schools teach students everything there is to know about cataloging in one semester (or even in two, if students opt to take an advanced course). How many of these employers found out whether the prospective employee had more than one cataloging course? Did they ask if the courses included OCLC experience—particularly the more "professional" tasks of profiling, making editing decisions, and setting up procedures for searching, inputting, and training nonprofessional personnel? Did they find out if the person was familiar with rare books, government documents, or special media? If these questions weren't asked or evidence produced to document competency, how can it be expected?

Teaching students the basics of cataloging monographic books (the curriculum in beginning cataloging courses in the six library schools in which I taught) can't prepare them to do original cataloging for other things—serials, nonbook materials, and so forth. It can't prepare them for the trickiest and most difficult materials, even if it includes an introduction to everything covered in AACR2, LCSH, and Dewey and LC classifications.

MYTH 8: WE DON'T HAVE TO HIRE INEXPERIENCED CATALOGERS

Another big myth held by personnel directors—especially in some large and prestigious libraries—is that they can acquire "turnkey catalogers" (see Myth 6) by hiring only experienced catalogers. Thus, they figure, someone else has done the training. This disregards everything common sense tells us about new jobs, new environments, and new situations. The larger the library and institutional setting, the more complex it is and the longer it takes a new employee to learn the ropes and adjust to it. This philosophy fails to take into account other factors that affect job performance: The person may still be getting used to a new neighborhood and new home or apartment—things psychologists tell us consume a great deal of a person's energy—as well as learning to live without the familiar places and people on whom he or she relied for companionship and support. One's family, friends, doctor, lawyer, hair stylist, druggist, and local librarian may be far away, and replacements or substitutes are needed before the person is 100 percent effective at work. It also ignores the need for every employee, experienced or not, to absorb local priorities, local politics, and local methods of getting things done.

Furthermore, it ignores a more pertinent issue, namely, that smaller, less research-oriented collections usually contain a far smaller proportion of esoteric materials requiring original cataloging. Experience with large numbers of difficult materials is hard to get in smaller libraries. Whether they like it or not, large, prestigious, research libraries have to spend a great deal of time, effort, *and* money training new catalogers until they achieve enough experience with the materials to feel confident confronting decisions that would discomfort a Salomon.

MYTH 9: COPY CATALOGERS DON'T NEED CATALOGING EDUCATION

The last notion I want to challenge is not a myth but a reality. It is the perception that paraprofessional copy catalogers don't need any preparation outside of what is provided by their supervisors. In truth, they need as much library school cataloging coursework as anyone else doing cataloging. I believe if they had it libraries might dispense with some costly revision processes and our network databases would be cleaner, contain higher quality information, and function more efficiently.

The problem with copy cataloging is that it requires high-level knowledge of certain kinds of detail that can be understood only in the context of theory. While copy catalogers don't need an MLS to do most of the work in run-of-the-mill public or college libraries, they always encounter a residue of material requiring professional decisions. Copy cataloging really can't be learned by imitating the entries found in network databases. Some entries are too old to be consistent with current standards while others suffer from lack of data or inaccuracies of various kinds.

So what can we do? That's easy. Send the cataloging clerk to library school for the one or two courses that will make him or her more effective on the job. In the long run the tuition for a course or two will not break the library budget, the trustees can boast about their generous staff development program, and, in the still longer run, the libraries and the networks to which they belong will reap the rewards in greater productivity and efficiency.

Another option, one that OCLC's PACNET experimented with in 1986, is for the networks to hold cataloging training sessions at the most basic level for nonprofessionals and professionals needing to upgrade their cataloging knowledge and skills. Library school faculty should teach such sessions, because what needs to be taught is not the latest change to the 007 field but the theories underlying AACR2, MARC, LCSH, and classification systems.

SUMMARY

To sum up: There are many myths about catalogers and cataloging. It is time to lay those myths to rest—especially among the library professionals who should know better.

- The myth is that catalogers are weak-kneed Milquetoasts. The reality is that catalogers have fallen from grace and are now lower paid than other types of librarians because of this perception. They need more than a big bite to become tigers. They need the same skills as others who succeed: knowledge and the talent to express it well, organization, foresight, and confidence.

- The myths are that cataloging courses are poorly taught and consist of only one kind of knowledge—either practical or theoretical, depending on where you are. The reality is that cataloging often is well taught, but it is a complex subject requiring more time than it is allotted in library school curriculums. Most cataloging professors try to teach a balance of theory and practice but lack the time in a single school term to provide students with important reinforcement and experience with a great many materials, something that can only be acquired over time.

- The myth is that practitioners can teach cataloging better than library school faculty. The reality is that full-time teachers also conduct research, counsel their students, and spend more time developing their teaching skills than practitioners. With few exceptions, I believe practitioners would lose to full-time faculty if they competed in a teach-off.

- The myth is that students hate cataloging. The reality is that cataloging is difficult and requires problem-solving and decision-making talent, both of which depend to a greater or lesser degree on knowledge, analytical skills, and confidence. Cataloging *is* intimidating, but it is an intellectual challenge furnishing many of the same satisfactions as solving puzzles and climbing mountains.

- The myths are that graduate librarians and/or experienced catalogers don't need on-the-job training. The reality is that they do, just like anyone else. Hiring someone cheap to do an expensive job is bound to fail. The MLS doesn't teach people institutional practices and politics, and knowledge takes time to acquire—all of which costs money. Large, prestigious libraries think they can avoid the issue by hiring people with experience. But there always are information gaps, and addressing them costs money.

- The final myth is that copy cataloging doesn't require cataloging knowledge. The reality is, it does.

6

Problems with the Catalog

I have been known to refer to the catalog as a great work of fiction. Supposedly the key to library holdings, the catalog sometimes betrays our trust. It leads us down blind alleys, helping to increase the frustration endemic in contemporary life and, all too often, in our encounters with bibliographic services. Sometimes the betrayal is our own fault—the result of a naive oversimplification of how cataloging information is disseminated.

For example, we say "the catalog" as if it were a monolith. We forget there are several parts to most libraries' catalogs and that no single one of them will satisfy Cutter's first object to show what the library has by an author, of a title, or on a subject. It would be less of a problem if each of the catalog's parts were relatively large, dividing the collection more or less equally. But that is rarely the case. Most often, monographic books comprise the preponderance of holdings and the catalog that contains information for them is much larger than those for other forms of material, e.g., serials, microforms, audiovisual materials, or special collections.

We forget that the boundaries of bibliographic units treated in cataloging records do not necessarily coincide with the boundaries of "works," if works are defined as intellectual units complete within themselves, capable of having authors, titles, and subjects. Application of the Rule of Three (i.e., if there are one, two, or three of something, such as authors, they are treated individually, but if there are more than three they are treated as a whole) limits the numbers of analytic added entries made for individual works contained in collections. When a book, recording, or micrographic set comprises many works—songs, poems, plays, stories, or books—it is tough enough to persuade catalogers to make contents notes listing the titles of individual works, let alone to trace each one. Budget-minded administrators would agree, since it is costly to make the notes and the added entries and to file and unfile them if the library still has manual catalogs. In addition, the added entries increase the size of the catalog, perhaps beyond what is efficient for the majority of searchers. (In truth, card catalogs in large libraries probably passed this magic measure, whatever it is, long ago.) Serials catalogs are designed to show only individual titles and library holdings for each, not the works contained within each issue. Periodical indexes provide that information, and we rely on bibliographic instruction courses to teach people about the indexes.

Both of these problems are explored further in chapters 22, 23, and 38, which focus on what could happen in a college library if a group of deteriorating materials was converted to microform sets without adequate bibliographic support. Not only can lay users become discombobulated, but even staff users may find their work affected by discontinuities in the catalog.

This chapter describes examples of catalog problems suffered by patrons and staff members in real libraries along with suggestions for solving some of them.

OFF-THE-SHELF PROBLEMS

A catalog record might or might not tell you when a book is off the shelf. (Our discussion applies equally to other items, but let's stick to books for now.)

There are several reasons why a book is not in its place when we go to retrieve it. It may be in circulation, returned but not yet reshelved, returned in such poor condition that it must be repaired or rebound before being reshelved, or removed — temporarily or otherwise — from the collection where we expected to find it (circulating, reference, reserves, adult, children's). For each of these alternatives, the average time that the book will continue to be off the shelf differs, as does the likelihood the library will alter its catalog record to inform persons trying to find it.

If a book is in circulation it is expected back by the end of the loan period, which varies from a week to a month in most libraries. For faculty loans at an academic library, the usual loan period is one term, or two to three months. The book might be renewed or held overdue. There always is a possibility it will never be brought back, although that happens to a relatively small proportion of circulating books.

Libraries generally do nothing to the catalog record of a borrowed book. Circulating books are supposed to be borrowed and, if one is not on the shelf, we can assume that someone has it out. But when a book is lent for a semester, shouldn't the catalog tell us that? If a library has an automated catalog integrated with its circulation control system or if the information is otherwise available, an estimate of a book's availability may be made. Still, it is only an estimate. Once a book leaves the library there are no guarantees about its return.

Some portion of every library's circulating collection is out at any one time — the larger the portion, the better — and, except for those few libraries with automated catalogs integrated with circulation, catalog records show no unavailability because they can't. When you want a new or popular item you expect it might be in use. If you are searching for an older book or one whose popularity passed long ago, you generally expect to find it waiting on the shelf. You might not bother to inquire about a new or popular book to see if it is overdue or lost. With an older book, however, you'll probably inquire about it. You may be surprised, sometimes, to find you have initiated a search process that goes on for weeks or months, again with no guarantee of success.

Circulation is considered a normal state, but repair and rebinding are not. (At least in the latter cases we can be pretty sure the item will come back; binderies usually return everything to the library, although they too may be late.) Sometimes catalog entries are flagged when books are sent to the bindery. In one library, color-coded cellophane wrappers are put over author and title cards when the last copies (or only copies) of the books are sent to the bindery. It is expensive to maintain such a service in large libraries with many books needing repair (especially if there are few titles with multiple copies), but it does allow searchers to make informed choices about whether to wait for an item's return. In other libraries, lists of books sent to the bindery are kept in the technical services department, the circulation desk, or both to answer inquiries from unsuccessful searchers. Libraries with automated systems can check books out to an artificial patron called "Bindery." The due date is set for six weeks, two months, or the average length of time for binding and return of the material. But if the circulation records are not tied in with the catalog entries, the catalog won't supply this information.

WHERE'S THE SHELF?

Libraries of all types may have special shelving set aside for new books. This fact is not usually indicated on the catalog record. The regular call number appears on the record and librarians assume everyone knows about the special location of new book sections. Casual searchers are likely to miss these books unless they happen on them by accident. The parameters for inclusion in special new book sections (or, conversely, for exclusion from them) are not always clearly defined. Sometimes new books are defined as all books published in the previous year or all books received within a specific period; sometimes only a selection of new books are kept apart from the regular shelves. How selections are made and whether the weeding and reshelving of books is done religiously are things we don't always know. The catalog entry is usually silent on these subjects, too.

Relocating books from the collection in which they were originally housed is another discontinuity that the catalog may or may not reflect. I am thinking particularly about college and university libraries, in which books are taken off circulating shelves and put on reserve for a term but no changes are made to the catalog record. If you needed one of those books for a different class, you would not know to search the reserve lists to find it. For the duration of the class for which it is a reserve item, that book probably is lost to you.

Public libraries have their own kinds of relocations, the favorite one being the new book shelves. They intend to make selected items more visible, but the result may make it trickier than ever to find something using just the catalog and common sense. For instance, in one public library young adult fiction is interfiled with the children's fiction collection, while young adult nonfiction is interfiled with the adult nonfiction collection. The call number doesn't reflect the difference, since it is only the normal class number preceded by *YA*. The logic of the relocation escapes me now, but I am sure there was a reason when it was inaugurated. Someone using the catalog for young adult literature might assume there is a young adult section in the library, but there isn't. A person asking about young adult fiction might erroneously assume that nonfiction is found in the same general area, but it isn't.

Another library changed its policy on classifying biographies from giving them all *B* for Biography, to intershelving them with the biographees' associated disciplines, shifting almost all of the existing collection. While the new policy was consistent with current classification trends, catalog records were never updated, leaving patrons to fend for themselves.

The same library, because it was planning a move from a card file to an online catalog, stopped pulling the catalog entries for discards several years before the online catalog was finally implemented. Imagine the confusion about that!

Even when the catalog shows a correct call number, it is no guarantee a book will be easily found. Do the shelves in your local library run from 000 to 999 without interruption? Or from A to Z if the library uses the Library of Congress classification? How about those mixed classification libraries that switched from Dewey to LC in the 1960s or 1970s but never got around to reclassifying the old books?

Is it clear which mysteries are shelved in the mystery section and which in the fiction section? In the public library where I once worked, the catalog gave call numbers accurately enough, *M* for the mystery section and *Fic* for fiction, but patrons who thought they had found all of Agatha Christie's books in the mystery section were surprised to find different titles on the fiction shelves and still others in the short story collection. The difference in that library was the presence of a dead body. If there wasn't a dead body, a book didn't qualify as a mystery even if it was by an author whose other works were all shelved as mysteries. And, of course, if there were more than three stories in a book, it went to the short story shelves.

PUNISHMENTS THAT FIT
THE CRIMES

Most libraries are content to live with the errors of omission and commission that creep into their catalogs over time—errors in filing, entries for discarded or lost books that are not removed, entries for books owned that wait in backlogs to be filed, errors in call numbers and headings, cross-references that lead nowhere, and other similar phenomena. But each error represents a betrayal of searchers' trust that the catalog—the key to the collections—will lead them to the books they want. These are information service's little crimes. They may be misdemeanors perpetrated under the most extenuating circumstances, but cumulatively they undermine the foundation on which information service rests. If you can't trust the catalog, what recourse is there?

Quality control in catalogs is often equated with authority control (an important component of quality, we would agree) and with professional catalogers' careful revision of filing done by clerical staff members, a time-honored procedure. These two quality control measures are supposed to insure that everything in the catalog is correctly entered and filed. What more can be done?

The following suggestions address the problems outlined above. Like authority control and revision of filing, they are not inexpensive to implement but they keep your catalog from lying to its users and destroying their trust. In the long run they should prove cost effective, since they help insure better service to both patrons and staff.

1. If you do not have computerized circulation and cataloging linked to provide status information with catalog entries, think about flagging the records of books that are removed from their rightful places for any length of time greater than an ordinary loan, including those shelved in a

special new book section, sent to the bindery, charged out to a professor for half the academic year, or relocated in a reserve collection for one school term or longer. It saves a lot of grief for the searcher who isn't savvy enough or persistent enough to track down the missing items.

Card entries for new books could bear a self-sticking removable label over the call number to indicate their temporary location. When the books go back to the regular stacks, the label can be peeled off. Use a good grade of label so when the time comes to peel them off there is no residue. Computer-based entries might have an appropriate notation programmed to self-destruct after a certain period of time or to be deleted easily with a single command. (This would also work for COM files that are updated often.)

Older books present more of a problem, but self-stick labels for cards marked "Removed for reserve" (or "binding," "term loan," etc.) or similar electronic notations for computer-based entries would nip unsuccessful shelf searches in the bud and lower the number of inquiries for missing materials at public service desks.

2.   Make shelf discontinuities clear in catalog records. If young adult fiction is shelved in a different department than young adult nonfiction, make it plain in the call number: YA Fiction (shelved in Children's Room); YA973 (shelved with adult books). This may give librarians reason to discontinue some of these artificial discontinuities. Take all that young adult literature and give it a home of its own or try intershelving it in one place or the other. Why further complicate an already over-complicated system?

Think about doing the same for related books split by the presence of two classification systems. Have both companion call numbers listed on each entry: 025.3 (see also Z695) and Z695 (see also 025.3). Having to create dual call numbers might well motivate you to plan for the elimination of the split within a reasonable period of time.

3.   Do a little continuing research on the number of errors in your catalogs. Decide what error rate you will tolerate and keep it to that level. Don't castigate the filers, revisers, inputters, or catalogers for mistakes. Remember they are human and are bound to commit some errors. Offer prizes to correct errors, not to discover them. One error may be compounded, e.g., one misfiled card will usually create a whole misfiled section behind it. Filing errors may be eliminated in computer-based files that rely on automatic filing, but computer-based files are not free of other kinds of errors, as we all discover sooner or later.

The extra costs of maintaining a high-quality catalog should be offset by greater efficiencies in searching, which in turn should affect the amount of reference work that has to be done. Here is an area for experimental research, perhaps for a dissertation. Librarians need to know if better cataloging is just spinning wheels or if it gives real value that can be measured in patron service. My money is on real service. What about yours?

Functional Inaccessibility
in Libraries

What is functional inaccessibility? I define it much like functional illiteracy. People who are functionally illiterate may have gone through school, taken the required number of courses, gone to the required number of classes, taken the tests, passed in the homework, and come out with diplomas or degrees. Nevertheless, for all practical purposes these people are illiterate. They can't read well enough to fill out forms, read the newspaper, or understand signs. Functionally illiterate people also may have trouble with simple mathematics, such as computing interest or making change. The admission by some well-known professional athletes that they learned nothing in four years of college despite receiving their baccalaureate diplomas attests to the fact that the problem of functional illiteracy goes beyond elementary or secondary education.

I contend that there are materials in libraries that are functionally inaccessible. These are materials that have gone through all of the library's traditional bibliographic processes, received typical bibliographic treatments, and have come out with all the trappings of accessibility—catalog records containing bibliographic descriptions, subject headings, and call numbers; spine labels; and cards and pockets or whatever computer-readable labels are used instead. Nevertheless, they cannot be retrieved from the catalog or from the shelf by ordinary library clients unaided by a librarian. And this inaccessibility sometimes continues even when the search is done by an expert, e.g., a reference librarian.

What kinds of functional inaccessibility are there? What causes these problems? What can be done about recognizing functional inaccessibility in our libraries? What can we do about it?

TYPES OF FUNCTIONAL INACCESSIBILITY

There may be and probably are many types of functional inaccessibility but, abiding by the librarians' traditional Rule of Three, I will mention only that many: works published together in groups; monographic works cataloged or classified as part of a series; and split files.

Works Published in Groups

Two distinct kinds of works are represented by this type of functional inaccessibility: works published as serial articles and works published in anthologies. In both instances, however, the result is the same. Library clients fail to have direct access to the individual works, regardless of their lengths or viability as complete intellectual entities, solely because they are published within the issues of a serial title or between the covers of an anthology. It used to be that when the number of works published together totaled only two or three, each work would be cataloged separately, but those treatments have all but disappeared in today's cataloging.

Monographic Works Cataloged or Classified as Part of a Series

Somewhere in the twilight zone between monographs and serials lies the monographic series—a hapless lot of monographs (i.e., finite publications) brought out in a somewhat less open-ended grouping than a serial (i.e., an infinite publication). When a library treats a monographic series on the series level, it indexes, classifies, and shelves the individual volumes in the series together under one group of headings or one call number assigned to the series as a whole. It doesn't matter whether these headings or numbers are appropriate to the individual volumes, and it is done despite the fact that each volume has its own title and is likely to constitute a distinct work in the minds of potential users.

Split Files

The opposite of dealing with many things under one umbrella, which roughly describes the first two types of functional inaccessibility, is dividing and separating things that belong together and are purported to be found together. The term *split files* as used here refers not only to runs of catalog records fragmented unintentionally into two or more author, title, or subject files, it also includes the unintentional and undesirable presence of two or more catalogs and multiple shelf-groups of materials that one would suppose are integrated into a unified whole. When searchers find one of the fragments they think they have the whole, investing functional inaccessibility upon the other fragments of the file, catalog, or shelf of materials.

CAUSES OF
FUNCTIONAL INACCESSIBILITY

The 3 x 5 Mentality

Maintaining a 3 x 5 mentality in the face of modern information production is one cause of functional inaccessibility.

For more than three-quarters of a century, from about 1900 until the advent of computer technology and online bibliographic systems in the 1980s, librarians dealt with bibliographic information displayed on 3 x 5 cards. Many librarians still handle bibliographic information in this form. Although the term *3 x 5 mentality* now stands for limited or diminished information, it is amazing how much data standard 3 x 5 catalog cards were able to carry. For the most part, complete bibliographic records for items—call numbers, tracings, full descriptions, headings, and control numbers—fit on a single card measuring approximately 15 square inches (minus the hole for the metal rod that anchored it into its drawer). Multiple cards for one item were rare, testimony to catalogers' abilities to condense and abbreviate data deemed essential for identification and retrieval of the item.

The key word here is *essential*.

Changes in the volume of publishing, publication patterns, and the physical formats in which intellectual works are manifested gave rise to changes in our perceptions of how much and what kinds of bibliographic data are essential. The 3 x 5 card was designed with books in mind—to be specific, books containing one work written by one author and confined to one subject. Contemporary literature being what it is we no longer deal solely with books nor, among the books we do handle, with works that can be described fully in a 3 x 5 space. Publications appear in many editions and physical forms, some of which take a great deal of space to describe adequately. Individual works may be about several topics or interdisciplinary topics and may be produced by collaborations among people sharing the same responsibilities or making contributions of different kinds. Physical formats have become so dense that one physical item can contain dozens, hundreds, or even thousands of works that if published individually might fill up several shelves or a library stack. Yet we continue to treat them all like books containing one work by one author on a single topic.

The Vise of Tradition

The 1990s librarian works in a transitional era, one in which traditional methods based on card technology still guide policies and procedures even for computer-based systems.

Observing the Rule of Three (still visible in the *Anglo-American Cataloguing Rules*, or AACR2R), failing to consider alternatives to summary-level bibliographic treatments, and assuming that once an item is cataloged or classified no further work ever needs to be done to enhance accessibility—all are evidence that we operate in the thrall of tradition. Given the potential for automatic filing and rapid retrieval of entries by computer, we could discard the Rule of Three or omit from AACR2R the complex rules for selection of primary and secondary entries that confuse catalogers and dirty our databases, yet we cling to these remnants of the card catalog era. Computer displays are contrived to resemble the ones that appear on 3 x 5 cards, and search options beyond the three types mandated by Charles A. Cutter in 1876 (i.e., author, title, and subject) are not exactly ubiquitous. Do librarians really believe that members of the public will be paralyzed by catalog records exceeding the 3 x 5 inch boundary?

While it is foolish to expect that traditional methods will disappear quickly, especially since card catalogs remain in use, some librarians—including this author—worry that they will linger indefinitely, hampering and slowing the adoption of a new, more client-centered perspective on bibliographic access and control.

The Penniless Librarian

Functional inaccessibility is perpetuated by slashed budgets and short-run accountability.

Nearly every remedy for functional inaccessibility costs more money than maintaining the status quo. Dollars are precious, practitioners tell me, too precious to waste on improvements to access systems. Librarians are too poor to recatalog or reclassify anything, too poor to buy computers if they don't have any (or better ones if they do), too poor to pay for the kind of programming that would enhance searching capabilities in the computer-based bibliographic systems they have, too poor to do complete retrospective conversions, too poor to do analytic cataloging, too poor to increase the number of cross-references, too poor to do anything that would diminish functional inaccessibility.

Catalog departments are judged on the size of their output, not the quality, understandability, or ease of use of their products. In a great many libraries any product will do. In the short term what counts are the numbers—units cataloged, classified, and shelved, measured against the cost of the resources to do it. The larger the number of units treated and the cheaper the resources used, the better.

Yet librarians assume people using libraries can make their way with minimal help from the experts. Reference librarians, who are busy selecting materials, planning programs, or doing the other things they are assigned so they don't just sit at the desk waiting for someone to approach them with a question, think people should be able to search catalogs alone and never mind the things that aren't in them; that showing clients how to use an index or two should educate them about using all indexes and never mind that even the simplest indexes contain idiosyncratic arrangements and peculiar terminology; that call numbers are easy to search and never mind that some items are shelved in special locations (new acquisitions, large print, oversized, reserve book room, request only) or are divided among old and new classifications (biographies, bibliographies, law materials) or reside in any one of several possible locations. I wonder if library administrators admit how much it costs to provide reference assistance for clients who can't make heads or tails of inadequate bibliographic systems? Have they looked carefully and objectively at the potential of better access systems? (Sharon Baker did just that and obtained hard data to show that classification for fiction was helpful to people using collections of certain sizes.[1])

RECOGNIZING
FUNCTIONAL INACCESSIBILITY

It is easy to recognize functional inaccessibility in your library. Just try walking in your clients' shoes. Search for things the way clients do. Keep a tally of every client request that begins, "I looked for _____ in the catalog (or on the shelves), but I didn't find it." Discover why people don't succeed with your bibliographic systems by trying them out yourselves. If the reason they fail is that the material isn't part of your collection, you can congratulate yourself. This will happen a good part of the time. But if the reason they fail is that the bibliographic unit is too small, that browsing isn't possible in a part of the stacks where material needs reclassification, that the desired item is part of a series classified differently, or that the catalog being searched only contains material cataloged after 1985, you have discovered functional inaccessibility in your library.

SOLVING THE PROBLEM OF
FUNCTIONAL INACCESSIBILITY

Don't assume it is a law of nature or a rule of information retrieval that one should not find a catalog record for a discrete work in the library's catalog because the work is one of several in an anthology or one title in a monographic series. Don't assume that ordinary people using libraries keep track of changes in catalog displays, classifications, shelving practices, subject descriptors, filing practices, or any of the other details of library organization.

Why should the library client always be wrong? Why should lay people have to think like librarians to use libraries? We can adopt an approach that has proved its worth in business and begin with the assumption that the customer (i.e., the library user) is always right. Instead of looking at things the way a librarian does we can try looking at them the way the customer does.

Instead of creating bibliographic records the way we do because that is what fits on the 3 x 5 card, for example, we can consider alternatives that make things easier for ordinary people. We might eliminate abbreviations. We could add many more analytic entries or do analytic cataloging for some types of materials. We might make tables of contents searchable, if not in the main catalog then in a special local index. We can pay for complete retrospective conversions and make integrated files a high priority. We could pay for more and better search capabilities in our computerized catalogs. We might take up Bates's suggestion to add a searchable Superthesaurus as a user-friendly front-end guide to online files using Library of Congress subject descriptors.[2] We can eliminate anomalies in shelving.

We can focus our attention on eliminating functional inaccessibility and reap some benefits in return. For one thing, it should enable us to make better use of the materials we own. Second, it will admit and address the fact that assistance from librarians is not always available or forthcoming. Third, it will help mitigate against embarrassing the sometime library client whose knowledge of libraries is limited or whose searching skills in a particular subject are inadequate. It seems to me that making materials accessible is a particularly professional task, something librarians know how to do and other people don't. Shouldn't we use that knowledge for the benefit of our clients?

And, for that matter, we can focus attention as a profession on eliminating functional illiteracy, too — something thought important enough a decade ago to be included in the list of high priority recommendations at the First White House Conference on Libraries and Information Services.[3]

NOTES

[1]Sharon L. Baker, "Will Fiction Classification Schemes Increase Use?" *RQ* 27 (Spring 1988):366-76.

[2]Marcia J. Bates, "Rethinking Subject Cataloging in the Online Environment," *Library Resources & Technical Services* 33 (Oct. 1989):400-412.

[3]White House Conference on Library and Information Services 1979. Resolutions (Washington, D.C.: U.S.G.P.O., 1980).

8

Dialectic Retrievalism: Looking Closely at the Objects of the Catalog

The objects of the catalog, formulated by Charles A. Cutter and used to introduce his *Rules for a Dictionary Catalog* in 1876, form the basic theory governing library cataloging and indexing rules and practice. After more than one hundred years, Cutter's objects are not dimmed in their vitality or influence. No theoretical article worth its salt dares begin without an iteration of the objects and an interpretation of findings within the context they set. For better or worse, Cutter's objects are what was, is, and very likely will be for some time to come *the* definitive statement of cataloging theory. The problem is that the objects are a dialectic and, like all dialectics, contain seeds of conflict within them.

Dialectic materialism, Karl Marx's socio-politico-economic theory of history that claimed that the capitalist system contained the seeds of its own destruction, furnishes an interesting comparison. Marx claimed that, over time historic phenomena could be understood in terms of a formula describing the dynamics of elemental forces, which might be expressed as

$$\text{Thesis x Antithesis} = \text{Synthesis}$$

or, in terms of developing socio-politico-economic behavior,

$$\text{Capitalism x Proletariat} = \text{Communism}$$

In everyday terms, Marx believed that the capitalist ruling class generated its own opposite, i.e., a unified group of the underclasses called the proletariat. Furthermore, the inevitable clash between the two was destined to result in a state of perfect balance or synthesis, which in Marx's view was Communism.

Unlike Marx, Cutter saw his objects not as a dialectic, but as a combination.

$$\text{Identification} + \text{Collocation} = \text{Catalog}$$

45

Lubetzky and subsequent theorists appear to agree. There is, however, a different way to view the objects. In this chapter the possibility that the objects follow the formula

$$\text{Identification x Collocation} = \text{Catalog}$$

is explored. I call this theory Dialectic Retrievalism, since the catalog is primarily a retrieval mechanism.

THESIS AND ANTITHESIS

The equation representing Cutter's combination theory implies that first the processes of identification are executed, then the processes of collocation are added, and voila! we have a catalog. No conflict is recognized. No problems are encountered. Librarians operate on these assumptions, but they do not reflect reality. True, in most original cataloging operations, descriptive cataloging precedes selection of entries and assignment of subject headings and classification numbers. This would seem to follow Cutter's formula of description plus collocation if you accept the notion that description equals identification and entries of all kinds equal collocation. A case can be made for equating description and identification. The theory breaks down when you try to equate entries with collocation.

The reason entries do not equal collocation has to do with the vagaries of publishing or producing and marketing. Obviously, if the cataloger wanted to maximize the identification value of entries, he or she would use the names and titles that appear on the item being cataloged as headings to represent it. Instead, catalogers usually translate the names and titles into their best-known forms—which may or may not coincide with what is printed on the item. Although titles proper, series titles, and alternative titles are transcribed as given on the item, they are not necessarily traced that way. The transcribed titles may be superseded by uniform titles or series titles that are traced differently.

The reason for doing these arcane things is to collocate both the items themselves and the works they represent under a single form of name or title rather than to disperse them throughout the catalog according to whether the publishers or producers choose to use Edwin Abbott or A. Square for the author of *Flatland*; *Alice in Wonderland* or *Alice's Adventures in Wonderland* for the title of the story; and H.D. or Hilda Doolittle for the name of the poet. Publishers, producers, and distributors probably use the forms of names and titles they believe are most likely to sell more of their product, whether that product is a book, film, video, microform, or software package. If I were selling a video of *Carmen* that was beautifully sung by Placido Domingo, I would certainly bring his name into the chief source of bibliographic information, perhaps calling the work *Placido Domingo's Carmen*. A modern publisher of a classic work written by a pseudonymous author may believe that using the author's real name lends scholarliness to the new edition and makes it more appealing to the college market.

Clearly, the processes that identify an item uniquely and those that bring the item and the work it embodies together with related works conflict. Steps taken to enhance identification, such as the transcription of titles proper and statements of responsibility exactly as they appear on title pages, may fragment related works. Steps taken to enhance collocation, such as using only one form of a name, title, series title, or descriptor, may obscure identification unless cross-references supply the missing links. While it is correct to say that we impose (I hesitate to use that naughty word *superimpose*) collocation upon identification, it is incorrect to call it a simple case of addition.

SYNTHESIS

I think most catalogers believe that the conflicts are resolved in the catalog. They believe the catalog is a synthesis or a perfect balance that transcends all conflict. Indeed, many conflicts might be resolved by cross-references, e.g., from one form of name to another or from one title spelling or wording to another. The cross-reference mechanism can furnish links between identification and collocation if it is employed to the fullest. Unfortunately, it is not usually so employed because there is never enough money to do the job and because if one spends cataloging budget on extensive authority work and syndetics, insufficient production results. There are other problems, too.

In the first place, definitions of *item* and *work* are not identical, although in cataloging we assume that they are. Cutter's objects are based on this false assumption. An item is a bibliographical unit — a physical manifestation of a work or works — while a work is an intellectual or artistic unit with a beginning, a middle, and an end — an intellectual representation that may or may not be contained within a single bibliographic unit. When libraries were made up of collections of books and when most individual books contained single works, catalogers did not have to worry much about discrepancies between works and items. There weren't many discrepancies and those that did exist, e.g., anthologies of poetry, essays, short stories, and so forth, could be squeezed into the one work equals one item model if they had collective titles, editors, and other trappings that could be analogized with the norm.

With few exceptions (most notably periodicals, which many libraries did not bother to catalog at all), the library as a collection of books persisted into the middle of the twentieth century. But as the number of informational media collected by libraries multiplied and, more recently, as the density of individual media increased immensely (that is, as the number of works likely to be contained in a single physical item multiplied from one work in a book to hundreds or thousands of works in a microform, a CD-ROM disk, or a database), catalogers were faced with a choice: treat the works or treat the items. Cataloging rules taught them to treat the items. Considering the circumstances of library cataloging — decreasing budgets and staffs, increasing flow of materials — and the techniques in use, even at this writing — labor-intensive original cataloging and extensive editing of online cataloging copy — one cannot fault their decision.

To be sure, there are options for treating works as basic bibliographic units whether they are contained in a whole physical unit or only part of it, i.e., analytic cataloging, but these options are rarely exercised and in no way can they be thought of as mainstream practice. Whether a cataloger believes it to be right or wrong in theory, analytic cataloging is costly and therefore is unlikely to gain a large following. Without a large following, analytic cataloging is unlikely to be legitimized by cataloging or indexing rules. As a result, even though you know its author and title, you cannot retrieve most editions of Longfellow's "The

Midnight Ride of Paul Revere" in the catalog, simply because it is unlikely to be cataloged or even traced separately from other poems in an anthology.

The inescapable conclusion is that the library catalog is not designed to show what works are in the library but what books and other bibliographic units are there. Librarians rely on commercial indexes to poems, songs, plays, and other short works collected in anthologies to guide them to the individual works. Because these indexes are purchased and used primarily by librarians who work directly with the public, they constitute a reference tool controlled and evaluated by reference librarians and have nothing whatever to do with the library's catalog or the people who manage it.

Practical matters, especially the cost of cataloging and the time it takes, interfere with and destroy Cutter's combination theory. Those practical matters are translated into the rules we make, e.g., the Rule of Three. Application of the Rule of Three insures that you will *not* find a work for which more than three persons or corporate bodies are responsible if you know only the names of its authors. Application of the Rule of Three allows catalogers to drop the names of subsequent authors from any mention at all in a catalog entry, thereby eliminating any possibility of linking their names and works through the catalog, even if someone succeeded in retrieving the work by title, subject, or first author.

Differences among physical media create wide differences in bibliographic treatment, too. In Cutter's day people walked into a library expecting to find Shakespeare's *Othello* in print form. There might be several versions, e.g., a book or one item in an anthology of Shakespeare's works. Today, however, people find *Othello* in at least three media—print, sound, and film/video—and each media group might have several different versions. For example, in sound recordings you might find the whole play or excerpts; in films or videos you might find the play as Shakespeare might have staged it or as a modern production. Practicality also dictates that, because some catalogers can examine nonprint items that require playback equipment while catalogers without the equipment cannot, both must be accommodated with different but equally valid sources of bibliographic data. Thus, even if two libraries have the same item they may catalog them differently, depending on which source of bibliographic information is used—the title and credits screens (for the catalogers with a VCR or projector) or the labels and accompanying textual material (for the cataloger without hardware). Failure to add uniform titles results in a lack of collocation.

Failure to do authority work virtually insures that the catalog will fail to collocate all the works of an author using more than one name, all editions of a title given more than one title proper, and all works on a subject. Even more distressing, studies repeatedly show that when subject authority work *is* carefully done, all works on a topic are not located with the use of only one subject heading. This occurs for a variety of reasons. The more specific one's descriptors, the more they will fragment a particular body of related literature. Furthermore, when catalogs are divided by medium they fragment more than just the material on a topic; they also fragment the works of authors as well as editions and versions of titles. Perfectly collocated files for authors, titles, and subjects are not without their retrieval problems, either. If searchers make one pass at a catalog and give up whether or not they succeed in finding what they want, which is typical, even a fully developed system of cross-references will fail. In plain words: If the entry says *See* _____ and the searcher refuses to make the effort to see it, Cutter's first object—simple identification—is destroyed. Also, if the searcher's vocabulary does not match the vocabulary of the catalog and no entry exists for the term the searcher is using, failure is certain.

CONCLUSION

The foregoing discussion demonstrated that the objects of the catalog are essentially in conflict. It also showed that the work needed to resolve the conflicts, being costly and time-consuming, is likely to go undone. For some searchers, even a perfectly identified and collocated file fails to furnish perfect retrieval success. Do we need a new theory of the catalog? Perhaps. The idea is explored in the next chapter.

Solutions for
Dialectic Retrievalism

The previous chapter discussed the possibility that Cutter's vision of the library catalog as a combination of identification (which we call description) and collocation (which we call access—both descriptive and subject) might be incorrect. It suggested that the catalog operates instead as a dialectic in which the activities that promote identification inhibit collocation and vice versa. Examples of the conflict included the inability to retrieve the works of an author when the works don't coincide with cataloging units (for example, individual works collected in a single book) and the inability to retrieve all the works of an author or on a subject when multiple names or subject headings are used without cross-references from unused forms or, when references were present, when searchers failed to follow through. I named this essential conflict Dialectic Retrievalism and claimed that the work needed to resolve it—analytic cataloging, careful and consistent authority work for access points, and copious cross-references—is likely to go undone because it is costly and time-consuming.

What can be done? We might look for a new theory of the catalog. This chapter explores three possible theories: the Probabilistic Catalog, the Relative Catalog, and the Bifurcated Catalog.

THE PROBABILISTIC CATALOG

One solution is that librarians cease subscribing to the fiction that the catalog is the key to all library collections and accept that it is an incomplete tool capable of producing varying degrees of retrieval success depending on a number of factors. I call this the Probabilistic Catalog. The job of experts in bibliographic access would be to assign the probabilities that searches will be successful. This could be done for individual searching parameters by doing research and developing theories that relate to the various elements of retrieval.

Instead of teaching young clients that the catalog contains records for all library holdings and that they can find anything if they know its author, title, or subject, children and adults learning about access to the information resources of libraries would be taught that the catalog contains records for many—perhaps most, but definitely not all—of the library's holdings and that they can find a portion of the records if they know the authors, titles, or subjects. The important lesson is the more information they can contribute to the search, the higher their success rate will be, provided the desired item is there to be found. If searchers know only one part of the retrieval combination — author, title, or subject — they should know what their odds are of success or failure in locating the desired material. Furthermore, beginning searchers should be made aware of the varying efficiencies of searching the names of authors versus titles versus subjects, instead of being led to believe that the three types of access points are equally effective or that authors' names are always the first to search. Titles generally are more efficient access points and they certainly are a better place to look for books that have many authors or editors, few of whom will be traced. Compilers of bibliographies and other kinds of reading lists should be made aware of the value of unique identifiers as retrieval aids (ISBNs, LCCNs, OCLC and RLIN control numbers), particularly in online catalogs, and they should be urged to include them as potential access points whenever possible.

In the real world of Probabilistic Catalogs, if you look for a book by a single author who writes under only one form of name, the probability is high — perhaps even 100 percent — that the search will be successful. If you look for a Beatles' song on a sound recording anthology titled *Greatest Hits of the 'Sixties*, the probability is very low that the search will be successful. The probabilities of success in performing various types of searches can be calculated in much the same way we calculate odds for any other set of alternatives, from the toss of a coin to getting caught in the rain on a cloudy day. Catalog research can determine the likelihood of finding various kinds of materials using different search strategies. Library clients can be taught about success rates for each type of search and they can approach the catalog much more knowledgeably.

The probabilistic solution will not be satisfying for those librarians who have grown accustomed to believing in the Perfect Catalog. For, despite all the complaints of reference librarians about the inadequacies of the catalog, frequently joined by acquisition librarians in pre-order searching units, a united front is presented to clients about the catalog's infallibility. We have created a Frankenstein and by doing so we have made members of the public feel foolish and frustrated when they fail at the catalog. Most important of all, we've made them believe it is all their fault.

THE RELATIVE CATALOG

Einstein's theory of relativity states a relationship between energy and matter: Energy equals matter times the speed of light squared, or

$$E = mc^2$$

This theory enabled Einstein to predict that huge amounts of energy could be released from within very tiny bits of matter multiplied by the exponential constant. Unfortunately for Einstein, this equation doesn't relate all forces in the universe to one another. Although Einstein and other mathematicians and physicists have searched for such a unified theory, none has been found.

Applying similar principles to a new Theory of the Catalog, we might say that retrieval equals information times accuracy times fullness divided by presence of the item in a particular database, collection, or catalog, or

$$R = Iaf/P$$

where P equals 1 if a particular item is present in the database, collection, or catalog and P equals 0 when it is absent. Absence of the item negates the physical reality of the answer.

Clearly, retrieval mushrooms when I, a, and f are positive whole numbers and decreases enormously when any of them are fractional or negative. I call this the Relative Catalog. While it doesn't integrate everything into the equation, such as the requirements of the searcher, this idea dramatizes the relative power of the elements it covers and allows us to continue searching for a unified theory of retrieval.

The Relative Catalog recognizes that it takes more than information to effect retrieval. It takes full and accurate information *and* the presence of the desired item in the database, collection, or catalog to maximize retrieval. It demonstrates that retrieval is negated by the absence of the item and that imperfection (i.e., fractionalization) in the elements of retrieval (information, accuracy, fullness) reduces but doesn't completely eliminate the possibility of retrieving something. This appears to be a more realistic representation of catalogs than Cutter's notion that information guarantees retrieval, regardless of its accuracy and fullness and regardless of the item's findability.

THE BIFURCATED CATALOG:
CATALOG AND INDEX

The Bifurcated Catalog is exactly what the name implies: a divided, forked, or twinned catalog. The bifurcation is simple: The catalog's twin or secondary version is an index in which the information likely to be missing or unavailable from the catalog is given. Both catalog and index must be available to the public and both must be used to maximize searching success.

Librarians are accustomed to using indexes to locate certain kinds of library materials—articles in periodicals; individual poems, plays, or stories in anthologies; or reviews in review digests; and so forth. These are used, however, for classes of items that are not customarily cataloged at all. Librarians are not accustomed to having indexes to the catalog itself. We think the catalog is the index to the library. Librarians must rethink this notion and begin to appreciate the value of catalog indexes to the public.

One of the main differences between library catalogs and other types of bibliographic lists is that the former usually include only the holdings of their institutions, not those of other libraries. Of course, this is not true of commercial indexes or databases. While commercial indexes to periodicals and to anthologies may be marked to show which of the titles indexed are held by the library, this cannot be done online for databases. In fact, one of the criticisms of searching giant online bibliographic databases is that so many of the items might be unavailable on the shelves of the local institution. Librarians should consider creating indexes to those items in the collection that are not sufficiently indexed in the catalog; these indexes could be created not on an item-by-item basis but according to the category of material. The catalog would be replaced by the combination catalog-and-index or, as I call it, the Bifurcated Catalog. You may think that this duplicates the coverage of commercial indexes and to some degree it does. The primary difference is that what appears in the local library's index is immediately available to the public, whereas what appears in commercial indexes may be inaccessible. The main benefit is the ability to exploit the materials owned by the library more fully.

Librarians are trained specialists in the science of information storage and retrieval. Yet we do a superficial, summary-level job of storage and then expect clients to do their own retrieval. What kind of professional information service is that? The Bifurcated Catalog could give local librarians a chance to do what they are trained to do — create information products and services — instead of leaving that creative part to commercial publishers and database producers. Some very valuable information retrieval tools began as local projects of ambitious, far-sighted, service-oriented librarians, e.g., *Poole's Index* and the *Dewey Decimal Classification*. These days, if an information tool isn't prepared for librarians, marketed to librarians, reviewed in a library periodical, and demanded by the public whose needs librarians are supposed to anticipate and serve, librarians might ignore it.

CONCLUSION

All three solutions to Dialectic Retrievalism have one thing in common: they regard the catalog as the imperfect tool it is. The Probabilistic Catalog suggests making the imperfections clear to all who enter our hallowed halls, in effect warning them to look beyond the catalog for comprehensive retrieval. Indeed, comprehensive retrieval itself may be a fiction. The Probabilistic Catalog assigns a passive role to catalogers, who merely measure success rates for a tool that is a given in the equation.

The Relative Catalog explains the principles underlying the whole retrieval process. When clients search the catalog with imperfect information they are destined to fall below the threshold of potential total success; only full and accurate information are likely to insure it. The Relative Catalog puts the burden of effort squarely on the searcher, who must be precise, accurate, and in tune with the catalog to get the best results. Again the cataloger is cast in a passive role, but this time offering a warning: *Caveat Lector!*

The Bifurcated Catalog recognizes that catalogs as we know them today are no longer able to fulfill Cutter's objects without the addition of supplementary indexes. It also sounds a clarion call to librarians as information storage and retrieval specialists to be more creative in solving local problems and in achieving easy and effective access geared to their own clients and holdings.

All three ideas of the catalog avoid depending on the Library of Congress or anyone else to do the job for local catalogers. A century of debate about the differing needs of school, public, college, university, and special library users as well as the differences among urban, suburban, and rural populations, young and old, educated and uneducated, dedicated and casual library clients, and so on, should be proof enough that no outside entity can produce a single tool for all of these populations. No catalog intended for the most sophisticated searchers in the country can be equally effective for use by very young children, newly literate adults, or a host of other people who are excellent library clients who deserve a catalog they can use easily and well. Local catalogs need to be made effective for local searchers by local catalogers who know the territory. The helpful searching tools created by local librarians, including the indexes of the Bifurcated Catalog and the list of success rates of the Probabilistic Catalog, must relate to specific collections and populations.

All of these solutions imply that librarians are responsible for doing more for the public than merely pointing out the catalog. At the very least, librarians must explain what the catalog can't do and what clients can do to improve their success in using it. At best, librarians can enrich the catalog, interpret it, add to it, and generally perform the functions for which library school prepared them.

10
The Case for AACR3

The Joint Steering Committee for the Revision of the *Anglo-American Cataloguing Rules* (JSC) and the bodies they represent — library associations and national libraries of the English-speaking countries who sponsor and publish AACR2, our standard rules for descriptive cataloging — issued a new version of the code in 1988. The updated AACR2 incorporated all of the many changes approved by the committee since 1978 (which were issued in three packages of supplementary pages in 1982, 1983, and 1985) as well as other changes approved between 1985 and 1987 that had appeared in the United States only in the pages of the Library of Congress *Cataloging Service Bulletin* (*CSB*). Not only was the new AACR2 more efficient to use than the combination of publications previously required — main text, supplements, and *CSB*s — but it appeared in loose-leaf format as well as the standard hardcover and paperback bindings, making it much easier to update as subsequent changes required.

One of the more interesting things about the publication was its official name, first rumored to be called the *consolidated second edition* but changed to *second edition, revised*. Librarians had to wait until the publication appeared to be certain that the codemakers had not changed the title again before sending it to press, since the committee was as secretive about the final rendition as government officials are about defense systems.

Speculating on the secrecy surrounding the new edition statement just before it appeared — and noting it was not a new title, after all — led me to pose a series of questions and hypothetical answers. Here is the stream of consciousness that resulted.

THE BIG SECRET

The first question was, "Why should secrecy be necessary?" The obvious answer was, "To keep something hidden." That immediately spawned a second question, "Assuming it is necessary to hide something, *what* is it that needs to be kept hidden?" For a moment, I decided to put the *What* aside and go back to the *Why*. (Remember, I said this was stream of consciousness.) People attempt to keep secrets for many reasons, including a somewhat immature desire to know something that others don't. Two reasons that frequently underlie business or government secrets are to maintain exclusive control of something valuable for as long as possible or to prevent others from throwing a monkey wrench into the plan until it is realized. In considering the possibilities, I realized I had to deal immediately with the *What* again.

Two possible *Whats* occurred to me: the name of the new AACR2 and its contents. I ruminated on these alternatives for a while. Suppose the name was the critical *What*. Is it likely that someone would benefit from maintaining exclusive control over that for as long as possible? I couldn't see this logic and didn't like to think that my colleagues on the JSC—highly intelligent, respected professionals—were playing a game of "I Know Something You Don't." But I could see the logic of wanting to prevent others from reacting to the name in a way that might endanger its implementation. Why would someone want to prevent implementation? Because the name implied something fearful and undesirable—something sounding like AACR3. I still recall many an article in which library administrators, budgets still smarting from implementing AACR2, violently ruled out AACR3 as something with no hope of survival.

I shifted gears and supposed that the *What* was the content of the new AACR2. What benefit could be realized from maintaining exclusive control over it as long as possible? If knowledge of the content leaked before publication, it might eliminate at least part of the market for the publication itself. After all, virtually all of the information contained in the new version was already available to anyone with an old AACR2 kept up-to-date by inserting all the revisions from the supplements and CSBs. Librarians may forget or ignore it, but income from the sale of the new version must cover the costs of its production, including support for the activities of the JSC. That seemed logical, but I couldn't see anyone building up a lot of steam over the notion that a few hundred catalogers wouldn't bother to purchase the new AACR2 but merely keep revising their old ones. If I were a library director, I wouldn't want a cataloger I employed spending valuable time updating the old book unless the price of the new version was so outrageous I couldn't recover it within a reasonable period of time or unless the new version wasn't much of an improvement over the old one.

A much more compelling idea was the notion that early revelation of the content might engender sufficient disagreement to prevent publication altogether. If indeed the content could be interpreted as sufficiently different than expected—very different, for example, than the documents we had in hand—the new edition might have triggered a revolt against AACR itself. Again, this idea was based on the assumption that any text one could reasonably call AACR3 was totally unacceptable to the library community.

This speculation could only point to one idea, namely, that if this AACR2 1/2 (as I couldn't help calling the new consolidation) could be construed even remotely as AACR3, it would bring the sky down.

All this got me to thinking about AACR3. What's so dreadful about the idea of a third edition? Why does it raise hackles and stir up such emotional reaction? Since librarians seem to accept the idea that cataloging codes are not static documents and that they evolve over time, why isn't it a natural and acceptable thing to expect a third edition of AACR at some point? Isn't this much like expecting new editions of *Library of Congress Subject Headings* or *Dewey Decimal Classification*—changes we not only expect but demand?

WHY AN AACR3?

Librarians recognize that cataloging rules must relate to the materials to which they apply. It would be silly to have rules that assumed book covers or colophons were the most important sources of bibliographic data, because they aren't. Had early printers and publishers decided to put the names of authors, illustrators, editors, etc. as well as titles and imprints in either of those places, rather than on title pages, our rules would reflect this by naming covers or colophons as the chief sources for bibliographic information. In order to be useful, the principles on which cataloging rules are based must reflect reality, and individual rules must work in practice. One of our difficulties is the evolution from an ideal past when one uniform type of work emanating from the brain of one author was contained in one physical item—a book—to the current state of affairs in which many different types of works emanating from multiple sources are contained in a variety of physical manifestations.

What principles underlie AACR2? One begins with Cutter, whose two objectives—the locational and collocational functions of the catalog—are served by bibliographic descriptions and headings. The Paris Principles elaborated on those fundamentals and changed their specifications somewhat but did not alter them. AACR2 orders catalogers to transcribe data exactly from prescribed sources of information, mistakes and all. The principle preserved by such rules is that of identifying a particular item in hand. AACR2's organization, too, implies that an item's physical manifestation is of primary importance. The underlying principle to which one might point is that the medium is at least part of the message. The ISBD format and punctuation incorporated into AACR2 serves the principle of uniformity and interchangeability of bibliographic records, whether they differ in language or physical manifestation.

Though some might disagree, most catalogers believe that the changes between AACR1 and AACR2 were positive, adhering to the principles outlined above and enhancing the potential of the catalog for service in several ways. First, AACR2 accommodated the variety of materials in which information appeared and insured uniform products that could be integrated into one catalog. Second, the inversion of the processes of description and access enabled catalogers to draw a clear picture of the item they were cataloging before making decisions about the ways they wanted to search it (i.e., the choice of entries). Third, AACR2's records carry the ISBD structure, making them grist for the Universal Bibliographic Control mill, which appears to be coming to fruition as more and more national libraries enter their records into network databases. Thus, AACR2 was more comprehensive and more easily applied in the field than its predecessor.

Time does not stand still, however, and since the appearance of AACR2 information production has changed. These changes can be seen in the rise of computer-based information media, including electronic publishing; in the continuing increase in the number of research and artistic teams who share the authorship of products; and in the discovery and use of very dense storage media that handle sound, pictures, and text, together or separately, in very large quantities. Many, if not most, of the recent changes to AACR2 may be attributed to ongoing changes in the techniques of producing and transmitting information (defined in its broadest sense). Three of the best examples of such changes are the new chapter 9, altered to account for microcomputing and compact disk storage technology, and additions to chapters 6 and 7 that account for sound compact discs and videodiscs.

The question people ought to think about and should be starting to ask is, "Will making incremental changes to AACR2 solve the difficulties in describing these new media, or are more far reaching changes needed?"

THE CASE FOR AACR3

I believe there are at least two issues on which a case can be made for moving to AACR3 rather than continuing to "fix" AACR2. The media groups defined within AACR2's chapters no longer obtain, making its organization obsolete, and the bibliographic unit needs to be rethought in terms of new, dense storage media, rejecting the traditional idea that one work equals one book, one film, or one score.

Remember the media groups in AACR1? They divided visual materials quite differently than AACR2, putting all the film-based materials together whether or not they depicted motion. AACR2, on the other hand, draws the distinction between visual media that create an image of motion and those that do not. The result, in 1978, was two mutually exclusive groups: motion pictures and stills. Along came video. At the start videos seemed to be just another kind of motion medium. Now, however, there are videodiscs containing thousands of still images that don't pretend to portray motion; yet AACR2 has us describe them using the rules for motion-image media rather than the rules for still images. Music videos and videos of concerts present another problem: Are they sound media or motion media? Video games present more problems: Are they videos or games? Computer games are sometimes defined as computer files and sometimes defined as games. The list of problems is much longer, but this is a good start.

AACR2's media groups are no longer unambiguous and mutually exclusive, and catalogers are troubled in choosing which chapters of rules apply to particular items and how to interpret individual rules. We need a whole new organization for the code—one, perhaps, that does not separate existing media further but unifies them.

The other issue is analysis—the cataloging of parts of something we define as a bibliographic unit. Analytic cataloging has long been anomalous. A new perception is long overdue. Newly developed media for information storage hold many of what we define as full-length works. What has happened with microforms (which have been around for a long time, relatively speaking) ought to illustrate the difficulties that will obtain if catalogers continue to ignore the issue of storage density. Analytic cataloging must be seen as a mainstream path. The chapter on analysis must somehow be integrated with the rest of the rules, e.g., by applying the famous Rule of Three into an instruction that states: *Optionally*, if a bibliographic unit contains more than three full-length works, catalog it analytically. The meaning of *full-length* in this context would be a matter for interpretation by LC's Office for Descriptive Cataloging Policy or by each individual cataloger.

WHY NOT AN AACR3?

Which brings me back to an earlier question: "Why *not* have a third edition of the cataloging code?" The answer is simple: "Because library directors, especially directors of large libraries with major investments in existing catalogs, might be expected to reject it, possibly dumping standard rules (which they never liked) entirely." The reason behind their rejection is the incredibly poor precedent set by AACR2's implementation costs — costs measured not only in dollars and cents but also in loss of service, degradation of staff morale, and other psychological debits. If another edition of AACR is issued, it might require a total disguise just to be acceptable. The codemakers may be thinking of this in their desire to remove all suspicion that the forthcoming issue is AACR3.

If evolution of the code is ongoing, however, how long can librarians be fooled into thinking they have stopped progress? Will all subsequent editions of AACR be named *second edition plus*? Why should they have to be fooled at all? Does anyone think cataloging rules can work when they fail to reflect the realities of information production and distribution? Or when they fail to meet the needs of catalog users? If you believe as I do that AACR3 (in whatever guise) is inevitable, perhaps even overdue already, then you must prepare for it.

PLANNING FOR AACR3

Two things can be done to prepare for AACR3: acknowledge implementation as part of the process of catalog rule revision and design cost-effective implementation plans. Thus far the JSC has not accepted any responsibility for the implementation of the results of their work, incorporating rule revisions, additions, or deletions into existing catalogs. That state of affairs should not be allowed to continue. Clearly, rule changes, however welcome intellectually, cause financial repercussions within individual libraries. Codemakers must think about the monetary implications of changed rules along with the other noncataloging issues they acknowledge, e.g., the political implications of alternative actions.

If the JSC members believe themselves to be at a disadvantage in the area of financial management and control, a knowledgeable subcommittee should be appointed to coordinate the cost of the various alternatives they have under consideration. The subcommittee could report the estimated cost of implementing each alternative before votes are taken. Naturally, the subcommittee should be peopled with directors of large research libraries.

Librarians, too, must acknowledge that ongoing rule revision costs money (this is equally true of dynamic subject heading lists and classification schemes) and that one cannot simply assume changes to existing cataloging will never have to be made. Some factor for recataloging to account for rule changes must be included in the cost of cataloging and processing.

Beyond acknowledging that rule changes have associated costs and attempting to deal with them at some level, the JSC needs to ask directors and public service librarians for their reactions to potential rule changes. Catalogers, on whom the JSC relies for feedback, have too personal an interest in cataloging to be objective. Naturally, directors and public service librarians cannot be expected to accept lengthy, single-spaced, pencil-amended documents written in a totally incomprehensible jargon (such as, "12.7B3c: in the penultimate sentence insert 'and accompanying matter' between 'this' and 'that'") to be critiqued and returned within forty-eight hours—something catalogers seem willing to do—but JSC members would have to translate their efforts into something ordinary people could understand and evaluate. This might be a boon for everyone.

Clearly, keeping the JSC and AACR unsullied with practicality and untouched by ordinary librarians behind prickly barriers of cataloging intellectualism has had unfortunate consequences. Pretending that cataloging never changes has, too. It is way past time to try something different.

The American Subject
Cataloging Rules (ASCR)

The literature is full of references to a subject heading code—a sort of *Anglo-American Cataloguing Rules* for subject cataloging. The subject heading code was on the conference agenda of the American Library Association's Subject Analysis Committee a few years ago. It actually appeared there twice. More recently, the Subject Analysis Committee sponsored a program on the subject. William Studwell and Paule Rolland-Thomas, two authors who have written extensively on the subject, published a series of articles in major cataloging journals proposing and describing their ideas about a code of rules to help users of *Library of Congress Subject Headings* (LCSH) assign subject headings with greater accuracy, precision, and consistency, and less time-consuming effort and confusion. Studwell writes a bimonthly column in *Technicalities* devoted primarily to subject headings, and much of his material relates to a subject code.

Studwell and Thomas are not alone in writing about the subject heading code. Lois Mai Chan also has considered its possibilities. Other groups, public and private, have been discussing the new code: Should there be one? If not, why not? If so, what should it look like? Who should be responsible for it? What should it cover?

It may just be a matter of time until a subject heading code materializes. No doubt members of the Subject Analysis Committee, the Library of Congress, the bibliographic utilities, and other interested groups will send representatives to a body somewhat like the Joint Steering Committee for Revision of AACR and the body will be empowered to devise the first code. An editor or two will be chosen. The committee will meet for a long while, possibly years. Eventually a draft code will emerge, be circulated among the cognoscenti for comment, be criticized in the literature as the best and the worst thing for subject access, be revised ad nauseum, and, finally, be published. If this code runs true to form, its publication will create an uproar as grassroots librarians grapple with the problems its application will cause in their work flow.

For all that grassroots librarians want change in LCSH—more current terminology, modern orthography, faster adoption of new terms, consistency in term structure, names for peoples that do not offend or impose judgment, nonsexist language—when changes actually occur, they cost money to implement. Money isn't a philosophical or a theoretical matter. The plain truth is that the grassroots librarian will be given a bad time when cataloging production falls off and backlogs build despite more or less constant funding levels.

The director will demand to know, "What is going on? What are you doing? Why is this happening?"

What is the librarian supposed to say? "It's happening because I finally got some of the changes in subject headings that I wanted for patrons. It's happening because LCSH has been improved, but I don't know how to manage the changes." Of course not. Instead, the response will go something like this: "*They* have gone and changed all our subject headings and now we have to redo everything we've done in this library since before I came to work here. I don't know why *they* have to impose *their* harebrained schemes on us. *They* have their heads in the clouds and *they* just don't understand what real people in real libraries need."

I can just imagine the mess that implementation of the subject heading code will cause.

Why should librarians even consider having a subject heading code? Perhaps the best course of action is to nip this subject heading code talk in the bud. Maybe real librarians should storm the meeting halls and demand an end to this nonsense before it gets out of hand and they are forced to conform to an ASCR—an *American Subject Cataloging Rules*, just as they had to conform to AACR and AACR2. Who needs an ASCR?

SUBJECT SEARCHING AND THE
NEED FOR ASCR

Searching for a known item—an item for which the author or title is known—should pose few challenges for either librarians or ordinary patrons. The form of names appearing in the catalog is the "most commonly known" and good catalogers will make cross-references from other forms known but not used in the catalog. Titles are transcribed as they appear on the item, so the main problem with title searching is in remembering the exact words in their proper order. Studies show that the main reason for failure in known-item searching is that the item is not part of the collection and therefore an entry for it is not to be found in the catalog.

Subject searching, on the other hand, is much less predictable despite the heroic efforts of the Library of Congress to minimize variations in subject headings by publishing LCSH, nicknamed "The Red Book." Problems with subject searching abound, caused in part by changes that occur over time in subjects themselves, by changes in terminology and common usage in the English language, and by the fact that people's approaches to subject searching may be general or specific, comprehensive or selective, well-defined or fuzzy.

Reference librarians know that patrons often have trouble articulating what they really want. Patrons may ask for books about the moon when what they really want is information about Neil Armstrong's lunar landing. One of the key elements in the reference librarian's repertoire is that mysterious interface known as the reference interview—an interchange during which the librarian finds out what the patron *really* wants. Sometimes the librarian can go directly to the shelves for desired material; sometimes the subject catalog must be consulted. Experience in searching for all sorts of topics arms the professional searcher with the knowledge that MOTION PICTURES must be consulted for materials about films, movies, or cinema and that COOKERY is what the subject catalog calls cooking, cookbooks, cuisine, and recipes. The longer a librarian works in a subject area, the more appropriate his or her subject catalog vocabulary becomes. But when faced with a totally unfamiliar topic in which the first attempts fail to produce any entries, the professional undoubtedly turns to the Red Book to see what term LC has decided to use for the topic, while the lay searcher may just assume there aren't any relevant materials in the library and give up.

Good reference librarians may show their clients the Red Book, explain its contents and how it works, and expect them to do their own subject heading legwork. However, all that LCSH can do is furnish the more than 280,000 terms that LC has used or referenced. If you look up a word that is not in the Red Book, you have to try to figure what other terms might be used instead. LCSH doesn't include every possible word or combination of words that users think up for subject headings. It is merely a finite list of terms, some of which are usable and some of which are not. The choice of one term over another doesn't follow any well-defined principles that could lead someone using the list to anticipate the correct form of other terms. For example, a few years ago when the subject heading for films was MOVING PICTURES and someone wanted a book about the music in films, they would not have found it under MOVING PICTURES – MUSIC or MOVING PICTURE MUSIC or MUSIC – MOVING PICTURES or MUSIC IN MOVING PICTURES, as you might think, extrapolating from the term used for films. Unfortunately for the searcher, this topic was called MOTION PICTURE MUSIC for no reason that justified its departure from more consistent possibilities. Now, of course, MOVING PIC-TURES has been changed to MOTION PICTURES, making it easier to find film music but not CHILDREN'S FILMS, FEATURE FILMS, COMEDY FILMS, or any of the dozens of other related headings based on the word *films* instead of *motion pictures*. This is just one simple example of the Red Book's lack of consistency. There are many more, including, but not limited to, the following:

- the choice of direct or indirect word order in multiword headings, e.g., TROUT FISHING versus FISHING, TROUT;

- the choice of spellings, e.g., AEROPLANES versus AIRPLANES or NON-PRINT versus NONPRINT;

- the choice of one term from among several alternatives, e.g., ESKIMOS, a pejorative term to the people it represents, versus INUIT, the more accurate and acceptable term;

- the choice between an English or foreign language, e.g., LAISSEZ FAIRE versus FREE TRADE; and

- the choice between a technical or commonly used term, e.g., SPIDERS versus ARACHNIDA, or CARDIAC INFARCTION versus HEART ATTACK.

The principles that govern the choice of terms in LCSH, formalized by Charles A. Cutter in the nineteenth century and interpreted by David Judson Haykin in the 1950s, sound simple but are difficult to apply. They are

- the reader as focus—use terms readers will recognize;

- unity—use terms that bring related materials together; and

- direct and specific entry—use a specific term directly, not as a subordinate phrase under a broader heading, e.g., use WHALES, not MAMMALS—WHALES. (Note that this is distinct from direct or indirect order of words in a multiword heading.)

In reality, these principles have been applied and interpreted differently by the various people responsible for LC's subject cataloging division. The result is an enormous and unwieldy hodgepodge of terms established following different guidelines at different times—namely, LCSH.

Here are the real reasons underlying the call for ASCR: a genuine desire to bring this barbarian Red Book under control; to make it conform to valid principles that will insure subject heading consistency, accuracy, precision, and relevance; to ease the task of local catalogers who truly wish to apply LCSH in the "proper" manner; and to enhance the potential retrieval success for searchers who use entries containing LCSH in library and information center catalogs.

Librarians have recognized these problems and desired their solution for a long time. Why should Studwell, Thomas, Chan, and others rush to create a subject heading code now?

WHY NOW?

There is a good and relatively simple reason why the present is the right time for a subject heading code. Before a great project can be undertaken the people involved in its planning and execution must have some hope of success. Until now, the idea of revamping more than a quarter-million LCSH headings and making the changes required in the millions of bibliographic records containing them was more than a dream. It was an exorbitant, impossible dream. Now, however, LCSH-mr, the computerized version of LCSH, is a reality and LC's MARC file, its file of machine-readable records, has matured. Computers and computerized manipulation of data have brought the hope of success to ventures intended to control and normalize LC's subject headings according to a set of preordained rules.

The question should not be "why now?" It should be "what set of preordained rules?"

WHAT PRINCIPLES SHOULD GUIDE
THE ASCR?

Studwell and Thomas suggest an AACR-like format for ASCR. They believe it should have two sections, the second section being more or less a condensation of LC's *Subject Cataloging Manual: Subject Headings* and the first section giving an "explication of the basic theory behind LC subject headings ... specific rules or guidelines that apply to subject headings as a whole ... [and] a number of subsections specifically concerned with special subject areas, e.g., art, literature, music, or sciences."[1] Let us consider the first part—the basic theory—in greater depth.

Some of the principles codified by Cutter and Haykin are no longer viable, e.g., what Haykin called "the reader as focus" and Cutter termed "the convenience of the public." This is not because they are bad principles but because catalog users have changed and cannot be characterized according to one profile. The library user and subject searcher is not uniformly white, male, Anglo-Saxon, educated, and Protestant, as might have been true in the nineteenth century. Subject searchers might belong to all these groups, but they are equally likely to be women and children; nonwhite, non-Anglo, and non-native; adherents of all religions; less than well-educated; and, when educated, novices to the subjects they are searching. How can a uniform vocabulary serve all these needs? Technical terms are not equally understood by expert and novice users. "Common" usage isn't common among all groups. (An example of the generation gap that caused some family consternation not long ago: When my husband says "bike," he means "bicycle;" when my youngest daughter says it, she means "motorcycle." Take it from me, there is a big difference.) These days usage changes rapidly, as a glance at any of William Safire's "On Language" columns in the Sunday *New York Times Magazine* will demonstrate.

The principle of specific and direct entry works against the principle of unity by differentiating among subjects that are related but not identical. Today we worry because the muddying of the lines between disciplines has exacerbated problems of defining where one subject ends and another begins. Furthermore, idiosyncrasies of format—the proliferation of books on multiple subjects and the production of information products other than books—makes it difficult to specify and unify materials by subject headings.

What principles are identifiable? One principle that seems straightforward is that of using direct order of words in multiword headings. The fact that, at the moment, some headings are inverted while others are not is not a principle, it is merely coincidence. Some people may believe inversion is beneficial to searchers, but there is a problem with mandating it as a basic principle. Some headings could be logically inverted in any of several places, e.g., a heading such as FRENCH MOTION PICTURE PRODUCERS AND PRODUCING could be inverted either as MOTION PICTURE PRODUCERS AND PRODUCING, FRENCH or PRODUCERS AND PRODUCING, FRENCH MOTION PICTURE. For that matter, MOTION PICTURES could become PICTURES, MOTION; every two-word heading could be a candidate for inversion. Even inversion's devotees recognize the nightmare this would create.

The idea behind inversion—bringing together materials on the topic of the word brought to the filing position—is a faulty one, since what inversion does is promote one relationship at the expense of others. For example, inversion brings together all works on art, regardless of their geography, by inverting JAPANESE ART to ART, JAPANESE and FRENCH ART to ART, FRENCH, etc. This is nice for art majors, but it doesn't help the area studies majors who would prefer to see FRENCH ART, FRENCH COOKERY, FRENCH LITERATURE, and FRENCH MOTION PICTURES. Who can say that it is better to collocate ART, ANCIENT; ART, JAPANESE; and ART, STYLES OF instead of ANCIENT ART, ANCIENT HISTORY, and ANCIENT MUSIC? (Of course, there always is the possibility that definitions of "ancient" could vary depending on the context—art, history, or music—so ANCIENT ART might cover art from the earliest times to 1000 B.C. while ANCIENT HISTORY might cover history from 2000 B.C. to A.D. 500 and ANCIENT MUSIC might cover music from A.D. 200 to 1850. Chronological terms probably need separate principles of definition.)

Where geographic areas are involved, inversion may be a good way to collocate materials on the same subject whose only differences are the location where the subject occurs. While it is easy to accept a single exception for geographic modifiers to the direct word order principle, it would have to be consistently applied. We now have such inconsistent constructions as ART, BRAZILIAN in the same catalog with AGRICULTURE – BRAZIL. Why not change the latter to AGRICULTURE, BRAZILIAN or the former to ART – BRAZIL? There are no compelling linguistic reasons why art should take an adjectival modifier (and be an unsubdivided term) while agriculture takes a noun (and is, thus, subdivided). With a single uniform rule, one could predict with some confidence how to search any topic subdivided geographically. Better yet, just use direct word order and collocate BRAZILIAN AGRICULTURE, BRAZILIAN ART, etc.

Maturing subjects outgrow inversion. When libraries had very few books about popular music, collocating them with other music books by inverting the heading to MUSIC, POPULAR made some sense. Now, however, differentiating popular music from other types of music helps limit the length of the MUSIC file, making both it and the POPULAR MUSIC file more efficient to search. As it is, the MUSIC file is extremely long because it has many modifiers and subheadings. Inversions that also bring MUSIC to the filing position simply add to the congestion. How likely is it that the same researcher will want to have materials on popular music brought together with Japanese music, Baroque music, and recorder music in a subject file with the following inversions—MUSIC, BAROQUE; MUSIC, JAPANESE; MUSIC, POPULAR; and MUSIC, RECORDER?

Figuring out principles that can be applied consistently to provide a more orderly structure for subject headings is not an easy task. Before moving ahead to consider other principles, perhaps subject analysts should go back and examine what should be the focus for all subject heading principles: observations about search behavior and the expectations of subject heading users.

NOTES

[1]William E. Studwell and Paule Rolland-Thomas, "The Form and Structure of a Subject Heading Code," *Library Resources & Technical Services* 32 (April 1988):167-69.

12

Subject Heading Terminology

How many of you recall *The Trouble With Harry*? It was a late Hitchcock motion picture in which Harry was dead. How he got that way, who perpetrated the crime, and so forth were the basis for this droll mystery, all of which brings me to this chapter's central theme: subject heading terminology. Let's begin again.

Subject heading terminology is a critical issue with many complex facets. Cutter dealt with it very simply, however, claiming that the language of the user should be preferred over other choices. When librarians dealt with a single, relatively well-defined and homogeneous user group, Cutter's recommendation was sensible and effective. Since Cutter's users were English-speaking, it made sense to use the English-language versions of words: ART OBJECTS, not OBJETS D'ART; MACARONI PRODUCTS, not PASTA; PANCAKES, WAFFLES, ETC., not CREPES. Since they were American, it made sense to use the American-English versions of words: ELEVATOR, not LIFT; TRUCK, not LORRY; TOILET, not WATER-CLOSET. Since they were scholars, it made sense to use technical terms: ARACHNIDA, not SPIDERS; PUERPERIUM, not POST PARTUM PERIOD; ANECDOTES, FACETIAE, ETC., not HUMOR or FUNNY STUFF. Nonetheless, Cutter made exceptions to his rules: LAISSEZ-FAIRE was preferred over any English-language translation, such as FREE ENTERPRISE, as was MAITRE D'S (headwaiters), STURM UND DRANG MOVEMENT (Storm and stress movement), and many other non-English terms in the current subject heading lists that owe their precedents to Cutter. In another exception to Cutter's rules, commonly used equivalents sometimes replace technical terms: STURGEONS are preferred over ACIPENSERIDAE.

Theoretically, integrity of terminology for any subject heading list demands that some rules be established to tell users how to choose one term over others if several terms are available to represent a topic, e.g., CINEMA, FILM, MOTION PICTURE, MOVIE, or MOVING PICTURE. When should a foreign term be chosen in place of its English equivalent? When should a vernacular word be selected over the technical alternative? If all things are equal in terms of precision of meaning and frequency of usage, how should the choice be made?

Choosing one term from among several alternatives is just the one of a number of issues relating to terminology. Selecting one term assumes that all alternative terms are equally available and appealing at the moment one must be chosen. Sometimes usage changes over time and the term that seemed best at moment A is no longer preferred at moment B—remember ELECTRONIC DATA PROCESSING? Or the spelling of the term may have changed—remember AEROPLANES? There should be rules that govern when enough is enough and AEROPLANES should be changed to AIRPLANES or MOVING PICTURES to MOTION PICTURES. One would hope that the determining factor would not be having a mutinous frustration level in the user community.

Which word to choose? When to change it? These are two of the most basic problems in subject terminology, though they are by no means the only ones.

WHICH WORD TO CHOOSE?

Before the twentieth century, the notion of cataloging standards with national applicability was still young, nationally distributed cataloging was not yet a reality, and most libraries did their own cataloging in-house. The internal integrity of an individual library's catalog was all that was at stake. If one library used BULLETS in its subject catalog while another library used AMMUNITION for the same subject, not much happened. Perhaps that explains why, before the dawn of national bibliographic networks, two different lists of terms gained national popularity in the United States: *Library of Congress Subject Headings* (LCSH) and *Sears List of Subject Headings* (Sears). Each of these lists is based on a different user image and uses terminology designed to suit that vision.

The basic difference between the two lists, it seems to me, is that for Sears the ideal user is a child or youth while for LCSH it is an adult. Sears favors vernacular over technical terms (SPIDERS, not ARACHNIDA) as well as terms with broader definitions, serving the user who not only doesn't know the more technical terms but who doesn't want such a detailed breakdown of subjects. Ostensibly, it was meant for nonscholars using small general libraries, i.e., school and public libraries.

LCSH visualized a knowledgeable adult user in a large general library. It seems to favor the use of technically accurate terms over simpler or commonly used alternatives and more specific words as well as broad ones. The result is to break down a large group of items into several different subject files rather than drawing them all together.

This last characteristic—to consist of fewer, broader terms instead of a larger number of more specific terms—is an important one. Sears designers recognized that its much smaller list of broad terms might not serve some collections where there were many items on one subject, so they allowed the cataloger to add terms from other sources as needed. Similarly, the designers of LCSH recognized that its enormous list of scholarly terms might not serve collections used mainly by young people, so they devised an alternate list of terms to be applied to children's materials. As technical and specific as it was, LCSH was neither precise nor specific enough to serve medical searchers, so the National Library of Medicine devised a separate list of terms called *Medical Subject Headings* (MeSH).

According to Cutter, subject terms for any list must exhibit at least four characteristics: accuracy of meaning, precision, appropriate specificity, and the acceptability that comes from general use. First, a word has to be an accurate term for the subject matter it represents: When someone is jumpy, excitable, and easily enraged, we might say they are having apoplexy, but APOPLEXY is not an accurate subject term for that particular behavior. In fact, the definition of apoplexy includes losing consciousness—not at all what was described.

Second, a word has to be precise enough to be understood: A set of repulsive-looking pictures might be called REVOLTING, but the term is not sufficiently precise and could be understood as the process of rebellion against authority. (Furthermore, beauty is in the eye of the beholder and what is repulsive to me might well be sad, moving, or exciting to you.)

Third, a word has to have the right amount of specificity to suit the catalog in which it is used—enough to bring several items together but not too many. In most public libraries, the subject heading FICTION, if applied to individual works of fiction, would fill a file few would care to search. In a special science library, however, such a heading might be just right for identifying a small group of novels.

Fourth, a word used as a subject term should be commonly used: COMPUTER, not ELECTRONIC DIGITAL PROCESSOR; CLOTHES or CLOTHING, not RAIMENT or GARB. Usage isn't everything, however, and subject words should not be faddish jargon or slang likely to be dropped or outdated quickly: JAIL, not SLAMMER, COOLER, or BIG HOUSE; APARTMENT, not PAD, PIED-A-TERRE, or DIGS.

A subject cataloging code would have to address all of these issues and devise a list of priorities for use when each possibility for a particular subject term satisfies some but not all of the desired features. Take the choice between SEDAN and FAMILY CAR. SEDAN is defined as an enclosed automobile with front and back seats. Few people other than automobile salespeople use the word "sedan" any more; instead, most people refer to all enclosed cars as "cars" whether or not they have back seats. (They might distinguish cars without a roof as "convertibles." People never say, "I bought a car without a roof." They say, "WOWEE! I bought a convertible.") FAMILY CAR, on the other hand, incorporates the more commonly used term "car" and denotes an automobile large and safe enough to hold a family. Presumably, a family car must have more than just a front seat to accommodate the children and a roof for safety, so it is applicable to the same concept as SEDAN. All right: SEDAN is more precise but FAMILY CAR is more commonly used. Both represent an automobile with front and back seats and a roof. Which should be preferred?

Literary warrant—the use of terms because they appear in the literature—is a time-honored way of choosing terms for a subject heading list. In automatic indexing systems one way to determine whether a word should be selected as an indexing term is to count the number of times it appears. When dealing with a limited amount of literature in a limited time period, this is a promising way to decide which of several alternatives is the best term to select to represent a topic. But, if literature is defined broadly to encompass all media—including newspapers, magazine and journal articles, books, and audiovisual forms—over an extended period of time, the counting method is not only difficult to implement but too variable in its results to be useful.

A logical application of literary warrant that could be especially effective for naming new topics is to designate a particular body of literature for deriving subject headings. For example, a subject heading code might dictate that terms used in *The New York Times, Newsday,* or *The Christian Science Monitor* will be preferred over others. (Why those? No reason; they are a random selection of well-known, reputable, up-to-date, general periodicals.)

Another method might designate a particular unabridged dictionary or ency-clopedia as an authoritative source of terms. Words that do not appear there might be considered unacceptable as subject heading terms. Words that do are fair game. These kinds of authorities would identify preferred spellings, too.

The value of such rules is clear and simple. Any indexer encountering a topical concept for the first time could establish a subject heading for it in the same fashion, coming up with the same term as any other cataloger. It would no longer matter if the Library of Congress did not own any titles on the topic and therefore did not establish a subject heading for it.

Isn't that the idea behind our descriptive cataloging rules?

WHEN TO CHANGE IT?

While established subject heading terminology is relatively stable over time, changes in the words themselves or their spellings do occur. Orthographical pro-gress is unpredictable and doesn't always move in a straight line, as those who championed the change from AEROPLANES to AIRPLANES might think. The change from hyphenated forms such as AUDIO-VISUAL, NON-BOOK, and NON-PRINT to their unhyphenated equivalents—a battle won relatively recently—was to reverse itself still more recently with a directive to LCSH users to hyphenate once again. If it was progress to move *away* from hyphenation, what is this? Should MICROCOMPUTERS be hyphenated? What about COOPERATIVES, TRANSATLANTIC, and INTERDISCIPLINARY? What should be the basis for deciding? A designated authority? The demands of pro-gramming in an automated system? After all, a good many words fall between CO-OPERATIVES and COOPERATIVES in a large catalog. A subject heading code would have rules that address these and other word formatting issues.

LC finally changed MOVING PICTURES to MOTION PICTURES after years of user grumbling and conflict with related headings like MOTION PIC-TURE MUSIC and MOTION PICTURE PRODUCERS. LC's reluctance to replace ESKIMO with INUIT and NEGROES with AFRO-AMERICANS and BLACKS (which have their own problems, to be sure) until the general outcry against the old terms reached monumental proportions was attributed to the high costs of altering huge numbers of catalog cards to conform to the new headings. Nevertheless, a good many LCSH terms changed in the last decade even before LC's online catalog was fully implemented. The changes resulted from the unflag-ging efforts of Sanford Berman, Joan K. Marshall, and others—primarily through ALA's Social Responsibilities Round Table and Subject Analysis Com-mittee (SRRT and SAC)—to replace sexist, racist, or otherwise offensive headings relating to people with more desirable terms or, at least, with neutral terms free of pejorative connotations.

Fixing only the squeaky wheels, however, and doing it only under duress seems to negate the logic and organization of the storage-and-retrieval process. Terms used in the catalog are supposed to be accurate, precise, and commonly used by scholarly searchers. ESKIMOS and HOTTENTOTS would not fit the bill, being unscholarly and inaccurate. Why did they appear in LCSH in the first place? Would a subject code have kept them out? Should the rules of a subject code include SRRT and SAC recommendations designed to prevent terms from being established that denigrate persons or perpetuate inaccurate representations?

Are terms that categorize *people* the only terms that require such sensitivity? What about other categories that require special care? Would it be unsatisfactory to call animals used for hauling and farming BEASTS OF BURDEN? Or to call birds that eat carrion BIRDS OF PREY? Is it pejorative to use the term GAMBLERS to describe people who spend their time and money betting? Who should decide what is acceptable? How should they decide?

CONCLUSION

This chapter asks only some of the questions that might be raised concerning the selection of subject terms and the alteration or replacement of existing terms. The range of issues that must be considered are both broad and complex. Yet can anyone charged with planning and implementing information storage-and-retrieval systems fail to consider them? Can librarians continue to work effectively without trying to resolve the most pressing problems in reasonable ways? Can a randomly driven machine (as the current implementation pattern of LCSH as a subject vocabulary might be described) survive on today's crowded highways? Even more important, would a subject code help to define the whole area of subject headings, organize it logically, and address the difficulties of appropriate and disciplined yet flexible terminology?

CHAPTER
13

The Fiction of Access to Fiction

Librarians, as information professionals — people with links to the social sciences and education — like to think they are rational, objective, thinking beings who are guilty of fooling themselves only rarely, if ever. Yet for years we librarians have subscribed to the fiction that we furnish the best access to fictional materials by shelving them according to their authors' surnames in special sections of the stacks, often without any call number identification in their catalog entries and without assigning them subject headings. Our commonly used classification schemes, the Library of Congress and Dewey Decimal classifications, do not do much better. Using Dewey, all contemporary American fiction gets 813.54, making the cutter number the critical factor in arranging it. This produces an alphabetical arrangement by main entry that is identical with simple alphabetization without a class number. LC classification treats fiction in much the same way but with far more hospitality: The basic class number — PSnnnn — reflects not only the work's nationality or language (American), the genre, and the time period, but also the initial letter of the author's surname. The cutter number begins with the second letter of the author's surname, which allows the greater fine-tuning of the alphabetic arrangement that this schedule is intended to produce.

If alphabetizing were the only way fiction was treated, perhaps people would have less trouble locating it, but it isn't. A public library visited recently by one of my students shelves English-language fiction in seventeen places, taking into account a variety of unclassified genres, adult and juvenile fiction, new and old fiction, rental fiction, and a small group of classified fiction in which the text is graced by biographical and/or critical notes. College and university libraries do better by classifying fiction according to its nationality or language groups, time periods, etc. and organizing it into a unified alphabetic arrangement; these pockets of fiction can be found in predicted places in the overall scheme. The only problem in searching such arrangements is finding all the works of authors who live in many places and work in several languages (Vladimir Nabokov or Isaac Bashevis Singer, for example) or who span several time periods. Fortunately, this problem applies only to a few authors and it can always be addressed through descriptive collocation in the catalog.

Two problems exist here: the issue of classification and shelf arrangement and the issue of subject headings.

CLASSIFICATION PROBLEMS

"People like it that way," I hear from colleagues and from students repeating what colleagues tell them about the physical arrangement of fiction. Frankly, I don't. If I really believed that people liked things better that way, I would recommend that we scrap all our classification numbers in favor of a Reader Interest Classification or some other bookstore-like model for all our materials, nonfiction as well as fiction. Why should I spend half a semester teaching students how to assign classification numbers carefully and accurately only to hear that people really prefer plain alphabetization better, so long as the thousands of volumes related only by their language and literary genre are grouped together?

Why not group the disciplines the same way? Why not have a mathematics area, an education area, a computer area, a history area, and shelve all the materials on these topics alphabetically by their authors' surnames? Would it make these materials less accessible? Probably not, judging by the prevalence of the mark-it-and-park-it style classification practiced in the field today. More important, why should libraries spend a lot of money and person-power classifying all their materials and then training pages to decipher all the inscrutable classification notation in order to shelve material properly? Everybody knows the alphabet. No one needs training to use it. What great advantage do we gain from separating books about marketing for food (TX356/641.31) from those about food preparation and service (TX645-953/641.5-642.5)? Why not have a grouping for FOOD and then alphabetize all these materials in it? Every book still has its individual shelf location, provided by careful cuttering and other shelf marks. The class numbers disappear and FOOD is substituted in their places. FOOD is understandable to anyone looking at it, unlike TX645 or 641.5, and easily remembered, too, so that trips to the shelves do not have to be preceded by transcribing (often incorrectly) a list of complicated call numbers.

"Our collection is so large we must have very specific classifications." Next time you go to a large bookstore, tell them that. Tell it, too, to the thousands of urban public libraries with current English-language fiction collections that run fifty thousand to one hundred thousand titles or more, all shelved as F, FIC, or something equally specific.

What, after all, is the purpose of classification? It is two-fold: to collocate items with related subject matter and to provide an expression of subject content (which we use to locate it on the shelves) for each item. Classification enables searchers to browse through groups of materials and to find desired materials serendipitously. Would alphabetic arrangements within broadly defined subject or disciplinary areas conflict with this goal? I doubt it. Library of Congress classification often relies on alphabetizing through the assignment of cutter numbers as part of the classification to subarrange a large body of materials.

Instead of wrestling with the difficulty of satisfying both objectives at once, i.e., identification and collocation, we would plant both feet firmly in the camp of identification and its resulting advantages for searchers. Alphabetization works. Take it from the telephone company, from the publishers of reference tools, and from Cutter himself. Instead of pulling fiction out of the classification system, throw away the classification system and put nonfiction into a similar order on the shelves. I daresay it would not cause any more instances of clients unable to locate any particular book, video, film, or sound recording (whether an audiotape or phonodisc) than our current shelving practices. It would go some way toward resolving the problems of classifying interdisciplinary materials and, perhaps, a bit toward resolving the problems of producing overlong class numbers.

But back to fiction. We can continue to classify our English-language fiction in one or more alphabets, depending on whether we wish to separate British, Canadian, Australian, Tasmanian, and American English-language fiction as well as the various time periods in which works appear. But we rely on words to express the division, not symbols: TWENTIETH CENTURY AMERICAN FICTION is much better than 813.5, isn't it? The important thing is that all copies of *Moby Dick* should be in the same place. Some should not be in 813 or PS while others are in F, jF, or SS (for SEA STORIES). Multiple treatments confound access and work against searching success. Public librarians might have to give up their sacred divisions between children's and adult fiction, hardcover and paperback fiction, and so on. They might actually save some money that is now spent on unnecessary duplication of the same works in several collections.

If you are outraged at the thought of dispensing with Dewey or LC classification, then use it for fiction, too. What difference does it make if all the British fiction is in 823, PR, or BRITISH FICTION? Only that new, casual, or unindoctrinated searchers (who are not necessarily new or casual) can expect to find all of Dickens, Thackeray, or Waugh there. They will not have to traipse all over the building to make sure they have exhausted the possibilities before determining that they have to put in a request for a desired title missing from the shelves. We talk about collocation and then destroy it by fragmenting our fiction into different collections around the library (seventeen in the agency visited by my student, remember?).

SUBJECT HEADING PROBLEMS

The question of subject headings for fiction is quite a different issue. It is not a matter of logistics or consistency. It is a matter of our fundamental philosophy and belief system. What is fiction? My pocket dictionary says fiction is something, as a story, invented by the imagination (New Merriam-Webster Pocket Dictionary, New York: Pocket Books, 1971). How does it differ from nonfiction? The same little dictionary does not have a separate definition for nonfiction, but includes it in a list of words to which the prefix non- is attached, non- being defined as "not," "reverse of," or "absence of." Since something the reverse of being invented by imagination makes no sense, we can dispense with that definition. But something not invented by imagination or something invented *in the absence of* imagination has a very understandable meaning. It means something observable, palpable, real, true, or not requiring imagination to perceive. Here is an intellectual difference. Real or unreal, true or false, these are distinctions we can make and this is the primary distinction between fiction and nonfiction.

Based on the definition of fiction as not-real, not-true, or not-factual, I want to challenge two corollaries: first, that the feature of imagination alone is sufficient reason to treat fiction differently than nonfiction for subject access purposes and, second, that by definition nonfiction is real, true, and factual.

What is reality? Philosophers have debated this question deeply to little avail. Do observations or sensations reflect reality? The story of the blind people and the elephant belie that belief. Do creators of nonimaginative works have a corner on truth? Tell me they do in view of the many works proving that the earth is flat, that the universe revolves about the earth, or many other scientific "truths." Much of what we accept as factual, true, and real is merely theory. The theory may work for a while and, while it does, we believe it is reality. But if a theory fails just once, it is discredited. In fact, a researcher never proves a hypothesis is true but that it is not untrue for the situation of the proof. Research can prove something is false, but results that uphold a hypothesis do not prove that it is true, just that it is still possibly true.

Is nonfiction unimaginative? Tell me that it is after reading *The Double Helix* or some of the works of C. P. Snow or Barbara Tuchman. Truly good researchers are extremely imaginative people. It is precisely this quality that enables them to see things that the rest of us miss. Imagination permits researchers to think up hypotheses, theories, and methods by which to test their ideas. Just because they write about these ideas in a systematic, scholarly way does not remove the imagination from their work.

If you will accept for just a moment that nonfiction is not exactly, absolutely, positively true but may be imaginative, too, then you may also be persuaded to accept for just a moment that some fiction, while certainly imaginative, may not be entirely false, untrue, or unfactual. Many writers of fiction spend years researching their subjects and go to great lengths to retain a context of reality in their works. James Michener is a good example, and there are many more like him. When I took research methods as a doctoral student, our class was assigned to read *Daughter of Time*, a mystery novel about Richard III of England, in order to learn about the attributes of evidence. Tell me that this work of fiction is false but Ptolemy's science is true and I will have to tell you that you are wrong on both counts.

Furthermore, fiction is studied for many reasons, including its ability to reflect its milieu, to present views of life dramatically, to give its authors an outlet for their ideas, and to provide pleasure and beauty for its readers. Fiction is occasionally an outlet for ideas that cannot be expressed as fact, e.g., *The Gulag Archipelago*. Works of fiction may be considered dangerous, as was reported in a recent *New York Times* story about the novel *Exodus*, which was considered anti-Soviet. Its possession was sufficient reason for jailing several dissidents. Tell the men who served three years in Soviet prisons that fiction is unreal or frivolous.

What is the point? It is to sensitize librarians who make bibliographic policies that the basic assumption that fiction is false and nonfiction is true is extremely questionable. It is also a questionable assumption that people do not use fiction for serious educational purposes. My purpose is to challenge librarians with the idea that furnishing subject access to nonfiction but not to fiction based on these questionable assumptions is bad practice.

We accept the fact that children read fiction to explore subjects. In response, LC provides subject headings for children's fiction through its Annotated Card program. A child going to the hospital wants to read about the experience (or perhaps the child's parent wants to choose such a book for him or her). A child who likes to read about horses or planets is permitted to choose fiction as well as nonfiction works on these topics. Why not adults? Why do librarians make a fundamental judgment that subject access is not necessary for adult fiction? The value of subject headings for biographical and historical fiction is accepted, though somewhat grudgingly, I think. (Only didactic fiction, including biography and history, was considered acceptable two centuries ago. That is why many novels were written as biographies or histories. How old and entrenched is the bias against fiction!)

I could give more instances of the educational value of adult fiction besides the previously mentioned use of *Daughter of Time* for beginning researchers (which could also be valuable for someone exploring the life of Richard III). Why do librarians claim to furnish subject access to collections and then cut one-third to one-half of our holdings out of that glowing bibliographic picture? If, as current research seems to show, subject searching is becoming more important than ever, might we not serve our clients better if we reevaluated that policy?

CONCLUSION

Classification and subject headings for adult fiction should follow the same procedures and the same patterns used for all other library materials. It would be so much easier for everyone if libraries classified everything and shelved the A to Z or 000 to 999 sequences in that order, but I have yet to read of a library in which the stacks were designed to accommodate this shelving. As an alternative, they could use broad general classes within which materials are arranged in alphabetic order by main entry, saving the staff time and money now consumed by classifying most, but not all, of their materials—some of it not very well. Instead, the sequence of classified materials is riddled with anomalies and fiction is singled out for a variety of unique treatments, few of which offer a subject orientation. The closest we come to subject orientation for fiction is genre classification. For most adult fiction, the subject catalog offers nothing to lead a searcher to relevant topical headings for the content of the works.

I repeat: It is a fiction that librarians supply good access to fiction.

14

Access to Serials

Contrary to the claims of some of my colleagues, the library catalog does not furnish access to knowledge unless knowledge is defined in very superficial terms. Nor does the catalog offer access to everything in the library, at least not to all the things that might be considered discrete works in the literary sense. What the catalog usually does best is furnish access to the library's monographic books. In addition to providing a record of holdings of monographic books, library catalogs often include bibliographic records for monographic films, sound recordings, other audiovisual items, and serial titles.

For certain nonbook media, such as sound recordings, microforms, computer files, and especially serials, discrete physical items often contain more than one work in the literary sense. In this respect their content differs fundamentally from the content of books, in which each discrete physical item can be expected to contain one work.

DEFINING THE BIBLIOGRAPHIC UNIT

The first thing every cataloger must do is decide what is being cataloged so the correct chapter(s) of descriptive cataloging rules may be applied. In fact, however, this decision includes more than a choice of the medium to which the item belongs; it also is the choice of an appropriate bibliographic unit.

Cataloging rules are based on the assumption that bibliographic units can be equated with physical items and both of these with literary works. But equating one bibliographic unit with one item and one work—a perfectly useful rule-of-thumb for most monographic books—creates problems for single physical items that include multiple works or, conversely, for items that include less than a whole work in one physical unit. Unit definition problems occur most often with nonbook materials, especially with dense media in which a single physical unit can hold many discrete works, e.g., microforms or sound recordings. Even books can present such problems, since some monographs are published in several volumes, making each volume less than a complete work, while others are anthologies (multiple works gathered in one volume). Either way, the assumption of equity between bibliographic unit, individual book, and literary work does not hold, and special rules must be devised to help the cataloger resolve the anomaly.

The special problem of serials is that they almost always contain more than one work in the literary sense but less than a whole unit, which includes issues not yet published.

STANDARD DESCRIPTIVE CATALOGING UNITS

According to the *Anglo-American Cataloguing Rules*, second edition, 1988 revision (AACR2R), individual books that contain multiple works are cataloged as a single bibliographic unit, although there are provisions to catalog each of the individual works separately as parts of a larger whole (this is called *analytic* cataloging). The policy of the Library of Congress is to catalog a single book containing many poems, plays, or essays—an anthology—as one bibliographic unit. At one time the Library of Congress had special rules for multiwork sound recordings, cataloging each work separately and linking the records with "With" notes. However, some years ago the policy was abandoned and such recordings now are treated as a single unit.

AACR2R also has provisions for applying the opposite option to a collection of monographic titles in a series—that is, to catalog the series as a unit containing all the parts instead of cataloging each individual item with an added heading for the series title. The Library of Congress does not often choose to create a single record for a monographic series, however, as long as each book in the series has its own title in addition to the series title. But if Library of Congress catalogers were faced with three books, each entitled *The Complete Works of Shakespeare* and marked "Volume 1," "Volume 2," and "Volume 3," the books would be considered a single bibliographic unit and the one catalog record made for all three volumes would have "3 v." in its physical description.

PUBLICATION PATTERNS AND BIBLIOGRAPHIC UNITS

There are many dichotomies in our field, but for catalogers one of the most basic is that the universe of library materials can be divided into monographs and serials. The distinction between the two is that monographs are nonserial units that have preset, finite limits, even when they are published in parts (like the Shakespeare title in three volumes); serials by definition are published in parts intended to continue forever. As soon as a serial ceases publication, it can be treated monographically. Open dates can be closed and the physical description can be completed. Unfortunately for catalogers and cataloging budgets, however, serials that cease sometimes resurrect, making it necessary to revive the open-ended catalog record to indicate seriality.

In descriptive cataloging, monographic publication is considered the norm. Serials have a separate chapter of rules—chapter 12—following those for monographic items that fall into one of ten media groups: books, pamphlets, and printed sheets; cartographics; manuscripts; music; sound recordings; motion pictures and video recordings; graphics; computer files; three-dimensional materials; and microforms. In this way description of printed serials is separated from description of printed monographs by a great many chapters and pages.

This distancing could be a coincidence or it could be perceived as evidence that monographic nonbook items are closer to books, bibliographically speaking, than are printed serials.

AACR2R's chapter 12 makes it possible to create one catalog record that will stand for all the individual issues of a serial title with little ongoing maintenance. Dates are left open and a skeletal physical description is made that doesn't indicate the total number of pieces. Only those elements that apply to all parts of the serial are included. Since material in any type of physical format may be published in parts intended to go on forever, the cataloger is instructed to combine the serials chapter with appropriate chapters for the medium if the serial item to be cataloged is a nonprint item, making adjustments to both chapters as needed.

Cataloging an entire item as one bibliographic unit is considered the norm while analysis is the anomaly. Analytic cataloging is covered in AACR2R's chapter 13, the final, brief chapter of part 1. For serials, the typical bibliographic unit includes much more than the item in hand; it also includes all the parts not yet published. The assumptions implicit in AACR2R are that typical library materials are monographic publications cataloged as a whole. Based on this norm, the most atypical situation imaginable in descriptive cataloging is an analyzed serial. These are the realities of cataloging, but do they reflect either the realities of information production or the needs of information users?

REALITY 1:
INFORMATION PRODUCTION

If the complaints of collection development librarians are to be believed, new periodicals and serials are proliferating so rapidly that they are testing the abilities of library budgets to keep up. In contrast, the annual output of monographic books is holding fairly steady or perhaps dropping slightly as publishing house leadership is assumed by professional managers interested solely in maximizing profits and as independent publishing houses are taken over by multiproduct, multinational conglomerates also interested solely in high-profit titles. In either instance, books estimated to be marginally profitable or worse—unprofitable—are dropped from the list of prospective issues regardless of their literary value. Fewer and fewer presses can afford to sell less than 10,000 copies of a book or publish titles they know will never make it into best-seller lists, book-of-the-month-club selections, or television or movie screenplays.

One of the principal problems facing collection developers in libraries is how to gain control over the serials budget to prevent it from swallowing the entire budget for new materials. Some libraries have ordered a freeze on purchases of new monographic books in order to continue paying for ever more costly periodical subscriptions. Others have declared war on serials, putting ceilings on the cost of individual subscriptions, ordering a moratorium on initiating new subscriptions, conducting subscription elimination projects, or mandating that no new subscription can be started unless an old one is eliminated.

Not only do serials create budget problems they cost more money for the binding and processing needed to make them sufficiently book-like to be shelved in book stacks, and then they consume large amounts of that limited space.

The question is: Should serial titles that cost so much money and occupy so much space be cataloged as if they were a single monographic book? Doesn't this hinder exploitation of the resource? Doesn't this keep the catalog from adequately reflecting the range of the library's collections as well as the scope and breadth of the knowledge the collections contain?

REALITY 2:
NEEDS OF INFORMATION USERS

Which brings us to the second reality: the reality of users' information needs. People who come to a library seeking a particular item usually have no trouble (or only a little trouble) finding what they want. For any item there are three possibilities: the library owns the item and it is available; the library owns the item and it isn't available because it is in use, at the bindery, past due, or lost; or the item isn't part of the library's collection. But when a person comes to the library seeking information—something on a particular topic, readings to be used to write a paper, or something pleasant to while away leisure hours—there is cause for alarm. The patron seeking something good to read, hear, or view, something informative, or something to suit some personal purpose may fail at the catalog, fail at the shelves, fail altogether to find what they want. Part of the blame should be placed on the information seeker if he or she doesn't have the courage or take the time to ask the librarian for help. But much of the blame is inherent in the catalog, which fails to reveal what knowledge the library actually contains.

For works manifested in dense media, such as microforms, sound recordings, and serials, the catalog offers the least effective access. Who cares if the library catalog lists *The Best of the Beatles* or Beatles. Works. Selections, if the catalog record doesn't tell you whether "A Hard Day's Night" is one of the selections? And who cares if the library owns *Technicalities* if the catalog record for it doesn't say that "Interfaces" is one of its columns? Certainly, there is no catalog record for "Interfaces" and no listing under "Intner, Sheila S." Library patrons are supposed to know that these aren't things the catalog is designed to show.

"What's the matter with you?" you explode. "There are indexes that show this kind of information and patrons are supposed to use them to find it. Libraries have indexes for articles and columns in periodicals; indexes to individual poems, stories, and plays in anthologies; and indexes to individual songs on record albums. There are all sorts of finding tools for the information you are talking about without making the library spend a whole lot of money for extra cataloging that would just clutter up the catalog, after all!"

Quite right! Librarians have indexes, most of which they don't prepare and most of which show what the publishers think should be shown. Most are excellent sources of information to complement the catalog—provided one knows how to use them. Still, two problems remain. First, patrons have to make sophisticated judgments about the information they seek before beginning the search process—for example, is what they want going to be found in a book, serial, microform, or sound recording. Second, commercially prepared indexes don't show what an individual library has in its collections; they show what a group of titles contain, which means multiple look-ups are required to succeed at an index-based search.

CONCLUSION

The foregoing analysis doesn't prove anything, but it is intended to provoke some serious thought about the nature of bibliographic units appropriate for cataloging the library's serial holdings. Here are some questions to consider.

- Is it and should it be part of the library's job to provide better access to serials?

- Is it enough to own whatever indexes are available in relevant subject areas? Is it okay to say, in effect, "Let H. W. Wilson do it?"

- Or are library catalogs failing to perform their roles as the keys to the collection?

- Is it time to consider some changes?

- What might be more desirable than one summary-level catalog record for a serial title that costs thousands of dollars, occupies dozens of shelves, and contains thousands of individual works, hundreds of columns, reviews, profiles, and other features?

- Finally, if computers are releasing library catalogs from the confines of card files and printed books, what might they permit — even encourage — in more effective access to one of the library's greatest assets: the serials collection?

Serials Catalog Records:
Image and Reality

Many people consider a library's catalog to be the key to the library's collections. This image may match the reality for some materials in the collection but it doesn't hold for everything. The image doesn't match the reality for materials not listed in the catalog nor for materials for which the catalog records are overly abbreviated. Serials tend to fall into one of the two categories for which the image fails to match the reality. They are rarely described in detail by their catalog records.

"So what?" I hear you cry. "Tell me something I don't know."

In chapter 14 I discussed several reasons for expanding access to serials in local library catalogs, including the physical size, cost, and amount of information a serial run represents; the continuing expansion of serials publishing; and the burden that not doing so puts on searchers. I pointed out that library catalog records for serial titles omitted information that is likely to change from issue to issue; this is done to necessitate the least amount of updating. In place of detailed catalog records librarians rely on commercially produced finding aids to gain access to the information contained in serials, primarily by buying indexes like the *Readers' Guide*.

In this chapter I want to focus on the catalog records librarians prepare for serials, identify what they contain and omit, and examine the rationale for current rules and practices.

DESCRIPTIVE CATALOGING RULES
FOR SERIALS

AACR2R's chapter 12 contains rules for describing serial publications. In its scope statement, chapter 12 claims to cover all serial publications without regard to physical format and claims that its rules should be used in conjunction with whatever other chapter(s) covers a particular medium, along with chapter 1, general rules. However, chapter 12's opening rules, which cover the chief information source, apply solely to printed serials. This creates extra inconvenience for nonprint catalogers, who must flip back and forth through three or more chapters instead of the usual two.

Chapter 12's table of contents looks very much like those for other chapters, except that sections for "Items made up of several types of material," and "Facsimiles, photocopies, and other reproductions" are missing. Presumably, serials made up of several types of material and reproduced serials will be cataloged using the appropriate medium-specific chapters of AACR2R, as stated in the scope statement. Chapter 12 has a unique section toward the end titled "Sections of serials," which prohibits multilevel entries for serial parts. Instead, the instruction is to "describe such sections as separate serials" (AACR2R, p. 298). Since it isn't customary for U.S. catalogers to make multilevel records for any materials, I suppose this point is moot, but I can't help wondering what disaster occurs if one applies multilevel structures to serial parts, e.g.,

Level 1   Library journal. — Vol. 1, no. 1 (Jan. 1, 1876)-
           . — New York : [add pub. here], 1876- .
           v. ; 28 cm.

Level 2   Vol. 115, no. 3 (Feb. 15, 1990). — Cahners/Bowker, 1990. — 244 p. : ill. (some col.) ; 28 cm.

Level 3   Visions of the '90s : where we're headed in libraries, book publishing, and distribution / Judy Quinn, issue editor. — p. 137-162.

A different option suggested by AACR2R is to add a contents note to the main record for the title, i.e., "Library journal," indicating that it includes "Visions of the '90s" as an insert. This is an impractical solution because it means continuous revision of the record every time *LJ* tries out some new idea for a section. A very long and rambling record would result.

The only thing searchers get in most libraries is the information in the first level of the multilevel record above, which doesn't tell them much, certainly nothing that pertains to or leads a searcher to the special section in the February 15 issue devoted to future trends in publishing. On the other hand, if the section were issued separately, we would have been free to describe it with a separate record—not great but better than nothing. The catalog record might look like this

Library journal. Visions of the '90s : where
   we're headed in libraries, book publishing,
   and distribution. — [No. 1]- . — New York
   : Cahners/Bowker, 1989- .
   v. : col. ill. ; 28 cm.
   Irregular.

Special rules relating primarily to serial publications seem to be based on a guiding principle of omission. They start by interpreting whether acronyms and names of corporate bodies, which often appear to be part of periodical titles (see *JAMA*, the *Journal of the American Medical Association*, for example), belong in the title proper (AACR2R, p. 278). These rules tend to be *ex*clusive, not *in*clusive, since cover designers seem to like jazzy logos made up of such elements more than titles proper. But subsequent rules instruct catalogers to omit other doubtful additions and elements that are likely to vary from issue to issue, such as the numbering. And this principle of omission continues.

Rules for statements of responsibility instruct catalogers to omit names of editors (AACR2R, p. 281), since editors come and go. Edition-area transcriptions are limited to five types (local, special interest, special format, language, and reprint or reissue editions), while other edition data are relegated to the Specific Details or Note areas (AACR2R, p. 282). The Specific Details area contains numbering and chronological data omitted from the Title and Edition areas, but for continuing serials only the data for the first issue is recorded. This is followed by a hyphen to indicate that the data is unfinished, or "open." Similarly, in the Physical Description area, the extent of the item is left blank since, as issues arrive and volumes are completed, extent changes.

Idiosyncracies in the Note area begin with the first note, "frequency," substituting for the "nature of the work" note of other chapters. This is unfortunate because titles such as *Omni* or *The Atlantic Monthly* do not readily identify the nature of their contents. In place of "edition and history," the seventh note for serials establishes a title's relationship with other serials. This valuable note tells searchers that *National Daisy Chain Circular* is a continuation of *Daisy Chain News* and is itself continued by *U.S. Wildflower Quarterly*. So important is this data that two pages of examples follow the instruction for the note (AACR2R, pp. 292-94). Other unique notes relate to the numbering and chronological data, indexes, and the item described. This last is not the familiar "copy being described" note common to other chapters, also present for serials, but one in which the cataloger identifies the issue used to make the description when it is not the first. There is no dissertation note for serials (doctoral candidates take note!), and the "with" note is called "issued with."

In the Standard Number area, the ISSN is provided (if there is one) along with the key title for the serial; this acknowledges the title as an alternative identifier. I fail to see why, if there is no ISSN but the key title is available, it is not given. Wouldn't the alternative unique identifier be even more important if no ISSN were present?

THE BIBLIOGRAPHIC LEVELS

AACR2 has three bibliographic levels, all considered standard, containing varying amounts of data. Libraries may choose the level that suits their needs. First level description, the simplest standard, lacks general material designations, other title information, multiple statements of responsibility, data for multiple publishers, full physical descriptions, and series statements. This level is fine for very small collections or libraries where such additional data is rarely used. Second level description contains all of the elements omitted in first level plus a few more. Second level is usually applied to large collections in major universities and public libraries as well as smaller collections in institutions that pattern their cataloging after the bibliographic leaders.

It is unsettling to realize that the Library of Congress, the largest research library in the United States and the leader of leaders in cataloging, does only first level cataloging (with some additional enrichments) for serials. There are no subtitles in LC's serial records, for example, because subtitles are "other title information" and that is not required for first level cataloging. Never mind that subtitles are a handy way to distinguish serials with generic titles like *Proceedings*, *Newsletter*, or *Bulletin*. These titles are distinguished by adding a different identifying term to a uniform title heading.

The choice of a term to identify generically named serials presents problems like those posed by generically named conference proceedings. One of the most disheartening arguments among cataloging rulemakers I ever heard regarded the merits of preferring the place of publication over sponsoring body as the identifying element for generically titled conferences. Although the people representing public service librarians made a strong case for sponsoring bodies, place of publication won the day because it was so much easier for catalogers. The decision was later reconsidered and still is a source of debate.

The point here is that any library considering second level cataloging for serials is thinking about outdoing LC. Isn't that reason enough to disdain the notion?

THE MARC FORMAT VERSUS CATALOG CARDS FOR SERIALS

Libraries that automate their bibliographic data using the MARC format gain something in the conversion besides the change from cards to computer screens, namely, a significant amount of additional information. Perhaps the most important addition in MARC serial records are the extensive index notes (field 510) that show where the title's contents are indexed. Title variants are given in fields of their own, and languages and certain subject contents are recorded in code. The symbols of holding libraries may be displayed. There is no question that the MARC serial record is a cut above its 3 x 5 counterpart.

Yet, when libraries automate with insufficient funds to do the whole job, they sometimes eliminate the serials holdings from the initial conversion under the mistaken notion that commercial indexes furnish all the information patrons need. The same argument is used to exclude serial titles from the card catalog. Those actions are unfortunate and short-sighted. Librarians who do so abdicate their responsibility to provide bibliographic access to a significant portion of the library's collections.

SUBJECT ANALYSIS FOR SERIALS

It is a hardy cataloging department that undertakes to assign subject headings to serials. A great many serials are quite broad in scope, some so truly general that any subject in the LCSH list might be applicable to some of its articles, papers, or columns. Although librarians are beginning to realize that nothing binds them to Cutter's ideal of a single subject heading for each item cataloged or to the Rule of Three in assigning subject headings (unless, of course, they use Sears), total conversion to a freewheeling mindset still lags far behind technical capabilities to enhance intellectual access to serials. The additional expense of subject cataloging, the additional entries in the subject file, and the notion that commercially vended indexes "do it all" are powerful inducements to neglect subject cataloging for serials.

Searchers in the subject catalog, who might be very well satisfied by the contents of a particular serial title, will not find serials along with monographs on a topic unless subject headings have been assigned. Put this piece of information together with the assumption usually made about searchers, i.e., that novice or less knowledgeable searchers use the subject catalog while experts tend to do author or title searches, and you see that failure to include subject headings for serials poses the greatest problem for the least knowledgeable searchers – people who might have difficulty searching indexes, too. Shouldn't these people get all the help they can from the library's main finding tool, the catalog?

Classification of serials is difficult, time-consuming, and costly. So librarians have created a myth to justify not classifying serials. Without the hint of a wink or a smile they say, "People don't want us to classify serials; they only look for them by title." Of course they only look for them by title – libraries shelve them that way! This silly, self-fulfilling prophesy has come true, all right, and it eliminates the need to do anything more than shelve the serial runs somewhere in alphabetic order by title.

The folk wisdom about shelving ignores the variety of problems alpha-shelving creates. These include

- problems of alphabetizing, e.g., if you are searching *JAMA*, the *Journal of the American Medical Association*, do you go to "Ja ... " or "Jo ..."?

- problems of serial parts. AACR2R has two fine examples: *Journal of Polymer Science. Part A. General Papers* and *Progress in Nuclear Energy. Series II. Reactors*. Should they or shouldn't they be shelved with their parent titles? Should the words *Part* and *Series* be regarded?

- problems of many identical generic titles.

- most important, problems for browsers, who will not find serial titles intershelved with other materials on a topic.

In a large library with eight thousand to ten thousand serial titles, miles of shelving are consumed by serial runs. It is not easy to maintain them in one unit. In one library I used, pre-1950 volumes were located in a sub-sub-basement; 1950–1959 volumes were located a floor above; 1960–1969 volumes were located in the basement; 1970–1979 volumes were shelved in a section of ground-floor book stacks, and more recent issues were in the reference department. Tracking a topic through the decades demanded real determination and physical stamina.

CONCLUSION

Serial titles usually are larger and more costly than monographic titles, but their catalog records are simplified in both descriptive and subject aspects. First level enriched descriptions are all that the Library of Congress does for serials, while second level descriptions or better are the norm for monographs. Assignment of added entries for editors and other details that change over the life of a serial run is rare. Subject headings may not be assigned to serial titles at all, even though it is through the subject catalog that novice searchers are most likely to seek information. Lack of subject-oriented classifications for serial titles means that browsers will overlook relevant serials in perusing the stacks in a subject area. And problems associated with maintaining and shelving serial titles make even alpha-shelving complicated.

What can be done? The next chapter examines strategies for treating serials more like books, bibliographically speaking, and affording them equivalent accessibility through the library's catalog.

16

Modern Serials Cataloging

Catalogers have always been attracted to practical solutions to problems in bibliographic access. This chapter offers suggestions for a new, modern perspective on serials cataloging that will enable librarians to accomplish two things: justify their serials budget expenditures and assist library patrons in making full use of serials collections. Now that's a positive strategy. It won't make patrons unhappy by cutting out titles they want the library to buy. It won't make subscription agents or publishers unhappy by cutting their business. What it will do is make the serials that are bought more accessible and thereby more used. More use means increasing the amount of information service serials provide and improving their cost-benefit ratio. This ratio must be improved if we are to avoid foregoing serials altogether. Since librarians have proved ineffective in lowering serials costs, increasing the benefits seems the only alternative. I think the proposed solution is practical as well as positive.

The assumptions on which my suggestions are based are simple. First, an entire serial run is too large a bibliographic unit for effective access; second, it is desirable to break a serial title into monograph-like units for cataloging purposes; and third, in general a serial volume is the equivalent of a monograph, and sometimes a serial issue is the equivalent of a monograph. The conventional wisdom that the entire serial run is the appropriate bibliographic unit for cataloging is counterproductive.

CATALOGERS' DECISIONS

In view of the assumptions stated above, the cataloger's first decision in cataloging a serial the modern way would be to determine the nature of the bibliographic unit, i.e., whether to treat the issue or the volume as the primary unit. The critical difference between traditional cataloging and the new method is that serial titles would no longer be treated in their entirety by a single bibliographic record.

Could two catalogers make different choices? Of course they could, and they should. The demands of a library's clients, the size of its collections, and the relevance of serial holdings to catalog search requests should govern the choice of an appropriate bibliographic unit in much the same way that these factors should govern the choice of an appropriate level of bibliographic description. Different levels of bibliographic description furnish varying amounts and types of information in the descriptive portion of bibliographic records. The choice of serial unit for cataloging purposes impacts all parts of the record, including subject headings and classification and other types of inventory control. (My experience indicates that part of the difficulty in exerting control over serials inventory lies in having only one catalog record for the whole run — translating into one inventory record. Wouldn't it make more sense to have one catalog entry and inventory record per unit of use?)

Each unit (read: issue or volume) of the serial could still be collocated with all other units of the whole title on a master record or meta-record that coordinates all of the subordinate units and holding libraries in an abbreviated form for the national network.

Monthlies and more frequently issued titles would be good candidates for volume-level cataloging. Issue-level cataloging would make sense for annuals, semi-annuals, irregulars, and quarterlies, especially scholarly journals whose individual issues tend toward book length and for which access to individual articles is of major importance to library patrons. (For annuals, volume-level and issue-level treatment would be identical, since the one issue per year often is an annual volume.) Public libraries would be relieved of the burden of cataloging scholarly journals or proceedings: They don't buy them, so they wouldn't have to catalog them.

Once the cataloger decides whether to treat issues or volumes of a serial title as the bibliographic unit, cataloging would proceed in the usual way, with some exceptions, e.g., open entries would become unnecessary except as temporary records of volumes in progress. Editors could be traced, as could columns and columnists, authors and titles of major articles, and features considered important by the cataloging agency. An automatic indexing system using existing standards could be employed to keep track of the levels of physical hierarchy (i.e., titles, volumes, numbers, issues, dates, articles, pages, etc.).

Other policy decisions would emulate those for monographic series or nonprint items, e.g., whether to index and class them together or individually and whether to intershelve them with monographs or shelve them separately.

WON'T THIS COST A FORTUNE?

Currently, the costs saved by cataloging serial titles as single units are far outweighed by the costs of the indexes required to access the serials' contents plus the cost of reference assistance to help patrons wend their way through the bibliographic maze: find and search index; locate title, volume, and issue; determine whether library owns it; find physical item; locate correct pages; find article. I still hold my breath when I finally reach what I think is the correct page for a citation located through *Library Literature*, never certain that I copied the citation without error, located the correct volume, and will indeed find the article on the designated page. When I don't — and it happens two or three times in ten — I must retrace my steps to find the glitch. At least once out of every two or three misses, when I cannot find the flaw in my search-and-retrieve process, I am forced to believe that the index citation was at fault. (Was it a different journal? A different author? A different title? A different volume? A different page?) And I am a professional librarian — a trained searcher. Imagine how it must be for nonlibrarians.

ADVANTAGES AND DISADVANTAGES

For patrons, one advantage of the new kind of serials cataloging I propose is that locally controlled products will be made available for each booklike unit of a serial title. Local controls ought to result in catalog products with greater relevance to patrons' needs. For example, critics who decry the use of AACR abbreviations in catalog records on the grounds that patrons can't decipher them should have a look in a Wilson index to appreciate the heights to which the art of abbreviation can be raised. In AACR cataloging, at least, titles proper are transcribed in full and cannot be abbreviated until the sixth word. If some uninstructed patron fails to realize that "ill." in the physical description means the item is illustrated, it isn't as crucial an error as failing to realize that *Am Lib Con* is *American Library Contracting*, not *American Liberty and Constitution*. (I made up that example, good reader. Don't go looking for it in *Library Literature*.)

More important, under the new method a librarian must actually handle the material to catalog it, thereby becoming more knowledgeable about the works (and their authors, titles, and subjects) in the serials holdings. The value of handling materials to build expertise cannot be underestimated. Not even the most dedicated librarians can be expected to read everything in an area of subject expertise, and reliance on commercially published indexes to collocate all information on a subject can be a terrible mistake. I am amazed by what indexers do not consider related materials as well as what they do not list at all.

If the library catalog is online I can let my fingers "do the walking" through the serials as well as the monographic holdings. I don't have to remember the commands for searching four or five different computer systems (one for the online catalog and one each for three or four different online and CD-ROM indexes) and, perhaps, four or five different thesaurus vocabularies for the same subject. Sure, I will get many more hits per subject request, but I can be much more specific and precise without failing to retrieve something of value.

Another advantage of making a record for a booklike unit of a serial is that more "works" by an author will be collocated in the catalog. When I want to read Michael Gorman's thinking about cataloging, using the catalog is a dud. All it lists is AACR2 (both full and concise editions), which won't give me any critical analyses. Gorman's valuable critiques of cataloging appear in a number of journals, some scholarly, and several proceedings. If I turn to *Library Literature*, I have to search at least ten of its volumes under several different headings and *see also* (which will probably yield at least one citation I will never locate). Wouldn't I like to have greater access to Gorman's scholarly writings on cataloging through the catalog? I certainly would.

This type of cataloging would help collection development librarians recognize theme issues of journals with monograph-like titles that are also marketed as monographic books. The savings on duplicate orders, purchases, and processing could enhance the cost-benefit ratio of modern serials cataloging.

Finally, library catalogs that contain records for local serials holdings only would not lead patrons to scads of items that their libraries do not have, which is my main complaint about periodical indexes, especially the online variety. Why is it that the article from *Zimbabwean Librarian*, to which my library does not subscribe, sounds like it has exactly the information I want, while citations to a dozen journals at hand miss the mark? My Hobson's choice is to forego the article while continuing to believe it is just what I need or to fill out several forms and wait a couple of weeks to discover, in seven out of ten instances, that the title is deceiving and the article is not what I thought it was—or what I wanted.

I foresee at least two problems cropping up in attempts to implement this notion of modern serials cataloging: increases in the volume of cataloging and justifying the purchase of serial indexes. Adopting modern serials cataloging does not mean a library should stop subscribing to serial indexes, it merely means the library should provide a better method of accessing local holdings. Any savings a library might realize would come from better use of local materials, fewer inter-library loans, and diminished need for reference librarians to assist patrons in finding information in serials holdings. On the other hand, separate serials departments might be absorbed into the cataloging department and provide the extra person-power needed to handle the load. Cataloging the smaller serial units would add much more interesting work to the serialists' routines of check-in, claiming, and binding. More important, the new status accorded to serials would give additional satisfaction to those who work with them.

CONCLUSION

The immediacy and vitality of information in serials is what makes them valuable for research. It is not unusual to read the same material appearing in a serial (sometimes reworked, sometimes not) two or three years later in a monograph. Publication in scholarly journals or conference proceedings often is the final step in the research process, so libraries that prefer to collect monographic books over serials may be foregoing one of the best sources of new knowledge. Can one be sure that "waiting until the book comes out" will not hamper one's public far more than spending money on the periodical version but not having the money to buy the book later on?

Two acquisitions librarians at the University of Rhode Island looked at the proportion of use of serials versus monographs reported in sixty-six research studies conducted since the 1950s. They found serials use to be as high as 93 percent in some disciplines.[1] They contend that an appropriate ratio for purchase of serials and monographs can be determined based on the characteristics of literature use for each discipline in which a library collects. I contend that the use of serials would rise still higher if the public could gain access to them through the library's catalog instead of having to go through a three-step search process (i.e., search index, search serials holdings catalog, search shelves) to find the information that serials contain.

The viability of the new perspective on serials cataloging depends on computer-based files. Modern serials cataloging probably would not work in a card catalog. The additional labor to catalog, duplicate, and file so many more cards would negate the benefits. However, librarians do not seem to be looking very hard for ways to make the computer-based catalog a better and more effective instrument than its paper counterpart has been. As a result, although the search process might be fancier, the online catalog doesn't tell us much more than the old card file did. One of the things librarians can do to make the online file a better tool is to put more information into it. I suggest that serials holdings represent the perfect body of literature for enhanced bibliographic information in online files. Devlin and Kellogg's research provides a priority list of disciplines for an experimental program of modern serials cataloging. How much might use increase and how much easier might it be to do the searching? Try it in one or two disciplines and see.

Although monographic books are not exploited as fully as they might be, bibliographically speaking, they are far and away treated more thoroughly than serials. Isn't it about time we looked for a better way to make the dollars spent on serials as beneficial as possible?

NOTES

[1]Robin B. Devlin and Martha Kellogg, "The Serial/Monograph Ratio in Research Libraries," *College & Research Libraries* (January 1990):46-54.

PART 3

ROCKY ROAD
Relationships Between Technical and Public Services

Ten Good Reasons Why Reference Librarians Would Make Good Catalogers

It has been said that the mindset needed for cataloging is quite different than that needed for reference work or management. But is this really true or is it merely another myth? Do librarians say it because it sounds good? Do they use it as an excuse to assuage their consciences when they offer lower pay to cataloging librarians than to other librarians? Does believing it make noncatalogers feel good, enhancing their status at the expense of colleagues who are normally out of sight?

The cataloging mindset is supposed include the ability to deal with detail, to understand complex sets of rules, to appreciate consistency and logic, and to be prepared to handle the processing of all sorts of materials—materials having unknown problems as well as previously encountered problems. This set of attributes sounds remarkably useful for reference librarians and managers, too; add in the abilities to communicate and to interact successfully with people, and you have the requisite skills for a good many positions in any one of these three areas.

Indeed, catalogers cannot be too bad at reference work, since a good many of them do it and are hired with the understanding that they have to put in a certain number of hours at the reference desk. On the other hand, many fewer reference librarians are hired with the understanding that they must put in a certain number of hours in the cataloging department, although this results in a loss of sorely needed expertise in the cataloging department for particular language or subject areas. Why is this so? Do employers believe reference librarians don't make good catalogers? Do they believe reference librarians haven't the correct mindset for cataloging?

This chapter offers ten good reasons why reference librarians would make good catalogers, along with a fervent plea to the administrators who devise job descriptions to consider altering the job descriptions of reference staff members. If the administrators can't implement the switch retroactively to affect those already on staff, they might try implementing it with new hires.

REASON 1:
PUBLIC INTERACTION

Reference librarians interact directly with the people using the library and can observe their information-seeking patterns directly.

The most obvious contribution of reference librarians to the cataloging operation is their direct knowledge of people's information-seeking behavior. In addition, they hear client complaints and are in a position to make suggestions or decisions based on what they hear and observe. If librarians truly believe that catalogers should produce user-friendly catalogs and be responsive to user needs, then knowledge of the public's behavior and criticisms is not merely nice to have—it is essential.

Is it really necessary for reference librarians to catalog materials in order to incorporate their knowledge of client behavior into the cataloging process? Why can't reference librarians merely report their observations and client complaints to members of the cataloging staff and let them handle the problems? The answer is simple: Having reference librarians tell catalogers what catalog users want without complete and thorough understanding of what the cataloging process is all about and the objectives it serves, and without having a stake in its success or failure, gives them the power to govern decision-making without taking responsibility. But if the same reference librarians are also catalogers, their knowledge of user behavior is integrated with their knowledge of cataloging principles and purposes and their decisions can be sensitive to potential conflicts and tradeoffs between competing demands.

REASON 2:
LANGUAGE OR SUBJECT EXPERTISE

Reference librarians often have valuable language or subject expertise.

Although the question of whether good reference librarians should be generalists or subject specialists is open to perennial debate, the fact is that almost all reference librarians have some area of special knowledge. In academic libraries they are expected to cover particular selection areas based on their language abilities, major interests as undergraduates, or specialization in graduate studies. In large academic libraries reference librarians either have a second master's degree in a subject area or are expected to get one in order to retain their positions and advance in the hierarchy. Isn't it a waste to expect the cataloging department to duplicate the talents and specializations of the reference department? Isn't it more effective management to pool the special expertise of the cataloging librarians with the special expertise of the reference staff and expand capabilities in both areas? Why not assign selection duties, public service, and cataloging to all of them according to their language or subject areas? Isn't this what dual assignments are all about?

REASON 3:
JOB SATISFACTION

Dual assignments in cataloging and reference make for more interesting and satisfying jobs.

Several recent graduates tell me they have or are actively seeking jobs with dual assignments. I commend them. I can't think of anything more deadly than having to sit at the same desk and catalog forty hours a week, except for the prospect of spending an equal number of hours a week running around answering questions at the public service desk. I love cataloging and I love doing reference work and have done them both, but I wouldn't want to do either one nonstop for my entire work week. Variety is not only the spice of life, it adds measurably to the pleasure of the work place, providing changes of pace and opportunities to hone many skills in the practice of one's profession.

REASON 4:
KNOWLEDGE OF REFERENCE SOURCES

Knowledge of reference sources is important for cataloging.

Authority work is just one of a cataloger's tasks that requires sophisticated knowledge of information sources identified primarily with reference work: biographical dictionaries or directories, atlases and gazetteers, directories of associations and government agencies, and so forth. Different types of headings require the use of different types of tools; this is child's play to the well-trained reference librarian, but it could be a tedious search through unfamiliar territory for the cataloger.

Knowledge of information production and publishing (the book trade) may be second nature to the reference librarian who deals with the review media and inspects titles obtained on approval. Although catalogers should be equally sophisticated in the book trade, they glean what they know from title pages — which are notoriously inscrutable if not downright misleading.

Cataloging has much to gain from librarians who have more exposure to and training in the use of reference tools and familiarity with publishing and distribution of informational materials.

REASON 5:
INTEGRATED DECISION-MAKING

Decision-making about the catalog is no longer a back-room affair but requires integration of knowledge about all the bibliographic services in the library.

When catalog cards were written in library hand and entered into monolithic card files, decisions about catalog entries affected only one tool — the local library catalog. Today, with the MARC-formatted catalog entry becoming the basis for a host of systems and bibliographic tools ranging from acquisitions and interlibrary loan to circulation control, one-sided knowledge and a one-sided perspective is a barrier to better service in all of these systems.

Fundamental to the function of the scholar's workstation is the ability to access bibliographic records as a first step in locating desired documents. When electronic publishing becomes more widespread, bibliographic systems will have to incorporate these elements in the web of universal bibliographic control being developed by local, regional, national, and international network links. Understanding of information retrieval and use is as vital in constructing these systems as is the understanding of information organization and storage.

The reference librarian (or the dual-assignment librarian) plays an essential role here. The more he or she combines knowledge of the input phase with knowledge of the output phase, the better the chance that developing systems will harmonize effectively.

REASON 6:
BIBLIOGRAPHIC INSTRUCTION

Teaching clients to use the library (i.e., bibliographic instruction) requires in-depth knowledge of the catalog: its organization and structure as well as its operation and use.

By working as catalogers, reference librarians contribute to the library's bibliographic organization, thereby enhancing their skills in teaching clients about it. If informal surveys among my students are to be believed, as undergraduates very few were taught to use the catalog well. Virtually none were taught more than how to recognize call numbers and access points (often, this information was library specific—e.g., the red print is a subject heading; the black print is a title; *B* means that book is in the branch library). Few were taught how to use the data provided in bibliographic descriptions, how to use tracings to broaden a search, or how to use the subject heading list to develop subject terms for a search.

It would be valuable for the library's lay public to understand the power of catalog entries to aid them in finding desired materials. Why bother to provide online catalogs with Boolean and keyword searching, index browsing, and other costly functions if you are not training the public to tap their potential?

Beyond the catalog itself lies the classification, shelf location, and circulation systems. The lay public understands these systems no more than they do the catalog and subject heading list, yet it is these systems that contain the information most library users really want, the answer to the question "Can I have this item?" As these systems are merged, the librarian who knows all of them well and can impart that knowledge has a valuable service to offer to the public.

REASON 7:
THE IMAGE OF THE
SCHOLAR-LIBRARIAN

The image of the scholar-librarian, currently a shadow (if not a specter) of its former brilliance, could be revitalized by reference librarians skilled in bibliographic organization.

Once upon a time, reference librarians were bibliographers and furnished bibliographic services, just like catalogers. Somehow, the twin purposes of bibliography, to identify and to organize literature, were dichotomized, just as reference librarians and cataloging librarians were split into disparate departments. I often wonder how much time reference librarians spend creating bibliographies or other bibliographic tools for their clients as opposed to doing ready reference for them or getting the clients started on doing it themselves. I know librarians who are told they may not spend more than ten minutes with a single client and others who are irritated when a client comes back for help again and again. With all the responsibilities heaped on reference librarians, perhaps they have lost their scholarly urges toward bibliography. These days, librarians are accustomed to having bibliographies produced by commercial publishers, not themselves.

How appropriate it would be to bring reference librarians back to the bibliographic fold, as it were, by encouraging them to create bibliographic entries and to contribute to bibliographic systems. It might motivate them to seek their roots in the great traditions of bibliography.

REASON 8:
FRESH PERSPECTIVES ON OLD PROBLEMS

Reference librarians might not believe it, but cataloging an item is a problem-solving exercise, just as doing reference work is. Their expertise at discovering clients' questions — what they really want as opposed to what they say they want — and then solving it by finding the right item would be exceptionally useful if applied to cataloging.

Furthermore, when a librarian has but one perspective, no matter how hard he or she tries, it is difficult to get outside that viewpoint to see things differently. Problem-solving in cataloging tends to move in predictable patterns and to serve a limited set of goals. If reference librarians came into the cataloging department, they could not help but see things from a different perspective and contribute that fresh viewpoint to both the solution of cataloging problems and the identification of new goals.

REASON 9:
TRAINING

Training new staff requires people skills — the reference librarian's forte.

If advertisements in the library press are any indication, hundreds — perhaps thousands — of catalogers are hired in libraries every year. Many of these people are new catalogers taking a professional library position for the first time. Others may be experienced but are moving to a new environment with a different game plan, cohorts, clients, missions, etc. All of these new catalogers have one thing in common: they have to be trained. How useful it would be to call into play the fabled people skills of the reference librarian in the implementation of the training program. What an asset to the cataloging department it would be to assign the new cataloger to a trainer whose patience in explaining things like the catalog and the shelving arrangement is honed by constant practice with those less knowledgeable than the new staff member (i.e., recipients of bibliographic instruction).

REASON 10:
CREATIVE NEW SERVICES

Creative new bibliographic services need input from people who see the catalog from the "other side."

Like problem-solving, the creation and development of new bibliographic services and systems needs fresh ideas, a different perspective, and an appreciation of the use side as well as the entry side of the catalog. When reference librarians contribute their ideas to system design without having had exposure to the cataloging department (as they have done in more than one library), they do so without an appreciation of the cataloging issues and implications. They contribute in a vacuum and, as a result, their contributions sometimes are set aside because they fail to accommodate some seemingly unalterable cataloging prerequisite. Or worse, their ideas are implemented over the objections of the catalogers and fail to produce the desired results. Such failures are costly indeed, wreaking double havoc by destroying traditional avenues of access without supplying alternatives while damaging the credibility of new systems. Clearly, the contribution of reference librarians is desirable in designing new systems only if they recognize and acknowledge the infrastructure into which the system must fit.

CONCLUSION

Here are ten good reasons why reference librarians should do cataloging. Think about it. Their presence in the cataloging department could spark a new interest in the work of the department, infuse new vitality into its operations, and inspire new visions of its products and services.

18

Public Service Librarians and the Catalog

What purposes does the catalog serve for public service librarians and what special problems caused by well-meaning technical service policies might hinder their work and prevent them from accomplishing those purposes?

Policies governing the catalog are usually carefully controlled by technical services staff. The twin objectives that catalog policies are designed to fulfill usually derive from Charles A. Cutter's 1876 statements: The catalog should show what the library owns, and it should bring together the works of an author or on a subject and all the editions of a title. Perfectly reasonable catalog policies serving these objectives, however, can create unusual problems for reference librarians and other public service staff members as well as for the public. The following story—an entirely hypothetical scenario—illustrates what I mean.

FRENCH LITERATURE IN UTOPIA

The administrators at respected old Utopia University Library, concerned about the physical state of its collections and impressed by new preservation and conservation techniques they hope will extend the life of the materials (some of which date back to the latter part of the nineteenth century), hire a well-credentialed and knowledgeable preservation officer who immediately goes to work evaluating the materials. Problem areas are identified and solutions devised. Two of the solutions are to convert some of the most fragile titles to microforms, which, luckily, are available, and to remove others from the shelves to await restorative treatment.

One portion of the university's deteriorating collection of early French literature is removed from the stacks and replaced with microform sets. These sets contain most of the removed titles, but not all of them, and also include some titles not previously owned. Another group of titles in slightly better condition and having some additional value as artifacts is set aside in storage to await restoration.

What happens in the catalog? All the entries for the titles removed from the shelves are pulled out of the catalog. After all, to allow them to remain in the catalog would work against the best interests of searchers, since these titles are no longer part of the university's active book collections, represented in the main catalog. Some of the old entries are held so they can be checked against the contents of the microform sets. Titles not included in the sets can be sent to the collection development officer to be added to the university's desiderata list. Entries belonging to the materials that will be restored are inserted into the books as they are removed and accompany them to their destinations. It may be a long time before they are fit for use again and even then they will not go back to the general stacks but will be sent to Special Collections.

Meanwhile, cataloging policies dictate that the microform sets are cataloged at the set level and the resulting entries filed in the microform catalog. Voila! There are no entries in any catalog for individual titles now available in microform, whether previously owned or new to the collection. Instead, the microform catalog has entries for the sets coupled with indexes available in that department for use in retrieving individual titles.

The reference librarians, of course, are aware of the change in physical formats and know that all of the materials are not gone from the collection. The French literature specialist even remembers most of the titles that were removed from the shelves, but can't be quite sure whether a particular title has been converted, stored, or is one of those lost titles unavailable on microform. Now, in order to locate an individual title belonging to the genre of early French literature for a patron who needs only that one item, the librarian cannot rely on the catalog, though it is still the first place searched, since some of the materials in fairly good condition remain on the shelves. When the catalog yields nothing the librarian sends the searcher to the Microform Department, another room on another floor (since microforms are not part of reference), telling the patron to consult the microform catalog. A lucky patron will do so successfully, locate the desired title, obtain it, find a reader, and have the time to sit there until they are finished. (For those searchers who do not consult the reference librarian, the subject catalog contains a guide screen that says "For early French imprints not listed here, consult the microform catalog." A more specific directive giving the exact microform set titles and locations is under consideration by the catalog department, but some of the catalogers believe no one will read a lengthy message on a guide screen.)

Along comes the collection development officer. This staff member consults with reference librarians as a matter of course but tends to rely first on personal shelf inspections and examinations of the catalog to determine collection strengths and weaknesses. The gap on the early French literature shelves is shocking and the corresponding gap in the catalog is devastating to the collection development officer until a reference librarian explains about the preservation project. The reference librarian suggests a consultation with the preservation officer.

The collection development officer is badly shaken by the knowledge that personal inspections of shelf and catalog are no longer reliable means to identify collection needs. What else has been missed by overlooking the microform catalog? Furthermore, what is the new French literature professor going to say after finding out that the marvelous book collection on which a course in historic French fiction was to be based is now a microform collection? What if the professor intends to put those titles on reserve? How will the circulation department cope with it? The collection development officer looks darkly at the public catalog, musing on its inscrutability, and wonders briefly why she or he was not consulted about all of this before the preservation plan was implemented.

PROBLEMS IN UTOPIA

Let us examine the public service purposes of the catalog and see how they are being thwarted by catalog policies adhered to, in good faith, by the technical services staff.

The first public service purpose of the catalog is that it reflect the holdings of the library. This purpose matches the first of Cutter's catalog objectives which, in turn, dictate catalog policy. Why are the objectives and policies in conflict?

The Problem of Bibliographic Units

When books are removed from the shelves, entries representing them are removed from the catalog. So far, so good. When the same titles are replaced in microform, this time with many books combined into a single set, entries for the sets are put into the catalog. Here is the first problem. Entries for the individual titles disappear with the change in medium. The bibliographic unit for books and microform sets should not be the same, but cataloging policy treats them as if they are because each represents one physical unit of the medium.

Cutter spoke about the catalog showing what the library has on its shelves. In Cutter's time that was primarily, if not entirely, books. Here is a second problem. Microform holdings, like other nonbook holdings, may not be part of the "shelves" or main stacks of the institution. They constitute holdings to be sure, but they are rarely mainstreamed, physically, with their book kin.

The Problem of Multiple Catalogs

Cutter's notion of the catalog implies a monolith. Most very large university libraries like Utopia University have multipart catalogs of which the main catalog contains entries only for books. When microform titles replace book titles, their entries shift from the main catalog to a secondary catalog that reflects microform holdings. Furthermore, when the restored books are reshelved in Utopia University's Special Collections Division, their entries will be refiled in yet another catalog, because Utopia's catalog policies permit special divisions to have their own catalogs and do not maintain a single complete union listing. No single portion of a multipart catalog shows all the holdings of a library; therefore, it cannot satisfy the public service need to see together all the titles of an author or on a subject, or all the editions of a title.

Some very large university libraries (and public libraries, for that matter) have turned to computerized catalogs to help them maintain control over their vast holdings. Many of them are monolithic in structure, containing in one display entries for books, microforms, and other nonbook media as well as special collections of various kinds. Those that are not monolithic fail to serve as complete finding lists despite all the money spent on hardware, software, user interfaces, authority control, and other expensive components of automated catalogs.

The reference librarians at Utopia University Library cannot tell searchers whether the early French imprints are available in microform or whether the imprints are unavailable because they were not reproduced on the microform sets or because they are in storage awaiting treatment. The disposition of individual titles has become a guessing game that the catalog is unable to resolve. Because the microform sets contain so many titles, they are the first alternative to which a searcher is directed, but for many people they are not the last. In addition, the reference librarians are unable to ascertain which new titles are available on microform, since they haven't worked with these titles. When the reference librarians are consulted by the collection development officer, they cannot provide much help in the area of early French literature except to refer the collection development officer to the Microform Department.

The Problem of Circulation Status

The collection development officer examines the catalog as a measuring stick of the collection. The presence or absence of a certain number of titles or certain specific titles is an indication of collection strengths or weaknesses. It is stunning when the catalog confirms the gap found on the shelves. People might deplete the shelves by borrowing the books, but the catalog has entries for materials owned whether or not they are actually present on the shelves. The collection development officer inspects the shelves and the catalog believing that they furnish reliable information. In reality, the inspections do not supply completely reliable data because they cannot.

Here is a third problem. Utopia University's catalog policies do not allow information about the actual location of an item (called status information) to be included with the catalog record. To be fair, not all library catalogs are capable of showing status information. In order to do it in a card catalog, the hundreds or thousands of daily transactions must somehow be recorded, continuously updated, or cleared from the entries. Only computerized catalogs with links to computer-based circulation control systems are able to accomplish such an enormous job. Only when circulation records are combined with catalog records can access data be considered complete (with a grain of salt added for human error, of course).

Utopia University Library's policies do direct technical service librarians to notify the collection developer when the last copy (usually the only copy) of a title is discarded unintentionally, such as occurs when the intended conversion of early French imprints to microform is incomplete. But being notified after the fact is not the same as having the information in anticipation of the conversion. Any library large enough to have separate preservation and collection development officers needs to consider consolidation of those two activities. The catalog, on which all staff should be able to rely for information about holdings, cannot tell either preservationists or collection developers what they need to know.

CONCLUSION

The most striking characteristic of the problems and processes explored in this scenario is the interrelatedness of the activities described, whether public or technical service activities. The impact of catalog policies changes as one or another procedure is implemented and, while there may have been perfectly good reasons for establishment of certain policies at one point, they may at another point work against the public service goals to which the catalog is supposed to be dedicated.

19

A Question of Medium

As fall approaches many libraries begin a new fiscal year with its accompanying full cup of budgetary allocations. Many of them, particularly libraries in the academic sector, but also public, school, and perhaps some special libraries, will launch new cycles of collection development and a new purchasing year. This may be an appropriate time to consider how the medium of a work affects its status in these cycles as well as in other aspects of policy and practice.

This chapter discusses how the factor of physical medium affects the way we plan for, acquire, catalog, and use indexes and abstracts. These common reference tools are available in book form (hard copy) and online as well as on CD-ROM disks, which are machine-readable but are not online. As you read, ask yourself if what you are reading sounds sensible and reasonable or whether we should revise our thinking about these tools in their various physical manifestations.

PLANNING ISSUES

I taught a class in collection development last year in which many of the students were staff members in libraries, some in professional positions. More than one wrote about development of reference collections in their term projects, but not a single one included anything about either the online or CD-ROM versions of indexes and abstracts. Naturally, I picked this up and we discussed it in class one day—a day when the lecture topic was information production. I asked the whole class why anyone planning for reference collections would leave out online systems and CD-ROM. The answer came without hesitation.

"Those aren't collections, they are services," came a chorus. They agreed that online services had no place in reference department collection development plans but rightfully belonged in planning for reference services or in some separate category for automation and automated services.

I was shocked and horrified. How can any reference department omit from its collection development planning the most important indexing and abstracting tools since *Poole's Index*? Online services and CD-ROM contain the same information that hard-copy indexes and abstracts do; students recognize the hard-copy versions and consider them in reference collection development planning. Why do they not consider the computer-based versions of these products? Putting them in compartments called Service or Automation doesn't negate the fact that they contain the same information that the hard-copy versions do — and sooner.

One person spoke up, "If we included the cost of online searching in our reference book budget, we wouldn't have any. The only way we can continue to buy reference books is to keep online services in a separate category. Besides, it *is* a service; it isn't part of our collection."

I countered, "Would you ever consider dropping the printed version of the index and keeping only the online service?"

"Oh, no — never," they replied, heads shaking in disbelief at my outrageous question.

"Why not?" I asked.

"That's easy," said one student. "Only one person can use the online service at a time, but lots of people can browse the indexes simultaneously. Also, online services cost much more."

"Why can only one person use the online service at a time?" I asked.

"Because we only have one terminal," said the student.

"And how much more does online cost?" I asked.

"Well, I don't know, really, but I know it's much, much more," came the reply.

The discussion continued at my prodding, forcing the students to consider the possibilities of adding more terminals or using microcomputer-based CD-ROMs as a third alternative to either online or print versions. What struck me first was that these neophyte librarians have been taught to compartmentalize so well that they fail to realize that DIALOG, BRS, SDC, and other online bibliographic services are reference tools containing the same information as the familiar booklike indexes. The difference between them is that the online services are more up-to-date than the books and much more extensive than the total index purchases of many libraries.

The second thing that struck me was that, even when they recognize that online services are faster and more comprehensive versions of the print indexes, these reference librarians write off the online services as someone else's department or as much, much more costly than books (although they don't know the actual cost) and as limited to one patron at a time (even though that is easily remedied by adding more terminals).

What are librarians really doing by failing to integrate the planning of online, CD-ROM, and print indexes into one process? Avoiding the question of medium, of course. What might they discover if they examined the alternatives without prejudice and weighed the objectively assigned value of the newfangled service opportunities against the full costs of the traditional service? Perhaps some librarians fear the answer.

An academic library director recently announced that he was giving up a host of journal subscriptions and turning to a commercial supplier of journal articles instead. This certainly responds to the complaint that libraries fail to provide patrons with the articles they find cited in indexes because the libraries cannot afford to subscribe to all of the indexed journals. It also enables the library to assign costs rather specifically to those users who incur them, should the library wish to recover costs. Another option is to subscribe to DIALOG's document delivery service along with the right to search hundreds of indexes on the same terminal; in this case, the cost of searching appears on the screen at the end of the search.

Many librarians fear that charging people for the information they provide means subverting professional ethics. They believe that libraries can give people books for free but must charge for computerized information. Is it true? I haven't seen any evidence of it. What I have seen is libraries full of books, not terminals. The only reason librarians believe book-based services can be given away free is that this is the way libraries have operated for more than one hundred years. It is accepted as a given that book-based services are cheap and computer-based services are dear. Suppose a new library was designed with lots of terminals instead of stacks and provided free online document delivery services instead of booklike indexes and printed journals? Might this be cost-effective? Who knows? Who has the audacity to try it?

ACQUISITION ISSUES

One would imagine that the administrators responsible for reference collections and services coordinate the acquisition of indexes and abstracts in all forms. Not true. The acquisition of computer-based systems are often, though not always, separate.

A crisis is taking place in reference departments as clients realize the difference in speed and comprehensiveness between book-based and computer-based services. When I was a student, I would have been glad to pay for the information I needed immediately, not next week or next month or when the journals came back from the bindery. In the whole picture of the cost of my degree, what would these additional charges have meant? Very little. Now that I teach, I am irritated that the book-based indexes are months or years behind the online versions and I have fits when the journals I and my students need (the previous year's issues) are sent to the bindery at the beginning of a semester. I would love to throw the whole print-based system out and install as many terminals as the savings would allow. (But I admit, I do tend to overreact.)

Reference librarians need to come to terms with the fact that acquisition of computer-based services should be coordinated with acquisition of book-based indexes or the waste of unnecessary duplication and the growth of a more popular computer-based information service department somewhere else will put them out of business. Technical service librarians need to be aware of this dichotomy when it exists; their work flow may change radically if coordination of acquisition requires their participation or if transfer of budget and responsibilities to another computer-based services department leaves them with fewer materials to collect for reference departments.

CATALOGING ISSUES

Everyone knows that you can't catalog something you don't have. The first principle of cataloging, according to Michael Gorman's marvelous distillation of AACR2's 620 pages into two fundamental rules, is to describe the item "in hand."[1] When there is no item in hand, there is nothing to describe for a catalog record. Right? Wrong! One of the many problems solved by the debate over computer file cataloging was how to treat files that didn't constitute an item in hand but that resided in a remote computer system. The ultimate bibliographic disposition for these items was simple and practical: One described what existed in the remote location (i.e., provide a file description) but didn't furnish a physical description since, obviously, there was no physical manifestation in hand to describe.

The three forms of an index provide a fine challenge to catalogers. The book form is simple, though it has its choices, too: whether to catalog the book (1) as a monograph, each edition complete in itself with its own record, or (2) as a serial, an ongoing publication without end. Most libraries I have used catalog ongoing indexes as serials with one catalog record for the whole entity—volumes past, present, and future. This takes care of both the individual issues, often appearing several times a year, and annual cumulations. It is neat and economical.

The online form of most indexes is ignored by catalogers. They don't catalog it because it isn't part of the library's collections. It would not make sense to catalog it any more than it would make sense to catalog another library's book because that book might be temporarily acquired on an ILL. The home library might have access to ILL books, but it doesn't own them. If it doesn't own them, it doesn't catalog them. Q.E.D. The home library has access to the online index, but it doesn't own it. If it doesn't own it, it doesn't catalog it. Q.E.D. Right? Unfortunately, right. This is the rationale behind OCLC's decision not to permit catalog records for such database services as DIALOG, SDC, or BRS and, presumably, for the individual databases they survey. The problem is that, as far as the person using the library is concerned, having ERIC online at a terminal through DIALOG or BRS is having ERIC available in the library. To someone who is computer literate, it isn't very different from having ERIC in a series of booklike volumes on the shelves. It is simply ERIC on the VDT screen instead of in print in a codex-style artifact.

Finally, what about the CD-ROM? Well, with the CD-ROM you have an item in hand (an item that, so far, is as stable as any book or journal issue). It can be cataloged using AACR2R's chapter 9. Does the library own it? Maybe it does and maybe not. What does the library do with its old disks? If it sends them back to the vendor in exchange for new versions, they are no more permanent than the online version. If the subscription ends, the library has nothing left, exactly as if they ended their online subscription. On the other hand, if the old disks are retained in the library, then all of the old volumes remain, exactly as occurs with the paper indexes. To catalog or not to catalog? Is it a question of medium or a question of ownership? What does a library own when it subscribes to CD-ROM indexes?

USE ISSUES

When it comes to using indexes in their various forms, several questions leap to mind. First, will all the media be located in the same place? Second, will libraries stick to having just one or two terminals placed in inaccessible locations or will they go for open public access to computer-based indexes? Third, will charges be instituted or continued, if they already exist, for online versions? for CD-ROM versions? but not for print versions? Fourth, will document delivery services accompany online services?

The first question, whether to base all indexes regardless of medium in the same location, is often not a matter of choice but a failure in planning or an accidental happening. Computer-based indexes may be located where the computers are, not where the rest of the reference books are. Computers may be found in the first department that showed an interest in them or in the computer center or media center, if there is one. Once ensconced, it is difficult to relocate them. Relocation may require a considerable investment in rewiring, relocating existing materials, and refurbishing the reference environment to accommodate computer-based indexes.

The old-style, staff-only terminal may have served the public when only a few knew people about computer-based indexes or when charges were relatively high for computer-based services. Now, young people are growing up with computers and the American Library Association is exhorting us to press for more access to computer-based service. If open access to computer-based indexes is desirable, will libraries buy more terminals and make it possible for people to use them? This course of action means making a considerable investment up front (computing always seems to require huge initial inputs of time and money) in order to provide a sufficient number of terminals for public access. Public access is impossible when the number of terminals is severely limited.

Public access is also limited when charges are extremely high compared to all other materials and services. And, speaking of charges, will there be a generally accepted solution to the issue of fee-based or free online service? What will librarians do if governing authorities prohibit charging for online indexes? Go back to paper exclusively? Drop paper in favor of online versions? Neither of those options are in the public's best interests. Planning for different allocation patterns to fund an optimum mix of paper- and computer-based indexes should be explored immediately and seriously in libraries where pay-as-you-go is not an option. Also, some consideration of charging for the use of paper-based indexes should be made, since these materials are not free, either, and often require mediation, too. The notion that a library's book purchase should cost nothing when its information is consumed but that same library's computer purchase should cost something when its information is consumed is utter nonsense, despite its being mouthed by some eminent librarians. Also nonsense is the idea that access to information on a screen is somehow very different than access to information in the pages of a book.

The last question concerns access to documents. While abstracts are the maximum that many computer-based indexes provide, this is changing rapidly and full-text is becoming the wave of the future. Until that wave is universal, however, the only documents most people can obtain quickly are those available from their library's journal collection. Judging from articles in the literature over the last year or two, librarians are spending more time figuring out which journals they can eliminate than how they can add to their list of subscriptions. Interlibrary loan, the usual next-best source, may take several days to two months, on average. If this is the best service libraries can provide free, perhaps the public is getting exactly what it pays for. If, however, document delivery services are offered along with the indexes, people might believe they are getting information services worth paying for.

CONCLUSION

What's in a medium? If one of the choices is in computer-readable form, plenty. The medium can determine location, administrative responsibility, development, cost, charges, access—in short, just about everything. All the solemn pronouncements in the world won't change the fact, however, that an index is an index, after all, whether it is bound in cloth or transmitted over a VDT terminal. To the person looking up a half-remembered citation, however, the VDT terminal offers many more possibilities than the silent, unresponsive pages of a book. The paperless society may be slow in coming to the fiction section of the library, but in the area of indexing and abstracting services, it is here (although our public services colleagues don't want to admit it). How about it, reference collection developers? Are you ready to interface with the jet set yet?

NOTES

[1]Michael Gorman, "The Most Concise AACR 2," *American Libraries* 12 (Sept. 1981):499.

20

Technical Services- Public Services: The National Networks

Two kinds of national network databases are available to library and information agencies: databases of the cataloging-support utilities, such as OCLC, RLIN, WLN, and Utlas; and databases of the reference-support utilities, such as DIALOG, SDC, and BRS. The differences between the two types of utilities parallel the differences between library catalogs and indexes (the catalog being a specific type of index). The growing list of similarities between the two types of network databases and the similarities between online versions of library catalogs and indexes is significant, too. What do these differences and similarities suggest? What do they reveal about their users?

DIFFERENCES BETWEEN NATIONAL BIBLIOGRAPHIC NETWORKS

Origins

Cataloging-support or technical service-support networks were a new response to an intolerable situation that evolved in large libraries in the 1960s: Cataloging departments were inundated by ever-larger purchases of materials with which they could not cope, and the costs of the whole process rose faster and faster. Simultaneously, more information was produced and few libraries had the dollars to collect enough of it to satisfy all their current and future needs. Pioneers in library automation believed that application of computers to problems of bibliographic control could help resolve them, introducing economies and opportunities for resource sharing on a new scale, too. This is the way the technical service-support networks, OCLC, RLIN, WLN, and Utlas, began. They became known as bibliographic utilities because they appeared to generate new bibliographic information. They were the creations of library administrators and are, for the most part, still influenced or run by library people.

In contrast, reference or public service networks arose to satisfy a very different need — that of scientists and engineers in government and industry for faster access to research information. For a profit-making company or a government agency, it can be more costly to fail to bring a project to a successful conclusion because of lack of information than to invest whatever it costs to get the needed information in time to outpace the competition. Beginning with the years of World War II, leaders of the military-industrial complex recognized that gaining and holding a competitive edge depended more and more on having the right information as quickly as possible — preferably before anyone else. Sharing the information with one's broadly based group of problem solvers was part of this new development equation. Computer networks of scientific and technical information, while costly to implement, paid off handsomely in terms of marketable new products and services as well as for their contributions to other projects. Thus DIALOG and SDC, two of the major reference-support or public service-support networks, were and are profit-making ventures, the creatures of Lockheed and Systems Development Corporation, respectively. It is interesting to note that both networks' sponsoring bodies are members of the American corporate economy, not the educational community.

Database Contents

Cataloging-support networks deal primarily with book titles, serial titles, and a small percentage of nonbook titles at the macro-bibliographic level, i.e., each book, serial, or nonbook title is a single unit in the system. In contrast, public service networks deal primarily with serial articles and research papers (which often appear as book chapters, too), operating at a micro-bibliographic level, i.e., treating units smaller than a whole book or serial title. The size of the bibliographic unit is a determining factor in the amount of access possible from a system — the system's access potential. DIALOG and SDC furnish not just a different sort of access but much more access potential than OCLC or RLIN.

Using a single serial title as an example, a monthly journal having ten articles in each issue over a ten-year period easily may have several thousand author, title, and subject access points in a DIALOG database. That same title in RLIN (chosen deliberately because it offers retrieval by subject heading) may have a dozen headings, if several subject headings and variant titles are traced.

Retrieval Options

The deeper access of reference-support databases is the result of more detailed indexing as well as treating a smaller bibliographic unit. Policies followed by library catalogers don't attempt to be exhaustive about headings, employing strategies such as the Rule of Three to justify limiting the total number of author and subject headings. The advent of computerized catalogs motivated some relaxation of the Rule of Three in the assignment of subject headings, but AACR2R's chapter 21 still mandates only two descriptive headings — one for the title and one for the first author — for a monographic item having four or more joint authors and no variant titles. Serial titles seldom are given personal author headings and rarely have more than one responsible corporate body, if any, to trace; some serials with no specific subject focus (e.g., *Life* or *Reader's Digest*) might not rate any subject headings at all. So a serial title would get just one entry—its title—in most library catalogs.

The policies of abstracting and indexing services, whose data are distributed by DIALOG and its competitors, appear far more generous. Usually many joint authors are accessible—in some services, as many as twenty are traced—and a much larger number of subject headings or descriptors are assigned. Instead of merely summarizing the items with which they deal, reference-support databases are likely to describe them in exhaustive detail. The more a citation is used, the greater the revenue it generates. The more relevant the information provided by the service is to a researcher, the more likely it will be consulted again and again. If you are selling information, it is good business to market an exhaustively described product.

PARALLELS WITH LIBRARY CATALOGS AND INDEXES

Library catalogs, like the cataloging databases from which they are derived, are concerned with macro-bibliographic units. Their purpose is to tell someone that a title is owned, not necessarily what information it contains. Bibliographic description in the catalog record is at the summary level and cataloging rules limit the number of author tracings to three or fewer. Ideally, one subject heading—a single noun coextensive with the item's subject—is all that needs to be assigned; however, if necessary, as many as five might be assigned, many of which consist of two or more words.

Economy was an unavoidable feature of book and card catalogs from which library catalogers haven't completely escaped. Many libraries still use OCLC or other cataloging networks solely for faster access to 3 x 5 cards, which are filed in banks of drawers. This manual operation is only one step removed from previous methods in which the cards were produced using a printing press, typewriter, or hand-lettering operation.

Unlike library catalogs, reference indexes are concerned with micro-bibliographic units, and they assign many more author and subject headings to individual articles or papers as a matter of policy than library cataloging policies allow.

Index makers sell access to information. Many of the best indexes are publications of for-profit corporations. Even those originating from nonprofit professional organizations are sold to support the group's activities. Library catalogs, on the other hand, are given away free, at least to the clients of each individual library. Perhaps if clients had to put a quarter into the library catalog for each search and if the library depended on that revenue to support its bibliographic services, the whole operation would fold from lack of customer satisfaction and repeat business. But the important parallel between these tools is that library catalogs are run by librarians for summary-level access in giveaway transactions while indexes are run by publishers outside the library field to furnish exhaustive amounts of information—as much as possible—to customers who will continue buying and using their products on an ongoing basis.

SIMILARITIES AMONG THE SYSTEMS

Putting catalogs online has had a beneficial effect on their access potential, at least in those places where the card catalog is not just duplicated in the computer. More subject headings and added entries are routinely assigned by some cataloging agencies because they no longer have to worry about adding too many cards to a set of tightly packed drawers. Computer systems have strict limits, too, but terminals don't occupy more space because they display more entries, and a larger number of entries can be manipulated with ease in a computer system than can be handled in a card file. Policies that mandate including annotations, summaries, and contents notes are being discussed by catalogers, and it may only be a matter of time before the Rule of Three is history. In these respects, online catalogs imitate online indexes.

Search features that have been available for some time in the reference-support networks were copied in the designs of online catalogs, e.g., combining search terms through the use of Boolean operators, searching on partial data by truncating terms, and searching every word in selected fields (i.e., free text searching). After more than fifteen years of operation without subject access, OCLC recognized the value of providing this and other features essential for end-user service and made its On-Line Union Catalog a DIALOG database with retrieval options common to all DIALOG databases. The crossover from technical support only to technical and reference support probably is the wave of the future.

OCLC, the oldest and largest U.S. bibliographic utility, began moving toward a more businesslike, corporate operating structure some years ago, instituting the sorts of controls accepted in the business world, such as copyrighting its database. Pricing structures and member contracts are always a matter of debate, and some OCLC libraries express the feeling that they have no more influence over network activities than the captive market of any large corporation. It may be that these developments were inevitable, given OCLC's immediate success and rapid expansion to a worldwide network. Nonetheless, it portends a future more like DIALOG's than like old-time library cooperatives. Utlas, the Canadian utility that began as the University of Toronto's library automation group, shed its nonprofit skin several years ago when it was purchased by Thompson International, a multinational corporation.

WHAT DOES IT ALL MEAN?

The most important inference that can be drawn from the foregoing discussion is that cataloging-support networks and the library catalogs derived from them are not concerned primarily with maximizing access for the end user. (Libraries must keep in mind that if they don't satisfy the end user — the client — they risk losing the client to competing information sources.) If people fail in library catalog searches, they can't complain they didn't get their money's worth, since the searches are free. There are no alternative sources for the information aside from asking for help from librarians or searching every inch of the stacks.

Public service-support networks and indexes try to maximize access for consumers, much like merchants marketing shoes or ships or companies selling airline travel or dry cleaning services. Information is the commodity and indexes are the medium in which it is packaged. The sellers (publishers of indexes in books or online systems) know that if their products fail to please, customers can turn to alternatives. Even if they are pleased, customers may be lured away by a competitor's lower prices or additional services. In the information business, user-friendly searching, longer hours, maintenance of private files, downloading data, special rates for off-hours, SDI, and a range of document delivery services may all be part of competitive marketing plans. Sometimes two advantages can be gained with one feature. For example, when Wilsonline was introduced, the ability to search up to eight databases simultaneously was highlighted as a cost-saving feature (it minimized the amount of contact time) as well as a convenience.

Currently, the idea that the consumer is an important customer to be wooed and won anew every time the product or service is used is utterly lacking in library catalogs or technical service products in general. Success at the catalog is an elusive thing, but, win or lose, one must return to the catalog in order to use library materials. This take-it-or-leave-it attitude is a constant, whether the user is a librarian or a member of the public.

The fact that the catalog's summary-level description of a title won't tell a searcher whether a copy is available for use — especially if the item in question is a specific issue of a serial — is another drawback. Links with circulation files can add this feature, but all library catalogs aren't equipped with this capability. Instead, multiple searches for a single item (one at the catalog, another at the shelves, perhaps a third inquiring at the circulation desk) are common. Compare this level of service with the ability to examine an item in a public-service database in short and full citation form as well as to read an abstract of its contents. In many instances, that's all a person needs; but if the item in full is desired, most services permit searchers to order copies (to be delivered by mail) with another command at the same keyboard, and some services provide the full text online immediately.

The idea that computerizing library catalogs brings them closer to their reference-support cousins in terms of service and access potential is important. It means that the vehicle, not the content — the computer, not the bibliographic data — underlies the change. Another motivating factor may be the enhanced expectations of librarians who have been exposed to reference-support networks. If *they* can have Boolean operators, truncation, free-text searching, and all those other goodies, why can't we?

REVELATIONS ABOUT THE
TWO KINDS OF SERVICES

What does all this reveal about technical and public services? For one thing, it shows that their purposes are miles apart. Catalogers provide a product that is never judged too harshly, since it is only out of kindness and a sense of duty that libraries provide catalogs at all. It is a free service and, perhaps, not worth more than its price. Catalogers send their products (read: entries) out into the world and, if users cannot decipher them, it shows how ignorant they are. If using the catalog requires several time-consuming searches, it isn't the cataloger's business. It doesn't take the cataloger's time or cause the cataloger a frustration headache.

The reference librarian (or reader's advisor or information service staff member), on the other hand, is directly accountable to clients. A dissatisfied client may complain to the library's administration or to the administration of the library's parent institution. "I pay your salary," is a familiar attack phrase from dissatisfied clients. However unfair those words are true, even though the path from taxpaying public to librarian's pocket may be indirect. How often are those words said to a cataloger who didn't enter a book under the word the client used but instead used an LC subject heading without a cross-reference?

Catalogers need not be concerned about the success or failure of their products. The libraries that generate cataloging copy do not sell it for profit. (For example, the Library of Congress sells its data at low prices designed to recover some costs, not to make a profit.) Catalogs do not generate any income nor even any good will.

Reference tools are often the product of nonlibrary corporations that must worry about the success or failure of their products. Their income depends on it. If they can merchandise their wares to new markets (e.g., direct service to end users without the intervention of librarian intermediaries), so much the better. They will make much more money serving millions of end users than thousands of libraries.

If you were an end user with a choice, what would you do? Would you use a product destined to give you insufficient information to answer your simplest queries ("Can I have this book?") or, given an alternative, would you switch? Beware the enterprising database builder who figures out a way to provide the alternative.

CHAPTER

21

Library-Produced Indexes

There seem to be two kinds of indexes: large, beautifully produced indexes by commercial publishers that get wide distribution and small, amateurish, unpublished indexes prepared by librarians that have virtually no distribution beyond the local reference desk. Why shouldn't librarians—who are, after all, trained as experts in information storage and retrieval—be the ones to prepare large, well-produced indexes? Why shouldn't librarians market their excellent indexes throughout the information world and reap the rewards? Why shouldn't librarians have, as a result, overflowing coffers and grateful customers? The ramblings in this chapter explore these intriguing questions.

FEELING THE NEED

One of the first things any publisher asks an author to provide, when ideas for a book are discussed, is a careful assessment of the need for the book, a profile of the people who would buy it and an estimate of how they would use it, a survey of other books available in the marketplace that address the same audience and need, and an explanation of how the author's book differs from those existing works. These are legitimate concerns that deserve consideration in the context of library-produced indexes. Do librarians have special opportunities to identify the need for new bibliographic tools or are they unlikely to be exposed to such perceptions?

Looking to library history for guidance in answering the last question, the instance of Poole's index seems instructive. William Frederick Poole began compiling his famous index because, while serving as librarian for his peers at the Brothers of Unity Library at Yale University,[1] he noticed there was no systematic method of determining which articles in the periodical literature were relevant to a particular course of study. He began his index to address that need.

There are recent accounts of similar experiences at local levels, with librarians deciding to index music and sound recording anthologies and, on a broader level, with research librarians who obtained a sizable grant to establish and implement a program for the analytic cataloging of microform sets.[2] These projects often are linked to the holdings of a particular collection or institution, which explains why so many of them are not marketable.

118

But librarians—particularly those who interact with the public and answer questions about available literature—seem to be in an ideal position to know what kinds of indexes are needed but not available. In fact, they are exactly the right people to identify the need for a new index as they strive to answer queries and locate specific works or particular pieces of data for their clients. If the problem is not just local but exists elsewhere, the index can be generalized for use by the population at large.

THE INFORMATION RETRIEVAL
SPECIALISTS

Public service librarians know a great deal about information retrieval. In bibliographic instruction programs they teach library clients how to search the library's indexes; they are the database searchers who specialize in mediating between end users and costly online indexes; and they select and administer appropriate user-friendly CD-ROM systems that end users can access by themselves. By looking at such public service-oriented systems as DIALOG, technical service librarians discovered it was a great idea to be able to search catalogs by keywords and Boolean operators, not just by Library of Congress descriptors; that catalog displays could be varied from a brief version giving author, title, and call number to a full MARC record, according to searchers' needs; that truncation was helpful; that browsing the indexes of the catalog could help searchers in their quests; that having abstracts of the work could sometimes obviate the need to handle the document itself; and a host of other important ideas about catalogs that go far beyond Cutter's traditional objectives.

It might sound obnoxious to admit it, but I suspect that without public service-oriented online databases to emulate, technical service librarians might not have had enough sophistication to expect their online catalogs to have these capabilities or other capabilities, such as links with acquisition and circulation files that answer the all-important question: "Can I have this book *now*?" (To digress a little, I always ask beginning cataloging students what information one gets from an entry in a card catalog. Most answer something along the lines of " ... that the book is in the library." They are much dismayed to discover that no such information can be gleaned from a card entry. All the card can tell the searcher is that the library once purchased the item and cataloged it, assigning it to a particular location on the shelves. The searcher must trek to the shelves or, if the stacks are closed, wait for the item to be paged before he or she learns whether the desired item still is there.)

THE INFORMATION STORAGE
SPECIALISTS

The difficulty of relying solely on public service librarians to inaugurate a major new index is that these librarians do not have the same expertise in information storage that they have in its retrieval. This may be the reason they are willing to leave it to the commercial sector to design indexes and make the entrepreneurial commitments to pay the up-front costs of getting the project going.

Instead, they should run to the back rooms, where technical service specialists toil, and work with these experts in organization and storage of information to design needed indexes for effective use.

Catalog librarians, who really are identifying and indexing library materials under the guise of doing original cataloging and classification, are true experts in information organization and storage. If this expertise is available under the library's own roof, why do public service librarians allow publishers to make the critical decisions about index organization, information storage, and display, when they know that publishers' motivations are to minimize the costs and maximize the market? To be fair, maximizing the market requires an index to be useful, efficient, and effective. It also requires investigating the market in some depth and insuring that its needs are carefully assessed so they can be met by the project under development. It isn't so bad, after all, to let a commercial publisher do that costly, hard work. But if one does, then it is only fair to let the commercial publisher control the parameters of the index and rake in the profits made on its sales. Ah, now here's the rub. Allowing commercial publishers to develop, produce, and market indexes means giving up any claims to the control of index parameters.

WHAT GOOD IS CONTROL?

Technical service librarians, particularly catalogers, should be sensitive to the subtler implications of giving up control over indexes, having experienced the results of losing control of public catalogs to administrators, public service or computer center staffs, automated systems vendors, or others outside the pale. What ultimately happens is that decisions made by others must be implemented by the cataloging staff even if those decisions represent conflicts with cataloging principles or with the well-being of the cataloging department and its staff. The decision makers rarely want to hear about either the conflicts or the principles. Their commitments are to the public, the library, or the parent institution, if not to other objectives remote from library interests.

With commercial indexes, other, more specific decisions that directly affect the arrangement of entries, coverage of materials, choice of terminology, choice of retrieval options, etc., are made by people outside the libraries where the index will be used — people who make guesses about what the folks in the library need and want. Shouldn't librarians eliminate the guesswork by jumping in and designing indexes themselves?

The value of control is simple and straightforward: it puts decision-making authority into the hands of the same experts who are responsible for implementing and using the system.

AND NOW, FOR THE
REST OF THE DEAL ...

This leaves the issue of making the initial investment, or planning for and covering the start-up costs to produce the product. If the experiences of entrepreneurial librarians like Poole or other enterprising librarians of the more recent past are any indication, their investments paid off handsomely. The examples are numerous: the University of Michigan professor who started Personal

Bibliographic Systems; the people from Pikes Peak Library who started Maggie's Place; or those from Brigham Young, Virginia Tech, Northwestern, and University of Toronto who began DYNIX, VTLS, NOTIS, and Utlas International, respectively.

All the modern projects named above are computer-based, and new indexes may be expected to be computer-based. Why would anyone attempt to produce a major index by hand when putting it into a computerized database makes it so much easier to organize, update, access, duplicate, and distribute?

The question is, should librarians get into the business of creating indexes? The only answer that makes sense is "Why not?" One might ask further, does the librarians' ethic of free service prohibit commerce in informational materials? In other words, if a librarian devises a nifty new index, does he or she have to give it away without charge—or at a cost-recovery-only charge—in order to remain within professional bounds? Answering "yes" clearly contravenes the facts. Librarians expect to get paid for their services. If "free service" were truly free, librarians should be prepared to work for nothing. (Wait a minute! Some librarians feel they do receive next to nothing for their efforts. Could earning more money be a spinoff benefit of a new index project?)

Few librarians are hired to devise their own tools, including the indexes they use. Instead, they are hired to buy information, including reference tools, such as periodical indexes; to process it at a summary level of organization and arrange it on shelves; to show people how to get what they want off the shelves; to answer questions; and to manage library buildings. For these activities professional librarians holding master's degrees accept rates of pay that factory workers would find wanting. In fact, it is difficult to understand why professional expertise is required to do some of these things. For example, why should a professional librarian have to deal with the heat, electricity, water, security, and cleaning systems in library buildings? A building superintendent without a reading knowledge of two modern European languages or an earned doctorate (preferred) in a subject discipline would be a better choice.

Why should a professional librarian be employed to show people how to read the numbers on book spines or how to find entries in alphabetic files? Certainly, some people need help with these activities, but does the helper really need a library degree to provide it? If high school pages can shelve books, why can't they help people locate them, too? If nonprofessional filers—sometimes high school graduates—can put entries into catalogs, why can't they help people get them out? In fact, if nonprofessional copy catalogers—sometimes college graduates, or persons with some college education—can create the entries in our catalogs and assign the call numbers to individual items for shelving purposes, why can't they explain to the public how to retrieve them? Perhaps those aren't the truly professional activities, after all.

What seems to demand professional training in library and information science are those activities that require knowing what information is out there and how to select it appropriately, put it together, and use it to achieve desired ends. How strange it is, then, that anticipating the need for information tools, designing them, and executing the designs appear to be outside the librarian's province. These activities are reserved for commercial publishers.

CONCLUSION

It is pure poppycock to think that only commercial publishers should be allowed to create, produce, and market indexes. This is an area in which librarians excel and in which they should be active, not as grateful consumers of someone else's product but as thoughtful initiators of their own products, not as users and mediators but as designers, producers, and distributors.

And here's how to do it: Pay a consultant to advise on the business end. Hire a layout artist to make a new index as attractive as possible. Write and publish an article or two in the professional literature describing what the new tool has to offer and why it is better than those already available on the market. Send out a mailing to professional colleagues to find out how many will buy the new index. Offer the new tool in a variety of formats. Package it the way librarians wish commercially produced indexes were packaged. Stop waiting for the for-profit sector to do the things librarians want, and start making profits. Librarians could raise enough money fill gaps in their budgets, to do things worth doing that cost more than most libraries have to spend. And if, as happened with several other institutions, the project makes so much money it is embarrassing, it can be spun off into a profit-making venture.

The entrepreneurial spirit should not be shut out of libraries and, indeed, it isn't. It is just that librarians appear to ignore it. Are technical service librarians so busy revising copy cataloging and filing that they can't put their minds to something more exciting? I hope not. Don't they know what needs to be done? They can ask the public service librarians—and then work with them to make it happen.

NOTES

[1]The Brothers of Unity was one of Yale University's fraternal societies, which provided its student members with residence and dining facilities as well as a library for scholarly support.

[2]Roy Leibman describes creating an index to individual musical works at California State University at Los Angeles in "The Media Index: Computer-Based Access to Nonprint Materials," *RQ* 21 (Spring 1981):291-299. A project to provide cataloging for materials preserved on microform is announced in "ARL Receives Grants for NRMM Recon Project," *Association of Research Libraries Newsletter* 130 (June 18, 1986):1.

22

The Self-Service Library: Implications for Bibliographic Instruction

Question: Who does bibliographic instruction in your library?

Answer: Reference or public services librarians.

The stereotypical response to any reference question begins, "Have you looked in the catalog?" This stereotype evolved from the all-too-accurate fact that people in libraries are expected to help themselves much of the time. Covering the reference desk, especially on evenings and weekends, often is assigned to student assistants, new librarians, others with less seniority, or volunteers whose skills and experience in developing and executing search strategies may be limited. They are expected to direct traffic and keep order, point out the location of various reference tools or library facilities, and send the rest to the catalog to fend for themselves as best they can. Even when reference desks are always staffed by successful and experienced reference professionals, the demand for services may exceed their abilities to give lengthy attention to any one person.

In their defense, I recognize that libraries have had a pretty difficult time just staying open in some neighborhoods, schools, and institutions of higher learning, because of more than a decade of budget cuts and economic retrenchment. Clients are often grateful to be able to enter the hallowed halls and borrow materials. They are content to use their libraries without having librarians make heroic efforts on their behalf, to help them find whatever it was they came for—research materials, a good read, librettos for the Saturday afternoon Metropolitan Opera broadcasts, literary criticism for an English class, a video for Saturday night, or whatever.

Public service librarians usually are not expected to do in-depth research for clients in any case, except perhaps in special libraries. The question of how long one should spend with a client is moot when the work of collection evaluation, selection, and departmental or intralibrary duties are added to (indeed, super-imposed over) the work of covering the desk and answering the telephone. Where library policies address it, the upper limits of time spent on individual answers is measured not in hours but in minutes.

Clients facing a plethora of informational materials and sophisticated storage and retrieval systems—perhaps involving direct interaction with a computer—are more in need of help than ever. Yet libraries have fewer staff hours to devote to the task. The result of this squeeze between need and response, demand and supply, is that in more libraries than ever clients do their own reference work or do without.

In *Foundation's Edge*, Isaac Asimov describes a library of the distant future in which one librarian presides over a mammoth collection that contains the accumulated knowledge of humanity produced on Earth plus all of the information produced in all of the galaxies of a universe-wide Foundation. The clients ask knowledgeably about what they need, receive some materials from the librarian, and proceed to find exactly what they want without fuss or bother. No wonder Asimov's work is called science fiction.

THE SELF-SERVICE LIBRARY
AND SOME OF ITS PROBLEMS

The most obvious implication of this combination of trends—more information, more complicated information storage and retrieval systems, and less staff time for client assistance—is that people have to operate in a self-service atmosphere. Enter the Self-Service Library. However, unlike other self-service operations designed for mass traffic (e.g., supermarkets, airports, discount department stores), the Self-Service Library is not geared for client self-help. In most academic, public, and school libraries there is very little signage, or what is there is very poorly done. There are inherent discontinuities in the classification systems used to arrange materials as well as imposed discontinuities in the progression of shelving from Dewey's 001 to 999 or LC's A1 to Z9999.

In the public library for which I worked, the Dewey 800s followed the 699s because all fine arts materials were located in special sections. Music was at one corner of the building, one floor down; art was at the opposite corner, on the main level with most other nonfiction materials. Clients were forever crisscrossing this twilight zone with bewildered looks in embarrassed silence until someone offered to help. As music librarian, I detested the elegant signs on the main level that tastefully (read: unobtrusively) explained the whereabouts of the circulating music materials in my charge. Many long-time regulars of the library never knew about the recorded sound or score collections until some library meeting or special errand brought them down through the music room, which was perched between a small meeting room and the young adult facility. (Others found it while searching for the lounges or the 700s.) Fiction and biography also were out of order—a common practice in public libraries—located together on the top floor with foreign-language materials and bound periodicals. Caveat Dewey Decimal user!

These groupings made sense from certain perspectives; readers of fiction and biography crossed the aisle separating their stacks quite often. Bound periodicals and foreign-language materials, which didn't attract much demand, appropriately occupied the most remote stacks in the library. But for clients trying to make their way alone through the nonfiction subjects in logical order, these anomalies presented traps from which they might never extricate themselves without human intervention in the person of a reference librarian. To this set of problems was added the peculiar location of oversized materials, audiovisuals, reference tools, and so forth, based on the library's unique tradition.

OTHER CLASSIFICATION PROBLEMS

Some barriers to self-service relate to the Dewey Decimal system itself and its offering of several choices for classification. For example, biographies may be located in the Biography section (B) or in a biography number within the discipline with which the biographee was associated or, if the work covers several people, in a collective biography section (92x); bibliographies may be located in the Bibliography section (016+) or in a bibliography number within their discipline; interdisciplinary topics, such as computers and computing, may be located in several dissimilar classes, such as generalia, mathematics, office management, or engineering; multitopic works may be located in the section for only one of the topics. In the public library in which I worked, there was evidence of both kinds of biography and bibliography classification, but most computer materials were gathered in the zero hundreds. Confounding the issue further, similar works receiving original classification could be assigned different numbers, e.g., American history (973) or American travel (917.3), word-processing as a computer subtopic (001.64 in those days) or as an office skill (658).

Add to these problems the complications of phoenix schedules and other wholesale relocations of materials into new or recycled numbers. Public librarians led by Sandy Berman have been trying to mutiny against what they perceive to be the cruel and unusual punishment heaped upon self-service library clients, while Dewey supporters point to the inexorable development of new topics and changed topical relationships.

LC classification has similar problems, as well as other problems inherent in a mixed notation scheme, not the least of which is numbers that are hard to remember. Lists of specially enumerated topics rarely are complete, and sometimes classifiers opt to avoid creating new ones for their libraries, lumping unenumerated topics in a broader, umbrella class and separating them from the more specific, enumerated categories.

Self-service is confounded by all of these practices and by varying local policies on cataloging and classification. Some libraries would rather fight than switch to a new edition of Dewey. Even if they switch, there is no guarantee that all older materials will be relocated immediately—or ever. Many libraries that switched from Dewey to LC in the 1960s and 1970s still have enormous stacks of Dewey materials as testimony to their traditions. Thus, self-service clients have to search both sets of stacks or miss possibly important materials. (Can you imagine any self-respecting supermarket leaving the old boxes of Corn Flakes in aisle 3 when they put new boxes in aisle 5?)

When Cutter urged librarians to consider the needs of clients as the highest priority, he could not envision either the diversity or the mobility of future American populations. Trying to describe the typical client in either an academic or public library setting is an exercise in futility, given the variety of backgrounds, interests, and levels of sophistication of clients in either type of library. Even if one succeeded in describing a particular set of clients for an individual institution, in a few years the profile would change.

Yuppies (young, upwardly mobile professionals) form a substantial proportion of library users during and after their educational careers. They move from school libraries (notable for their nonstandard cataloging and abridged classifications) and public libraries (over 90 percent are true to Dewey, though not necessarily the same editions or applications) to academic settings where they may have to learn LC classification, too. Then they move from job to job, using local libraries whose classification and shelving practices differ, making it impossible to transfer what they learn in one place to another.

This is no way to run a self-service library.

BIBLIOGRAPHIC INSTRUCTION
TO THE RESCUE

What keeps the system from breaking down utterly and completely are the services of reference librarians, however those services may be limited, and programs of bibliographic instruction. To test, in an informal and unscientific way, the pervasiveness and effectiveness of the latter, I asked a group of twenty-one library science students in a beginning cataloging class about the bibliographic instruction they had received — any where, any time, up to that moment. Their answers were revealing.

Four students said they had never received any bibliographic instruction at all, ever. One said, "Any bibliographic instruction I obtained was through my own stumbling. My reference class is helping me continue that stumbling." Two more said that their parents had showed them how to use the library. One of the two commented, "I had no formal bibliographic instruction as a student. I only learned when I asked. But my mother was a librarian and I was alphabetizing catalog cards when I was four years old and I still am mystified by some elements of the card catalog." The other said training was given at the local public library by her mother and, "When [I] came in contact with LC call numbers [I] was completely mystified. College — never set foot in [the library] until [I] started working there sophomore year — completely avoided any type of research as undergraduate." Six of the twenty-one graduate students had never received instruction in the use of the library as part of the normal course of their education.

On the brighter side, seventeen of the students reported having had library instruction. Nine were in elementary school when they got their first training, five in junior high, one in senior high, and two in college or university. Some of their comments indicated that a few people had several experiences reinforcing whatever training was given.

"Junior High: Very basic introduction to *Readers' Guide* and a few more indexes for short papers, book reports, etc. High School: A bit more. For Advanced Placement and honors classes, we were encouraged to use the libraries at Cal State Northridge and UCLA (they even got us temporary library cards!), but with *NO* instruction(s) for using an academic research library. So I learned the hard way before Undergrad work. College: Work at UCLA's URL [University Research Library] and [took] GSLIS 110." [Note: Emphasis in original.]

"Elementary—Public library; the librarians gave me some basic instruction. Undergraduate—All freshman English classes were given a resource-reference class relating to the library."

Nevertheless, some people were less than pleased with their overall experiences, as evidenced by this comment: "Junior high school English classes—remember in particular instruction in *Readers' Guide*. High school English Comp class—research paper instruction given. College research papers required—no instruction given. Learned more by working in cataloging department in college library, typing and filing cards and some bibliographic searching. Taught library use skills for six years in elementary school grades 1-6. At least those children will have a foundation in library use."

Unless reinforcement occurs somewhere along the line, early instruction may fade beyond recall. One student wrote the following: "I am pretty sure I got some library training in jr. high." Another said, "I had some very spotty bibliographic instruction in jr. high (i.e., 'This is the card catalog. You can look up a book under author or title to see if the library owns it, period.') during orientation. My best bibliographic instruction was from my supervisor (a librarian) when I got my first library clerk job eight years ago."

Exposure to bibliographic instruction in school libraries was not always the rule, and eight of the seventeen students who had formalized instruction first received it in the home, in a classroom, or in their local public libraries. Some of the students named English teachers or parents as providing the instruction, not librarians. One explained, "My dad, a historian, showed me how to use the card catalog in high school and explained subject headings." This same person said later in the reply, "During college, I was shown how to use the card catalog at the Library of Congress by a bibliographer. She explained every entry on the card. To be honest, I only really paid attention to title, subject, author and the tracings, although I didn't call them that nor did I fully understand how to use the cross-reference information."

Out of the entire group of twenty-one, only nine had bibliographic instruction courses in their undergraduate college or university. In many institutions, library tours and instructional courses are optional. New students are offered one or more opportunities, but it is up to them to take advantage of them.

INTERIM CONCLUSIONS

Though these responses are too few and from so specialized a group that they probably are not representative of the general population, they do demonstrate that bibliographic instruction is not universally obtained in the normal course of a person's education. They also show how large a variation there is in the timing, setting, and leadership of the programs that exist.

In addition to surveying students about their experiences, I surveyed a group of librarians about bibliographic instruction programs in their libraries. Six academic and four public librarians answered the inquiry. Five of the six academic libraries and three of the four public libraries had programs in place to teach clients library skills. These programs are varied in scope and depth, in the way they are administered and taught, and in the objectives they serve. All three of the public library programs, however, were under the authority of public service librarians. Responsibility for one academic library program was held by the head of technical services, but the other five were either part of public service units or separate instructional units.

The next chapter describes of each of these eight bibliographic instruction programs and offers an informal evaluation of how they address the needs of clients in the self-service library.

AUTHOR'S NOTE

If you wish to provide information about your library's instructional programs for an update to my initial survey, please send answers to the following three questions to the author, c/o Simmons College; Graduate School of Library & Information Science; 300 The Fenway; Boston, MA 02115-5898.

1. Who is responsible for BI in your library? (Public service departments/librarians, administrators, technical service departments/librarians, or others.)

2. What topics are covered in your course(s)?

3. If there is no BI program in your library, do you provide other, less formal services that substitute for it? If so, describe the alternative services.

Bibliographic Instruction: An Informal Survey

Recollections by a group of library school students—all post-baccalaureates—of their encounters with library instruction programs were described in the last chapter. Only a few people claimed they received what concerned librarians would consider satisfactory training in using the library, although only a handful had no training at all. Most students were given some form of bibliographic or library instruction (BI) by librarians, teachers, or parents. For the most part, they learned only some of the skills that BI might provide with very little emphasis on appropriate use of materials.

In an attempt to find out how librarians in the field viewed their BI programs, I sent an informal survey to several colleagues. The group included four public libraries located in large and small cities and six academic libraries in geographically and programmatically diverse colleges and universities. Each librarian was asked to answer three questions.

1. Who is responsible for BI in the library?

2. What topics are covered in the courses?

3. If they have no formal BI program, do they have informal alternatives?

All but two of the ten librarians surveyed claimed they had BI programs in their libraries. One of the four public librarians replied there was no library instruction program of any kind in her institution. One academic librarian said she was the newly appointed coordinator for bibliographic instruction but that at the moment there was no formal BI program or course. The reference department in her university conducted tours and other informal activities, primarily for freshmen, including explanation of services, hours, location of service stations, materials, catalogs, and the research process (this last was qualified, "briefly"). This respondent's job was to pull it all together into an organized program which, she said, might also include offering a credit-bearing course.

In all three public libraries with BI programs, public service professionals were in charge. In the academic libraries, reference or public service librarians were responsible for BI in three institutions. Interestingly, in the rest, technical service librarians shared BI duties with their public service colleagues (on a voluntary basis), though in all but one of them public service staff members appeared to be responsible for the programs. In one library, the head of cataloging was the BI course instructor.

PUBLIC LIBRARY PROGRAMS

Looking first at the public libraries, there were several notable differences between the three programs. In one small midwestern town, the Head of Adult Services was a member of a team of instructors. The BI class lasted six weeks, cost six dollars and was titled "Library Skills." It was part of a larger adult education program and was listed in its catalog of courses. The librarian wrote, "We have revised our approach this year ... and have a team effort with [S.H.] coordinating the team. [S.H.] attends each session, takes attendance, and introduces the staff member(s) responsible for that session.

"This fall we have sixteen enrolled with an average attendance of thirteen and, while we have not evaluated the team approach (will do so after the series is finished), the initial feedback is that this is a preferred method to having one staff member responsible for all six sessions.

"In addition ... we offer bibliographic instruction to individuals and to groups."

The description in the course catalog outlined the content of Library Skills class: "This course will introduce the student to the wide variety of materials available in and through his local library. Covered will be history, organization, library terms, indexes, card catalog and the total library as an information center. You will be amazed at the wealth of information located in your library."

Two-Pronged Approach

The library of a small West Coast city offered a two-pronged approach to BI, which was the responsibility of its Reference/Information Division. The first prong comprised what we think of as typical BI and was divided into four activities: (1) visits by local school classes, accompanied by teachers, who are assisted in doing subject-specific literature searching by a librarian who introduces the students to the tools (indexes, vertical files, catalog) they need to use in doing their assignment; (2) tours of the reference area, also for classes, with introductions to searching tools and equipment; (3) individual instruction for people of all ages who have never used the library or who need more help in a specific subject area; and (4) preparation of "basic guides which aid students in locating material in specific subject areas."

The second prong was an unusual, coordinated effort involving four branch libraries and the elementary schools in their neighborhoods. This effort was briefly described by one librarian, "For all intents and purposes, the four branches serve as the school library, complete with catalog use instruction, etc." An impressive, 108-page course guide outlined objectives and requirements for the cooperative program, gave suggestions for implementation and effective instruction, and furnished sample exercises and lesson plans for each grade level. The documentation included, in addition to the course guide (bound attractively in a spiral binding), lesson plans developed by the branch librarians with supporting bibliographies amounting to an additional 100 pages or so. It was a well-structured course, and both the project and its documentation were obviously designed with great care.

MONTHLY MINICOURSES

The third public library, in a suburb of a major East Coast city, had a varied BI program under the direction of the Information Services department. They advertised a class titled "Library Mini-Course" in the library's monthly calendar. Its description said, "Learn to use the library effectively. One-hour tour designed to answer individual questions meets at the Information Desk." This basic program was offered at 10:30 a.m. and 7:30 p.m. on the first Wednesday of every month. Tours and general instruction in the use of the library were available for individuals — adults and children — and for school classes. A locally produced Spanish-language library orientation videotape also was offered. Instruction in the use of library video equipment and production resources was a unique feature of this instructional program. Another interesting facet of this library's BI program was its "Research Paper Workshops," nine-hour courses that consisted of six sessions: three sessions about research resources and tools and three in which writing skills were taught. The sessions on research resources were taught by librarians, while the sessions on writing were taught by faculty members from a nearby university. Librarians might be expected to explain the proper use of materials in a course such as this.

ACADEMIC LIBRARY PROGRAMS

The Social Sciences librarian headed the BI program at one southeastern university. He wrote, "We have a multifaceted program that makes use of most of our reference librarians at some time or other. We conduct general group and individualized tours, one-shot bibliographic instruction seminars for specific courses in diverse subject areas, and we have a special arrangement with the English Department to take over two to three sessions of each of their ... composition and beginning research courses for bibliographic instruction. This last allows us to hit nearly all of the incoming freshmen.

"Most of our bibliographic lectures and seminars are based on compiled in-house bibliographies and are held in a classroom within the library."

BI Service Department

A more elaborate program was described by the department chairperson of Instructional Services at a state university in the midwest. "We have established a separate service unit whose primary responsibility is bibliographic instruction.... In addition to BI this unit is responsible for publications, exhibits, and public relations. Typically, this unit has 2.5 FTE faculty positions.

"In addition, 9 or 10 other librarians from both public service units and technical services units participate in our BI program.

"We are involved with one credit-producing course, which covers use of the catalog, indexes, abstracts, government publications, and, to a limited extent, production of audiovisual materials.

"We include search strategy as a concept and teach the theoretical application of search strategy to library information gathering.

"Content of other integrated and course-related instruction is negotiated between the librarian and the academic faculty member."

Course Outlines

A second midwestern state university librarian, this one head of cataloging, sent a three-page syllabus describing the objectives of a BI course he taught called "Using the Library." The objectives of the course, as stated in the syllabus, are, "At the successful completion of this course, the student should be familiar with the basic functions and structure of a library in general and the ... State University library in particular. He or she should be able to conduct a known-item search in either the author or title catalog; interpret information on main entry cards; use the subject catalog; use the serials list; identify and use reference sources; identify and master the indexes and abstracts in his or her subject area(s); use government documents; and develop logical search strategies." The syllabus also outlined a semester-long course calendar, assignments, textbooks, and grading scales. Unfortunately, no other information was included that explained if this was the only BI course or whether other courses, tours, and instructional activities were conducted simultaneously.

The head of the college library unit within the central library of a major East Coast university sent a brief outline of instructional activities for freshmen along with support materials developed for the program. She wrote that freshman composition classes "all have two scheduled meetings with a librarian. Session 1 is a general orientation of the catalogs, physical layout, etc.; Session 2 spends time on bibliographies, indexes, etc. plus subject catalog. We've just formalized this — we have a long detailed outline for all library instructors."

Two handouts matched the descriptions of the two sessions. The first included a list of all the different library units within the university with locations, hours, telephone extensions, and brief descriptions of the collections; a campus map; a two-page manual for the online catalog; and an illustrated guide to the card catalogs, including filing rules. An exercise was inserted into the booklet. The second one, which also had an exercise accompanying it, concentrated on explaining *Library of Congress Subject Headings* and periodical indexes; the handout also contained a bibliography of subject indexes and other basic reference tools. The two handouts totaled twenty-three pages.

Distributed System

The last library system surveyed was in a major West Coast university. The administrator with responsibility for Research and Instructional Services replied, "We have a 'distributed' program of bibliographic instruction. Each public service unit offers something in this line, but the scope and the content vary by unit, according to the needs of the users." She went on to describe six alternatives in the main program: a class session devoted to library instruction in each required freshman English course; a credit-bearing, term-long course offered by the university's graduate library school; individual courses taught by librarians at professors' requests; seminars on new materials in particular disciplines aimed at faculty and graduate students; online catalog instruction, required in every unit possessing a public terminal; and catalog information stations located in several branches.

Instructors for the English classes, the library school courses, and the online catalog demonstrations were volunteers who could come from any library unit or department. A small percentage of instructors in the graduate library school course were technical service librarians, but they were outnumbered more than four to one by reference librarians. Individual courses and seminars were taught primarily by the college or central research library's reference librarians and bibliographers, though subject specialists from branches might also serve as instructors. Online catalog training was given by librarians in each unit.

One of the graduate school libraries sent a separate reply indicating that public service librarians were responsible for BI in that unit. Research methods and strategies were the topics covered and subject-focused workshops and consultations were the modes of instruction.

Accompanying the replies from this university was a syllabus numbering more than two hundred pages used in the graduate library school BI course. The table of contents included all the usual topics, e.g., organizing a search, using resources, writing a research paper, etc., but each was broken down into detailed components and in each section there were examples, exercises, and bibliographies. The depth of this course was impressive.

CONCLUSION

The results of the survey corroborate the hypothesis that BI is primarily a public service activity in both public and academic libraries. BI programs vary widely, but all focus, at the very least, on where things are located and how the main tools — catalogs, indexes, and bibliographies — work. Some programs also emphasize writing and some teach search strategy, annotation, and other related skills. Several talked about the research process, although none of them mentioned plagiarism. Clearly, there is a fairly close consensus among the libraries surveyed about what BI programs should contain.

The last of the university programs to be described differed from the others mainly in its breadth, variety of approach, and flexibility. It also involved a great many more staff members, among them technical service librarians who volunteered for BI duty. Holding seminars to acquaint advanced researchers with new resources seemed a most effective service for users who are customarily considered too expert to need BI. Two of the public libraries channeled significant amounts of staff time into BI and supported varied types of instructional programs. City library branches that served also as school libraries were extremely thorough and focused in their approach to BI. Support materials for the public library-public school program were more than just lengthy; they were carefully thought out and professionally executed, as was the syllabus prepared by the graduate library school.

Technical service librarians might take note of how few of the respondents — only one out of ten — acted on the assumption that explanations of the catalog and other bibliographic tools required someone with special expertise. At the same time, studies show that a significant proportion of catalog searches end unsuccessfully. Whatever is being done to explain bibliographic systems to users of self-service libraries doesn't seem to be working well enough.

Bibliographic Instruction and the Technical Service Librarian

One of librarians' time-honored responsibilities is teaching clients how to use the resources provided by the library. In academic institutions, this can be an expensive and frenetic task marking the first onslaught of a new crop of undergraduates during orientation week. Often, it continues in some manner for the ensuing weeks until midterm examinations, after which students are left pretty much to their own devices. Librarians in elementary and secondary schools have more leisure to devote to teaching library skills, stretching their efforts over several years and encompassing a whole curriculum of activities. Public librarians generally do not do a great deal of formal bibliographic instruction, save for introductory work with classes from local schools. Some public library clients seeking help will get a quickie course in locating materials from especially good reference staff members, but there are no guarantees about this.

Most of the time, in most of these libraries, it is public service librarians who instruct the public in how to locate desired library materials. What difference should that make to technical service librarians? Why would anyone ever consider bibliographic instruction a technical service interest? It is a classic example of *public* service: face-to-face interaction between librarian and client. Nonetheless, I submit that bibliographic instruction is, in reality, a point of interface between public and technical services and that it should be shared by both kinds of librarians for maximum effectiveness. In this chapter, bibliographic instruction is broken down into its component parts to demonstrate that the knowledge required is not limited to public service librarians.

Courses of bibliographic instruction may include several components. Basic to all of them are lessons explaining how to use the catalog. Equally fundamental is acquainting people with bibliographies, indexes, and other tools that can help them find what materials have been published on a topic or by an author. A third component is describing how the library has physically arranged its holdings and the procedures clients must follow to use the holdings. Occasionally, training in using the materials — e.g., when and how to cite sources — may also be included. Explaining the research process and what constitutes original research, though somewhat peripheral to a course devoted primarily to learning about an individual library's collections and services, may be part of bibliographic instruction, too.

In the sections that follow each of these elements is examined with an eye toward who in the library is best qualified to understand and explain it to members of the lay public who have never been trained in library theory or practice.

DECIPHERING THE CATALOG

Training in finding, interpreting, and using catalog entries is central to the systematic use of library materials. In addition to a refresher course (unless it is the client's first encounter with a library) in identifying the elements of entries, clients must be taught to recognize the idiosyncratic practices that individual libraries overlay upon the standard rules for descriptive and subject cataloging.

In many libraries there are several catalogs, and each one may be different, compounding the number of rules, exceptions to rules, and unique applications that should be taught. Filing and display practices vary from one library to another, too.

Consider this incident: A college junior I knew who transferred from one eminent college that had a straight dictionary catalog to another equally distinguished institution that did not, was unaware that the catalog in his new school was divided into two sections, one for authors and titles and one for subject headings. Searching in the subject section for Shakespeare's *Othello*—as a topic under "O"—he found no entries. The title-as-subject was in the author-title section following the entries for all of the editions of the work itself. A successful search we did together in the "S" drawers of the author-title catalog turned up thirty-two English-language entries. The man confided that, while he was surprised that his original search was fruitless, considering the importance of Shakespeare in the curriculum, he had assumed the library did not have what he needed and so planned to purchase a copy of the play. He did not approach a reference librarian for assistance. He believed that he knew how to use all library catalogs, having had bibliographic instruction at his previous university. Only my accidental discovery of his failure and subsequent persistence in helping him find the proper location of entries for *Othello*-as-subject enabled this bright student to tap the wealth of resources available in his university library.

When filing rules, cataloging rules, or subject headings change, as they do over time, institutions differ in their response. Considerations other than conforming to standards often sway decisions; special consideration seems to be given to the amount of money available for recataloging, the number of staff members needed for the job, and the space that might be required for physical shifts of materials. When I took my first job in 1973 in a modern-looking, aggressively innovative, affluent, suburban public library, they were still filing by the 1949 rules and using an outdated edition of Dewey for classification. The decision makers believed it was too confusing and expensive to change. Years later, when the library began to accept the products of a standardized cataloging service, big changes had to be made because maintaining the older classification scheme proved even more costly than being up-to-date.

Who in a library is best qualified to know and understand the catalog, its changes, irregularities, and accommodations? Technical service librarians, especially catalogers, receive my vote. It is doubtful that average public service librarians expend much energy keeping up with the latest proposals to make changes to AACR2R or LCSH. They probably do not read *DC&, Additions & Changes, Cataloging Service Bulletin*, or the *LC Information Bulletin*. Technical service librarians should (although many don't) know about these proposals and read at least some of these publications. They should be aware of key issues concerning catalogs and cataloging and how their responses will affect local bibliographic tools.

LEARNING ABOUT
BIBLIOGRAPHIES AND INDEXES

Bibliographies and indexes — major tools of librarianship — are usually entrusted to the stewardship of reference librarians. Not only do they furnish reference staff with information that enables them to answer questions, locate desired materials, and perform other tasks in direct service to individuals, but these tools also aid them in the selection of appropriate new materials to add to the collections. These public services are such an important part of the library's mission, and physical control over bibliographies and indexes by the reference department is so much a part of its services, that we often forget the role of the same tools in the execution of technical service functions. Technical service staff members share major bibliographic tools like BIP, PTLA, and CBI with public service librarians. Often, this sharing is not figurative but literal; that is, because of the expense involved in duplicating the titles, both departments actually use one set of books (or disks, fiche, etc.). Although periodical indexes tend to be used exclusively by public service librarians, other bibliographic tools are not. Technical service librarians are as familiar with indexes and bibliographies and adept in their use as any public service colleague. Though I would give public service librarians my vote as the most expert in their knowledge of bibliographic tools, technical service librarians should be well qualified to instruct clients in the use of such tools, too.

ACQUAINTING CLIENTS WITH
ARRANGEMENT OF COLLECTIONS

Pointing out the location of reference materials, materials in various subject areas, special collections, and other resources available for client use is a third element in bibliographic instruction. All librarians should know the whereabouts of the library's materials. Classifiers should be particularly alert to the idiosyncrasies of whichever standard scheme is used to arrange library materials on the shelves, as well as local departures therefrom. This familiarity with the principles underlying shelf arrangement cannot help but add a measure of extra understanding and knowledge to technical service librarians' potential as teachers of bibliographic instruction.

Within the reference collection, naturally, reference specialists are most likely to know which items are secreted behind desks or inside offices. In one library it might be *Consumer Reports*, in another, the microform *Playboy* or the works of Sigmund Freud. However librarians decide to handle the problems of high demand or vandalism-prone titles, clients should be made aware of them.

Those who invent the rules—the public service professionals—know best how to enlighten people. Nonreference collections, however, are another thing. Stack maintenance staff are the most likely to know the vagaries of circulating collections, for example, when materials are relocated from the new book section to regular stacks or when items are put on reserve or removed for preservation microfilming.

While public service librarians may be well qualified to explain the physical location of the library's materials, any staff member should be able to do it. Some aspects of shelf arrangement are best known to technical service librarians, particularly local interpretations of the classification scheme or other departures from standard practice.

USING LIBRARY MATERIALS

Teaching clients how to use the materials they obtain from the library is not always included in courses in bibliographic instruction, since it is not strictly part of the library's services. In one sense, there is no obligation on the part of librarians to see to it that the materials they provide are used wisely or appropriately; it is enough that clients are helped to get them. (The words of a song by Tom Lehrer mocking renowned rocket scientist Wernher von Braun offer an apt analogy: "'Once the rockets are up, who cares where they come down? That's not my department,' says Werhner von Braun."[1])

Librarians may be correct in assuming that others—classroom teachers, for example—should be responsible for teaching young people the proper use of intellectual resources, which include books, periodicals, and other kinds of materials; however, the assumption often is a mistake. It is not even safe to assume that all young people are taught how to make a standard bibliographic citation, a fact I confirm each time I ask new students to complete an exercise in doing them or, if I haven't assigned such an exercise, the first time I receive a batch of term papers. Discussions of plagiarism were never heard in any classroom in which I sat as a student. Did my teachers assume it wasn't necessary? If they thought librarians clarified this touchy, tricky issue they were wrong; no librarian ever mentioned it. The only discussions of plagiarism to which I have been privy were in conversation with colleagues, referring in hushed tones to the rare embarrassment caused by the discovery of plagiarized research and subsequent withdrawal of doctoral degrees.

Teachers (and some librarians) do teach students to write book reports and synthesize information for term papers. They often do not clarify what constitutes appropriate quotation and paraphrase and what exceeds the bounds of propriety. Since no one is born knowing the difference between appropriate quotation or paraphrase and plagiarism, no one can be expected to use library materials correctly by instinct alone. A few years ago, a student sued to win back a baccalaureate that had been withdrawn by her university because of a plagiarized paper. She contended that, since her faculty advisor approved the paper and all sources were cited, the punishment was unjustified. She succeeded in retaining her degree only after a hard-fought battle that hinged on a legal technicality.

There is good reason for librarians to be responsible for proper use of library materials, just as physicians are responsible for the proper use of prescription drugs by their patients. Librarians should make clear which uses are appropriate and which are not in the same way a physician tells a patient to take two pills every four hours for a week. Despite instructions the person may go home and misuse the drugs (or the materials), but not out of ignorance. If librarians duplicate the lessons of classroom teachers it does no harm but it reinforces the principles of intellectual integrity and honesty.

Who among library staff are best qualified to teach how to cite sources and use materials properly? Any professional librarian should be able to do it. In earning their graduate degrees they should have had the experience of writing papers and bibliographies, citing sources, and using resource materials. Their experiences should have taught them how to make standard citations and understand the distinctions between use and misuse of sources.

EXPLAINING THE RESEARCH PROCESS

Related to the proper use of intellectual resources is explanation of the research process and the creation of new knowledge. The word *research* is bandied about by elementary and secondary school teachers without careful distinction between *original* research and simply searching through existing literature on a topic. Later on, undergraduates escape being taught the valid use of resource materials in the research process because they are supposed to know it already.

In library and information science programs, courses in research methods are either required or heavily touted as electives. Even if a formal course is not taken, library and information science students hear a great deal of talk about the research process. Understanding and being able to describe the development of new knowledge—the product of original research—may be assumed to be part of every librarian's education. Thus, any graduate librarian should be able to conduct this part of a course in bibliographic instruction.

WHO IS THE BEST BIBLIOGRAPHIC INSTRUCTOR?

Public service librarians are well qualified to teach every aspect of even the most broadly defined bibliographic instruction program. So are technical service librarians. Technical service librarians have special knowledge of catalogs and shelf arrangements. Public service librarians have special knowledge of reference tools and certain shelving problems. The best instruction would tap both kinds of expertise and involve both kinds of librarians. Ideally, clients should learn about the catalog from catalog specialists and about reference tools from reference specialists. It should not matter which kind of specialist teaches about physical arrangements and appropriate uses of materials.

Beyond any special knowledge or training, less tangible factors influence the exclusion of technical service librarians from programs of bibliographic instruction. An image persists of catalogers as reclusive pedants absorbed by arcane trivia worthy of medieval theologians. The notion that catalogers cannot deal easily and successfully with the public is one of those myths that refuses to die, yet no scientific studies confirm it. Just as anyone can point to individual catalogers with introverted, shy, and retiring personalities, they can point to some reference librarians whose brusque behavior is almost misanthropic and whose response to any query is a confrontational "Go look in the catalog!" Lonnie Beene's eloquent plea for an end to intraprofessional stereotyping is particularly relevant in this context.[2]

It is logical to suppose that new professionals consciously choose to work with the public or behind the scenes depending on their natural talents and inclinations, but it is not necessarily true. First jobs are taken just as often because of location, salary, or because they happen to be the only offer received by a recently graduated librarian anxious for a year or two of experience. Once in technical (or public) services, it is harder to land a higher level job in the other department.

Finally, though bibliographic instruction is not generally perceived as a high status service and assignments to teach it are rarely considered plums, it still is "turf," not willingly shared or given away. Technical service librarians who never thought about it before might not find bibliographic instruction a welcome addition to their list of responsibilities. They probably feel just as overworked and underappreciated as everyone else. Why should they accept, let alone seek out, more to do?

The more libraries rely on client self-service and self-help, the more important programs of bibliographic instruction become. Yet in libraries across the country, personnel officers are having to stretch fewer staff members across increasing numbers of tasks. Technical service librarians constitute a whole segment of the professional and paraprofessional staff that could be involved in helping people learn more about using their libraries.

NOTES

[1]Tom Lehrer, *Too Many Songs by Tom Lehrer with Not Enough Drawings* by Ronald Searle (New York: Pantheon, 1981), 125.

[2]See her letter in the "Reader Forum," *American Libraries*, 16 (July/August, 1985):468.

PART 4

FUTURE SHOCK
Policies for the
New Millennium

25

Differences Between
Access and Ownership

At a recent American Library Association annual conference, I had occasion to speak before a standing-room-only audience of about two hundred circulation librarians. This was the first program the group had ever sponsored — the Library Administration and Management Association Systems and Services Section's Circulation Services Committee (LAMA/SASS/CSC) — and I was honored to be included on the inaugural platform.

I was asked to speak about the theoretical framework underlying circulation services for the future, and I did. In part, I talked about differences in the nature of access to owned and unowned materials, and some of the questions from the audience that followed the formal presentations focused on these differences. Although my remarks were received with warm applause and followed by several gratifying letters telling me they were thought-provoking and much appreciated, I couldn't stop thinking about what was said, and not said, in the forty-five minutes or so allotted to me. In this chapter, I'll explore further some of the issues relating to access versus ownership.

Circulation services or, as I prefer them to be called, document delivery services, are an important part of the access versus ownership issue, but the most complex and intriguing aspects relate to collection development and cataloging and, beyond them, to the very core of our professional philosophy.

COLLECTION DEVELOPMENT ASPECTS

When librarians talk about access versus ownership, what do they mean? In this chapter, three kinds of materials are subsumed under an umbrella of accessed, not owned, materials: (1) interlibrary loan materials owned by other libraries; (2) computer databases located at remote sites and not under the library's control; and (3) materials whose ownership is shared among a group of partners, such as a film collection administered by a school district media center or county library on behalf of all the constituents.

Collection developers may not have to deal at all with subscriptions to computerized databases when they are considered services rather than materials. Students in my collection development classes who work in libraries say, "We don't deal with online databases and we never will. Database subscriptions would consume our entire budget," and they consider the question closed. These neophytes can be forgiven for forgetting that adding databases to their scope would bring database resources under their control, including space, staff, equipment, and material procurement allocations. But what about experienced professionals who say exactly the same thing? They are giving out a strong message that access to computerized databases is not equivalent to ownership of printed volumes containing nearly identical information.

In discussing microcomputers and the reference function in 1988, reference expert Elizabeth Futas said, "In some libraries, the distinction between manual and online tools is perceived as a difference between having real materials and contracting for services from outside sources, not as having the same information in different formats. This may splinter an already divided function [i.e., reference] even further, creating more confusion for patrons and the possible loss of control over online reference sources. Failing to come to grips with the issues of new technology will create an enormous disservice that may fulfill the gloomy prophecies of the 1970s about the withering away of the library."[1]

But what about interlibrary loan materials? Aren't they regarded in collection development policies? In theory they are, but in practice, policies or selection manuals rarely state explicitly that certain categories of material will be borrowed from other libraries rather than purchased. Only in the few places where cooperative collection development has developed beyond the "Gee, that would be a great idea!" stage—e.g., in Illinois, Pennsylvania, the Pacific Northwest, the CARL libraries in Colorado, the FLO libraries in Boston, and the LEAP libraries in southwestern Connecticut—has interlibrary loan become a significant collection development factor. In some libraries, loan applications are discouraged by hiding the interlibrary loan desk in a remote corner of the building; by excluding categories of patrons from service, such as children and youth or nonresident cardholders; by limiting the numbers of loan requests a patron can make; and by giving bad service that reflects the low priority of the service in the eyes of library decision makers.

Materials whose purchase is shared with partners and administered by a larger unit are regarded by collection developers to the extent that selection responsibilities also are shared. It is more likely that the administering unit itself will develop the collection, organize it, process it, house it, and maintain it, furnishing constituent members with catalogs and the opportunity to reserve items wanted by their patrons.

CATALOGING PROBLEMS

Libraries rarely catalog interlibrary loan materials. They simply circulate them, maintaining only an inventory record—often a bare-bones copy of the book card—in order to make a good faith effort to insure the eventual return of the material to the owning library. In connection with interlibrary loans, access—i.e., getting patrons something they want from another library—is not the same as ownership.

It might be difficult to justify spending the time and money of catalogers and other processing staff on entering bibliographic records for materials only temporarily under the library's roof. One rationale, however, is that entering the record, even temporarily, could alert other patrons who might want the same item that it was made available to a local patron and could be obtained for them, too. (If an item circulates once, what are its chances of circulating a second time?)

Shared materials also are rarely cataloged by local libraries, since part of administrative responsibilities are the organization and processing of individual items. Local libraries usually are supplied with a catalog or, at least, a list of items in the shared collection, from which local patrons can choose desired items. Problems occur when this special catalog is kept out of sight or when access to the shared collection is not well-publicized. Librarians often believe everyone knows about such services, but in reality, only library regulars might be expected to be aware of them.

If a library subscribes to the ERIC database through DIALOG, its catalogers are directed by OCLC not to catalog it in the OCLC system, although they customarily catalog the printed ERIC index online. If catalogers want to include the computer-based ERIC in their public catalog, they must type up a card, input a local record, or do whatever it is they do to present information about the subscription to the public. DIALOG and its constituent databases, including the computerized ERIC, are not "holdings" capable of inclusion in the OnLine Union Catalog. Holdings, according to the rules of the bibliographic utility, apparently must be corporeal, physical items that occupy shelf space somewhere.

Perhaps because they are still relatively new or perhaps because no one has complained and raised a fuss, computer-based indexes are rarely cataloged at all, locally or otherwise. By acts of omission or commission, catalogers are sending a strong message that access is not equivalent to ownership with regard to bibliographic services.

ACCESS/CIRCULATION/DOCUMENT DELIVERY SERVICES

I'm not sure whether it is a contemporary flirtation with *tech speak*[2] that has elicited alternative names for circulation services, or whether it is that the terms *access services* and *document delivery services* are truly more accurate and appropriate for the tasks of managing the borrowing of library materials. These days, just as it is not uncommon to find the reference desk renamed "Information Services," it also is likely the circulation desk has been renamed "Access Services" or "Document Delivery Services." What's in the name?

Access is a very tricky word. I know, because I had to research it for my doctoral dissertation, which was titled "Access to Media." On the surface *access* means *availability* and, presumably, lack of access means unavailability; but when you scratch the surface there are few guidelines for determining finer distinctions between perpetual availability and complete unavailability. Therein lies the rub: When does partial availability meet or fail to meet the test of access? Librarians should be familiar with this concept, since access to library materials often merely means the potential to borrow an item for a few hours, days, or weeks. It does not mean the item is guaranteed to be available at all, and a patron cannot keep it indefinitely (unless that patron is a faculty member abusing the traditional academic library perquisites of extended privileges). This fuzzy definition of access is not limited to libraries and librarians. Important people claim to have access to the president of the United States if they can speak to someone who can speak to someone who can to speak to the president.

Are circulation librarians the profession's availability specialists? The answer is "Certainly," since they operate the systems governing the shelves and shelving (clearly, determining the physical availability of materials), borrowing, trapping and holding materials not in hand to satisfy requesters, and tracking and punishing borrowers who make some items unavailable by not returning them on time.

But access has other meanings, too, and frequently is used by technical service librarians to refer to cataloging and classification. Bibliographic access is their concern and responsibility and, in fact, it was bibliographic access to which my dissertation title referred. *Access to information* is used to mean the right of citizens, rich or poor, to obtain information from libraries, government archives, computer databases, etc., and might imply, too, that no charges are paid in exercising that right, especially if the phrase used is *free access to information*.

Who knows what is meant by the word *access* used alone? No one. It is a word that requires qualification, definition, and precise specification.

What about document delivery? That's my choice. First, it implies a service activity. Second, it includes the word *document*, the commonly used generic term for the stuff being handled. Third, *delivery* specifies what happens to the stuff. Document delivery is better than circulation, because its scope goes beyond borrowable (i.e., circulating) materials to all acts of providing documents to people. It might include providing borrowed documents, such as interlibrary loans, and it might include providing rental items, such as McNaughton best sellers, or shared materials, such as commonly owned film circuit materials.

Suppose we take away the documents. Can there still be document delivery? I think not. Information delivery is not the same as document delivery. If the physical manifestation disappears, the function changes. When a patron receives information without documents, we are talking about reference work. Reference equals Information provision. Q.E.D. If you don't believe me, ask a reference librarian.

TROUBLING QUESTIONS

Aside from imaginative portrayals of the librarians of the distant future by Isaac Asimov and other science fiction writers (see Asimov's Foundation series), is there any truth to the proposition that a library can be a library without collections? If the "library" does not own or handle documents that comprise important and heavily used parts of the collection, is it really a library or does it become merely an information brokerage? Does "providing access" cease to be a function of libraries and librarians when there are no materials to be purchased, cataloged, and shelved? I wish I had answers to these troubling questions, but I have only the following suppositions and opinions to offer.

First, I think it is clear that librarians do not believe that access is equivalent to ownership of materials. Access is ignored by some and regarded with suspicion, if not rancor, by others in the library profession.

Second, provision of information without owned documents is commonly identified as a service, not an alternative collection. The literature reflects some discussion about computer-based versus printed indexes, but this does not mean that, within the walls of any library, decisions about these items are made by the same authorities. Access to documents online or from online services does not appear to replace or eliminate the need for library-owned documents. With few exceptions, owned documents clearly are the higher priority items and the preferred basis for library services.

Third, from my experience, lip service is being paid to access. Librarians know they can't own everything needed by their patrons, but they are going to try to buy it all anyway, even if it means cutting back on monographs with marginal demand, journal subscriptions with small followings, and costly or difficult-to-obtain materials.

Library materials fall into four categories: popular materials in heavy demand, purchased by everyone; materials enjoying some demand, purchased by nearly everyone; materials with marginal demand, purchased by only a few librarians; and mistakes—materials having no demand that remain unused on the shelves until they are weeded out and de-acquisitioned.

Outside of a nucleus of materials for which demand is highest (the 20 percent of the collections that satisfy 80 percent of the information requests), what should be purchased and owned is not what most other libraries are buying but exactly those marginally demanded monographs, journals, and other nonbook materials that can serve a library's unique public in areas to which there is no other access. Collection developers can expand access by increasing their purchases of database services, especially full text services, expanding their interlibrary loan activities and shared collecting agreements, and reserving their purchasing decisions for items that cannot be obtained except by owning them. When a category of materials is considered for purchase, the questions might be, Do we have to buy this? Is it part of our 20 percent must-have core collection? If not, can we settle for access to it? Can we get it through DIALOG, *Wilsonline*, or another computer-based service? Can we expect to obtain it through interlibrary loan? Can we share the purchase with neighboring libraries?

How might library collections vary from one school, university, or town to another if we eliminated some of the duplication of ownership in favor of access? How would collections change if materials budgets were not spent to purchase as many titles as possible from the same list of recommendations but instead were spent to purchase only the most essential ones, provide access to the others, and purchase a group of scarce titles tailored to the individual library's public?

NOTES

[1]Elizabeth Futas, "Collection Use: Reference Work with Hardware and Software," in *The Library Microcomputer Environment: Management Issues*, Sheila S. Intner and Jane Anne Hannigan, eds. (Phoenix, Ariz.: Oryx Press, 1988), 59.

[2]If the definition of this term is not obvious, see Edward Tenner's entertaining book, *Tech Speak, or How to Talk High Tech* (New York: Crown, 1986).

26

Requiem for a Database

Late in 1991 the Research Libraries Group (RLG) announced that it sought to end its role in support of shared cataloging. A few weeks later a follow-up announcement stated that negotiations with OCLC about taking over this role for RLG members had ended and all bets were off. Had the merger of RLG's cataloging database with OCLC's OnLine Union Catalog come to pass, it would have marked the end of an era. It also would have meant that librarians in the United States finally would have had a national network—but definitely not the way they imagined it.

This chapter speculates on some of the events and trends that might have led RLG to abandon the Research Libraries Information Network (RLIN) as a cataloging database and on the potential impact that RLIN's departure could have had on the national cataloging database. All of these speculations are, of course, personal opinion and in no way reflect any official knowledge of RLG or RLIN, or any other networks.

Before looking into RLIN's past, however, I should point out that RLIN wasn't the only shared cataloging database that was disappearing at that time. Like Wonderland's Cheshire cat, Utlas International, the Canadian network that helped pioneer computerized shared cataloging in the early 1960s, also was in the process of vanishing. Librarians now possess the smile. Although Utlas's merger talks with OCLC became sidetracked, one needn't be a pessimist to anticipate that a likely outcome eventually will mean its demise. Because Utlas has not been sufficiently profitable, either a buyer will be found in the near future—OCLC or another—or it will go to database heaven, phased out by its owner, a multinational corporation. (Those who monitor the library automation scene could have predicted Utlas's demise as soon as a profit-making company got into the act. Since when did anyone reap big profits from libraries? Libraries interpret nonprofit to mean that they don't make a profit. They give information away free. Librarians simply haven't the context, the tools, or the inclination to appreciate "sufficiently profitable.")

EARLY PROBLEMS THAT
COME BACK TO HAUNT

Personally, I always thought that RLIN's major problems were related to its hardware. In the early 1980s, I taught a library school course called "Library Information Networks" in which we compared the system structures, hardware, software, governance, services, costs and finances, and other distinctive features of the bibliographic utilities. For the purposes of the course, I covered four such entities: OCLC, RLIN, UTLAS (then still affiliated with the University of Toronto and rightfully an acronym for University of Toronto Libraries Automated System, not a word), and the Washington Library Network (then, as now, WLN). Some people might question including WLN with the other three networks, which were national in scope. Although WLN, then a part of Washington's state library unit, wasn't strictly national, it served libraries beyond the borders of the state of Washington and thus qualified as a multistate shared cataloging system. Within a year or two, it changed its name to Western Library Network and, in the more recent past, dissolved its relationship with the state of Washington.

Upon examining the networks, it quickly became clear that RLIN's greatest assets were its flexible, sophisticated software and a democratic governing structure. Its closest rival in software sophistication was WLN, which initiated computer-based activities around the same time (late 1970s) and had the same advantages of later hardware and knowledge of previous mistakes; none of its three competitors had anything resembling RLIN's one member-one vote democracy. RLIN's greatest flaws were its hardware and its finances, both of which were so limited that the utility could barely support the minimum levels of activity its members required.

Certain RLIN policies, ostensibly designed to insure the integrity of the database and its eventual value as a research tool (such as the higher cost of partial or inaccurate records), served to dampen database-building enthusiasts and data-entry activities to more supportable levels. Frequent periods of downtime accomplished the same thing less gracefully or predictably. System architecture was designed to maintain all cataloging records entered into the database online simultaneously, so members could access their own cataloging at any time (as well as everybody else's). It resulted in the need to provide and maintain huge amounts of storage space, at a time when storage space was much more costly than it is today, and the need to develop fancy algorithms to gather, group, and control for retrieval an enormous number of intentionally duplicate records.

While OCLC encouraged building its database throughout its early years, RLIN seemed to discourage it by making it costly to enter new cataloging, especially for East Coast institutions, which had to pay high telecommunications costs in addition to other charges. Since the lion's share of cataloging data in the initial phase of both networks came from loading LC's MARC database, it was particularly troubling that RLIN members had to pay so much to use the data. However, RLIN had some obvious virtues lacking in OCLC, such as subject retrieval and perpetual online access to local records.

Just as RLIN was beginning to grow and flourish, adding more flexible retrieval capabilities — such as keyword searching and Boolean operators; succeeding in handling Chinese, Japanese, and Korean scripts; and planning the implementation of additional nonroman scripts and authority control—its capacities were taxed anew by retrospective conversion. The system was expected to handle significantly larger data entry loads as members began computerizing bibliographic data for the huge collections that already existed when RLIN was launched—something that had been put off for a decade or more during which implementation of the network and new local systems were the more pressing concerns.

Other RLG projects designed to facilitate resource sharing and to promote preservation efforts, such as the Conspectus, began to assume more prominence and consume a larger share of total network resources. Shared collection development data like that available online via the Conspectus was not something other networks supplied, and RLG's special databases of archives and manuscripts, art materials, etc., also were unique among the bibliographic utilities. RLIN was first to establish a direct online link with the Library of Congress in its Linked Systems Project. However, despite these stellar accomplishments (or perhaps because of them), I don't recall ever hearing RLIN catalogers express satisfaction with system performance for cataloging. Costs remained high and downtime made departmental management difficult, to say the least.

MEANWHILE, BACK AT THE OTHER UTILITIES ...

In the meanwhile, OCLC, running hard to match increased expectations fueled by the accomplishments of RLIN, UTLAS, and WLN, found itself with the largest database of all the utilities. OCLC's OnLine Union Catalog (OLUC) was a multimillion record database in which members' original cataloging was the majority of data. As time passed, LC's contributions became an increasingly smaller proportion of the whole. More important, perhaps, OCLC had developed a huge membership that did an enormous amount of online searching, cataloging, interlibrary loaning, etc. OCLC's members paid less per unit for these activities than RLIN members but contributed much more in total dollars to the network's coffers because of the greater number of transactions. Uptime was good and steadily improving, retrospective conversion was encouraged, and OCLC continued to acquire and maintain the hardware it needed to support its much higher volume of activity.

In the recent past, OCLC did three things to insure its future survival. First, it funded a relatively large research and development unit (large, that is, by library and information science standards) and facilitated participation by outside scholars who devised projects of potential interest and use to the network and its members. Second, it continued to develop and build its hardware, software, and telecommunications systems to keep pace with a still-growing membership. Third, it varied the number of ways it could serve libraries by developing new products and services based on the OLUC.

Some of OCLC's new ventures failed, such as the search for a network-wide circulation control system and its foray into vending local systems. But others worked, such as offering the OLUC as a reference database on DIALOG, complete with subject searching and all the fancy retrieval modes available to DIALOG users. The service, known as EPIC, now is available either from an OCLC terminal or a DIALOG terminal. New products included subscriptions to a series of source databases on CD-ROM—subsets of the OCLC—which enabled libraries to minimize telecommunications charges and offered an alternative to full online cataloging. Another new product was a CD-ROM that could be used for collection evaluation; the disk contained records for a local library and up to three selected peer institutions for use in making collection comparisons. In addition, more sophisticated software for the online system was developed and implemented; this was known as the PRISM service. Nevertheless, individual library members sometimes found OCLC more bureaucratic and distant, paying lip service to user needs while really being attuned to the bottom line. The unpleasant fight over copyright of the OLUC was testament to the different perceptions of purpose on the part of the utility—now an international network—and some of its regional affiliates and local members. Promised changes seemed to occur very slowly and more layers of management separated local librarians and OCLC decision makers.

UTLAS, which early on chose a different path in its governance and relationships with participating libraries, almost immediately developed a varied product line to meet the needs and pocketbooks of its customers. Because it was based in Canada, UTLAS had to accommodate catalog records in French as well as English. Of all the networks, UTLAS was perceived as the most responsive to client needs and the most flexible. Before and since its purchase by Thomson International, UTLAS/Utlas International sought customers in the United States and seemed open to establishing links with local system vendors. These efforts seem to have met with only modest success.

WLN, on the other hand, was for many years the only utility to boast authority files linked with its bibliographic records and successful high-level quality control over cataloging. WLN decided at the start to remain regional, offering to provide its software to other libraries or networks instead of drawing them into WLN membership. Perhaps this effort not to bite off more than it could chew enabled WLN to survive. WLN also developed CD-ROM based cataloging products to aid small libraries in automating affordably, and its constituents in the lower forty-eight states and Alaska are fiercely loyal. (When, on one occasion, I neglected to discuss WLN's products and services adequately in an article on automated cataloging, I received letters from WLN users scolding me and describing the services at length in glowing terms.)

TROUBLESOME TRENDS

Two trends must have detracted from RLIN's willingness to offer shared cataloging services: progress in computing, which inevitably requires major changes in basic system hardware, software, and telecommunications; and continuing financial distress among research libraries, which causes them to seek major cost containment or cost reductions.

These trends are not mutually exclusive. OCLC's provision of new software to address old failings (such as lack of subject access), its incorporation of new processing and retrieval capabilities (such as Boolean operators, browsable indexes, and greatly improved editing techniques), and its introduction of newer, less costly alternatives to full access to the main online system (i.e., its CD-ROM products) are responses to the ongoing development in computing as well as efforts to save money and lower costs to members.

Two cost factors to be considered are telecommunications—always a considerable cost for the East Coast members of a West Coast utility like RLIN—and access to the whole online database. In moving to the PRISM service, OCLC radically changed its telecommunications systems to save money and keep members' charges low, but this required a major development initiative that might have been prohibitive for RLIN. In bringing out products that obviated the need to access the whole database online, OCLC enabled libraries to use the OLUC for a different kind of cataloging.

In addition, OCLC sought continuing growth in its client base. Development of CD-ROMs containing subsets of the OLUC for libraries that did not need or want all the data online enabled OCLC to serve more libraries and a greater variety of needs than were possible otherwise. These aims may go beyond RLG's intended purposes for RLIN or, while not being entirely undesirable, may be too low on the priority list to warrant an investment in their development.

RLIN never presented itself as a "people's" database. RLG fought a nasty lawsuit to enable RLIN to dump a group of California member public libraries. The libraries in question definitely were not research oriented but they were long-standing members of CLASS, the California regional network that distributed Stanford's BALLOTS system before it was chosen to become RLIN. The legal action certainly demonstrated RLG's firm commitment to serve only the tiny, elite community of scholarly libraries for which it was established. What the commitment means in monetary terms is that RLG libraries will pay much more for every service they receive, since the costs cannot be spread over a large membership. Apparently, the cost of cataloging was becoming less supportable. This begs the question, what about the cost of acquisitions and interlibrary loans? Are any RLIN functions supportable? Only time will tell.

SPECULATIONS ON THE FUTURE

If OCLC had become Our National Network (yes, capital letters intended), it would not only have replaced RLIN and Utlas, it also would have superseded the Library of Congress as everybody's source of original cataloging. The possibility still looms large. Perhaps it is inevitable that OCLC will become ONN.

When RLIN made its first announcement, OCLC didn't wait for the proverbial body to cool before announcing changes in its pricing structures to increase the financial burden on members who fail to add new data to the network. In a news item that appeared on the same page with RLIN's bombshell, OCLC said it was moving toward something called "contribution pricing" in which costs to searchers would rise while the rewards to contributors of original cataloging—who always received a token monetary thank you—would increase. Maybe that was simply coincidental, and maybe the result is less foreboding than one might think. (An article by Emerson College librarian David P. Miller reported that the new pricing structure actually lowered Emerson's OCLC costs.[1])

All these dramatic announcements of radical change followed fairly swiftly on the heels of announcements by the Library of Congress that it was starting to experiment with copy cataloging. Whose copy would be left if RLIN bowed out and Utlas was bought by OCLC? OCLC's, of course. Librarians shouldn't forget that OCLC was the network that pitched in and picked up the slack before, rescuing projects such as CONSER, Music Recon, and the Dewey Decimal

Classification, all of which seemed destined to perish for lack of a sponsor at some point in the last decade.

When the dust settles, OCLC could become the sole U.S. bibliographic utility—a clear monopoly with no real national competitors. Libraries could choose to use OCLC or fend for themselves. Or libraries might go back a hundred years to the time before shared cataloging, when every library did its own thing with locally designed cataloging systems. The notion of local control, local authorities, and local decision making is heady, indeed, but catalogers had better take care not to become intoxicated. Who knows what dangers lurk in the darkness of total local control? Yet who can even imagine what dangers lie in turning shared cataloging over to one utility? If local librarians thought they were powerless before, won't the monopoly make them still more insignificant? It may be a debate for the future or a moot issue. I'm not sure which choice is preferable and which should be most feared.

NOTES

[1]David P. Miller, "OCLC's New Contribution Pricing: How Does It Play Out in the Library," *Library Journal* 116 (Oct. 15, 1991):49-51.

Copy Cataloging and the Perfect Record Mentality

The idea behind network shared cataloging is that once someone has cataloged an item and contributed the bibliographic record to the shared database, no one else has to catalog it "from scratch." Others can copy the existing record from the database into their own catalogs, hence the name, copy cataloging. The result is supposed to be faster, less costly cataloging for all network members. This was the primary purpose of OCLC when it was established in the 1960s, although resource sharing also was an important goal. More recently, research and support of other service functions, such as acquisitions and serials control, have become important. RLIN, Utlas, WLN, and other networks also aim to provide faster, less costly cataloging for their participants.

NETWORKS, SAVINGS, AND COSTS

Common sense tells us that the more items an individual cataloging department must put into the database "from scratch," because they are the first to catalog them, the less they will benefit either from the speed or dollar savings to be had from network shared cataloging. Libraries that contribute unusually high percentages (e.g., more than 25 to 30 percent) of their catalog records as first-time entries might be called "net contributors" for the same reason that libraries are called "net lenders" when they lend more items to other libraries through interlibrary loan than they borrow from them. In recognition of their contributions to the database, OCLC gives a small monetary reward to libraries that enter a record for the first time. This reward is the same, however, for any library that contributes a new catalog record. It does not vary in size according to how many or what proportion of a library's records are first-time entries. Libraries that contribute more original records (i.e., first-time entries) earn more of a reward but not a larger reward per item.

No one, logic says, would hanker to become a net contributor under these circumstances. When library administrators consider joining OCLC or some other bibliographic network, they hope to get rid of all of their original cataloging once and for all. Some of the less knowledgeable administrators eliminate all of their professional cataloging staff when they join the network, thinking these staff will not be needed any more. Ruth Hafter documented the phenomenon in her 1986 book, *Academic Librarians and Cataloging Networks*,[1] and Liz Bishoff decried it a year later in an article appearing in *American Libraries*.[2] This is sheer foolishness, because it is rare that there will fail to be some proportion of materials, however small, that requires original cataloging. But for most general libraries that buy English-language trade books, the number of items not already cataloged by the Library of Congress or some other large research university that generates huge amounts of cataloging copy will be very small. It is clear that the shared cataloging network is the key to less work in general and, certainly, less work of a "professional" nature as well as some dollar savings. Using the network costs money, of course, but substituting nonprofessional staff for professional catalogers and doing less work overall should mean the library is saving something somewhere.

What is less obvious to network participants is that they reap the dollar benefits when network catalog records are accepted without alteration (or without much alteration) by the libraries that did not put them into the database. The more one tinkers with an existing record, the more time it takes a staff member — any staff member — to complete the cataloging for an item. More time results in more cost and fewer savings.[3] More importantly, perhaps, is the fact that the more one tinkers with certain parts of an existing record — namely, the parts that require skilled judgments to be made, judgments that depend upon professional knowledge — the more difficult it is to dispatch existing records quickly while still producing the same high-quality records for the local catalog that the professional cataloger's "from scratch" records could produce. Now, here's the rub: Does the library want to give up quality by accepting someone else's judgments without regard to their accuracy, or give up savings by spending more time and money tinkering?

THE QUALITY ISSUE

Most catalog managers find it extraordinarily difficult to give up quality, even when the catalog represents a very small general collection, isn't used as a research tool, and doesn't have numerous editions of individual titles requiring extensive data to tell them apart. And surprising though it may seem, it is equally difficult to get catalog managers for large research collections to consider risking local cataloging quality in favor of speedier production by minimizing or eliminating tinkering, even when their backlogs are growing at a frightening rate. I have argued for less tinkering to no avail with both professional and nonprofessional catalogers from all sorts of libraries. I always wonder how they can justify network participation if they can't let what they receive from it alone but insist on fixing field after field until they might as well have put in an entirely new record for the amount of effort and cost lavished on editing.

Conventional wisdom doesn't support the notion of accepting network records as is willy-nilly. Conventional wisdom says exactly the opposite, as the following bromides demonstrate:

- Do the best catalog record you can now, because fixing it up later on costs much more.

- A library's catalog should serve its users.

- The "mark-it-and-park-it" philosophy negates the purpose of classification to provide a browsable collection.

- Full, accurate cataloging in the network database makes the database more valuable to every library that uses it.

- Full, accurate cataloging pays for itself by enabling library clients to find materials faster without asking for help from public service librarians.

There are more such sayings, but these will do to make the point. I believe the sayings are true and I use them frequently in teaching, speaking, and writing. Why, then, am I arguing the opposite view? The answer is simple. Current trends in information service won't permit catalogers to continue keeping faith with the ideal of producing perfect catalogs made up of perfect catalog records. Remaining faithful to their ideals in the face of what is happening in the information field is worse than quixotic, it spells doom to the essence of cataloging and discredits what catalogers can and should be doing instead of creating perfect records.

WHY THE PERFECT CATALOG IS DOOMED

Three trends spell doom for perfect cataloging: the continuing information explosion, computerization of bibliographic services, and the real cost of perfect catalogers.

The Continuing Information Explosion

The information explosion that burst on the library scene in the latter half of the twentieth century now has become the status quo. There isn't anything strange about experiencing annual increases in the avalanche of publications in all formats—books, serials, microforms, videos, sound recordings, etc. That is standard for our times. If a year went by in which there wasn't a significant percentage of new journals, librarians would think something was wrong and would probably bemoan the lack of diversity in journal publication. Librarians probably would complain if a year passed without a new format or two combining computers, lasers, and time warps with the familiar audio, video, and alphanumerics. Everyone who uses information (which is just about everyone) has grown accustomed to the torrential outpouring from the information horn of plenty.

Now that everyone—including administrators, faculty, librarians, students, and just plain folks—understand and accept the fact that they can't keep up with the flood of information in their interest areas, they are resigned to falling behind. Thus, it is difficult for them to work up steam over the titles they can't read, view, or hear in the cataloging backlog, because they haven't got time to read, view, or hear all the titles that make it out of processing and onto the shelves.

It is far better simply to ignore the part of the flood that remains out of sight than to recognize it and become even more frustrated and depressed at the thought that one can't deal with it successfully. Research libraries are in no particular hurry to get it out on the shelves, anyway, since they haven't much shelf space left, and there is precious little interest in building bigger buildings every few years to cope with a never-ending flow of material.

Similarly, once one realizes that there is no hope of success in collection development, one stops trying to buy everything and settles for what one can get. The fact that it can't all be cataloged is a plus for collection developers, because it allows them to feel that they are able to more than satiate their libraries with purchases.

Computerization of Bibliographic Services

Computerization of bibliographic services has provided catalogers with two opportunities to create perfect catalogs: first, by inputting their own perfect records, and second, by editing other people's flawed records. But online public access catalogs (OPACs) also offer capabilities of storing and retrieving cataloged materials in ways we couldn't dream of without computers, e.g., by combining access points (Boolean operators), by retrieving terms that do not appear in the filing position in an access point (keyword searching), by retrieving terms that aren't even part of an access point but occur elsewhere in a record (full-text searching), by correcting the searcher's incorrect spellings ("forgiving" retrieval), and by searching on partial data (truncation), to name just a few. With these additional aids to searching and retrieving desired materials, having the perfect record in the database becomes less critical for achieving search success. If a title is garbled a bit (e.g., *Chaos, the Making of a New Science*, or *The Making of the New Science of Chaos*), it can still be located if it is searched by the keywords CHAOS and SCIENCE. Retrieval will be even easier if the searcher knows that the author is Richard Glueck, and the search won't be confounded when the name is misspelled "Gluek" if the OPAC is programmed to search for *ck* whenever a *k* alone is entered. Having every detail correct in the body of a record, or even in its designated access points, loses its importance when so many alternatives can be employed to aid the searcher in overcoming an error or two. Of course, not only do searchers have to understand how to use the aids, but library catalogs have to be programmed to support them. In my experience, very few OPACs have even the five mentioned here — Boolean operators, keyword searching, full-text searching, forgiving retrieval, and truncation — let alone others.

A second way computerization of bibliographic services has affected librarians' perceptions about the need for perfect records and perfect catalogers is the anticipation that within the next decade expert systems will be designed to produce virtually perfect records from a scan of covers, title pages, tables of contents, indexes, etc. Despite Ben Tucker's astute observations that human catalogers are needed to decipher bibliographic details that publishers try to obscure,[4] I believe the fullness and accuracy in records produced by machines will far outstrip those in records produced by the humans in most library cataloging departments, especially cataloging departments that have been stripped of their professional staff. My study of the fullness and accuracy of catalog records in OCLC and RLIN showed that both databases, with all of their quality control efforts, seem equally dirty.[5] If cataloging were removed from the hands of well-meaning but unschooled library staff and put into the realm of well-programmed automatic computerized production, it probably would improve immediately. Between trusting a host of different humans with different educations, backgrounds, biases, and capabilities, or a host of different computers all running the same expertly programmed system to do the best job of cataloging, I'll bet on the computers every time.

The Real Cost of Perfect Catalogers

Think about the real cost of a perfect cataloger. Try translating the salaries that graduates of library master's degree programs were paid in 1965, when librarians' salaries were more in tune with the salaries of other professionals, into current dollars, then add something for the higher amount that an experienced, truly excellent cataloger with several languages and demonstrated subject expertise—a perfect cataloger—should command. The results, somewhere in the neighborhood of $75,000 a year, boggle the mind. The librarians I know who receive such salaries are not catalogers but top-level administrators at a small number of institutions.

Assuming that things haven't changed since the last time I looked at job advertisements in *Library Journal* and *American Libraries*, libraries in most parts of the country are still trying to hire catalogers at somewhere between $18,000 and $28,000 a year, for which they still expect a year's experience, a foreign language, and subject training beyond the bachelor's degree. This is about $50,000 short of the real cost—and perhaps the real value—of a perfect cataloger. Clearly, perfect catalogers are far beyond the means of libraries as long as decision makers keep target salaries pegged at their current low marks. (Beginning librarian salaries compare well only with unskilled labor jobs. They are being or already have been overtaken by the salaries of sanitation workers, taxi drivers, corporate secretaries, and public school teachers.)

WHO CARES IF THE PERFECT CATALOG IS DOOMED?

Not I.

In view of the foregoing arguments, who should care if perfect catalogs in libraries are receding farther into the distance? No one, I believe. Extensive editing is a futile occupation that should be minimized as far as possible. Even today, without the realization of super-sophisticated OPACs or expert systems, the dollars-and-cents arguments of growing backlogs and shrinking catalog departments mandate the reevaluation and quick disposal of the case in favor of heavy editing of network records for local catalogs. Instead, editing should be avoided absolutely with very few exceptions, and bibliographic networks should be prodded to beef up their quality control efforts as value-added contributions to the database. Individual libraries aren't equipped to do it for them any longer, any more than they are equipped to develop software or maintain network equipment.

I firmly believe that it is better to have a flawed record in the database than to have no record at all. I also believe catalogers should stop hitting their heads against stone walls, by trying to turn out the best possible cataloging they can manage for whatever portion of purchases they can handle that way, and turn their attention to more productive and satisfying goals. These goals include making shared network cataloging work better, faster, and at a higher dollar value for their libraries and also acquiring the skills to function in the new world of cataloging that will come with the advent of expert systems and super-OPACs. These new skills include expertise in training, planning, budgeting, communicating, and designing organizational systems. By acquiring these skills, which are managerial skills, catalogers may find themselves moving into the ranks of higher level administrators, where they can begin to command salaries approaching what a perfect cataloger should be paid.

The essence of the issue lies in choosing the right goals and objectives — seeing and doing the job that needs doing, not a job that might have been significant at some point in the past. Instead of approaching their cataloging tasks on a book-by-book basis, deciding how to catalog each one appropriately, catalogers must approach them on a total job basis and figure out how to catalog everything that is acquired. No doubt the plan will require giving up a considerable amount of editing of network shared cataloging. (A case can even be made for accepting call numbers without change regardless of whether they contain Dewey or LC classification numbers. Quite a few academic libraries that switched from Dewey to LC in the 1960s or 1970s still have sizable remnants of their Dewey collections. Why not just mark 'em and park 'em in the appropriate collection? That's what public librarians do with conflicting editions of Dewey, and no one seems to put up a big fuss about it.)

Catalogers today have an opportunity to turn their seeming defeat into victory. By taking up the job they've been avoiding for years, they can convert serving an outmoded perfectionism into a vital role in the future of library service, thereby aspiring to more challenging work and better pay.

NOTES

[1] Ruth Hafter, *Academic Librarians and Cataloging Networks: Visibility, Quality Control and Professional Status* (Westport, Conn.: Greenwood Press, 1986).

[2] Lizbeth J. Bishoff, "Who Says We Don't Need Catalogers?" *American Libraries* 18 (September 1987):694-696.

[3] A fine discussion of "tinkering," which identifies the issues, policies, and procedures for catalog managers, is available in Arlene G. Taylor's *Cataloging with Copy*, 2d ed. (Littleton, Colo.: Libraries Unlimited, 1987).

[4] Ben R. Tucker, "The Limits of a Title Proper, or One Case Showing Why Human Beings, Not Machines, Must Do the Cataloging," *Library Resources & Technical Services* 34 (April 1990):240-245.

[5] Sheila S. Intner, "Much Ado about Nothing: OCLC and RLIN Cataloging Quality," *Library Journal* 114 (February 1, 1989):38-40.

28

The Education of
Copy Catalogers

Although it deserves the attention of educators, the education of copy catalogers is being neglected by U.S. library schools. Nor is lack of attention to paraprofessional education for library and information science limited to the cataloging department. Library schools outside the United States have programs to prepare technicians or library assistants, but in accredited U.S. library and information science programs, no one thinks much about formal education for those who work as para- or nonprofessional staff in libraries. Perhaps the whole idea is that they have not gone through a formal educational process; educating them in schools of library and information science might defeat the purpose of employing them as complements to those who have. Yet that idea flies in the face of the realities in other fields, such as law and medicine.

In my opinion, education for this paraprofessional specialty should differ from that of professional specialists in cataloging and bibliographic control. Two things seem obvious: copy cataloging doesn't require a master's degree, and it should include courses in cataloging and classification. However, those are hardly adequate specifications for desirable levels of education or appropriate curricula. In a paper delivered at the 1991 Congress on Cataloging Heresy at St. John's University, I examined the differing educational needs of catalogers who conform to cataloging standards and those who reject them.[1] The work for that paper made me begin to think about education for copy cataloging. This problem ought to have the same careful consideration, I believe, because copy catalogers are now ubiquitous throughout the library world, particularly in academic institutions. This chapter begins to examine the issues and problems of educating copy catalogers appropriately.

PARAPROFESSIONALS IN OTHER FIELDS

There are several levels of education and training for the law, from the juris doctor and higher degrees to training for support personnel like paralegals and legal stenographers or secretaries. In most places, the graduate degree of juris doctor is required before one can enter the practice of law by taking the bar examination, and passing the bar is the credential needed to represent clients in court. (Until a few years ago, one did not need a university degree to qualify for the bar examination. One could "read" with a practitioner until one felt ready to take the examination. But I am told that this is no longer true, at least in the states with which my informants are familiar.)

If one needs legal advice or representation, one goes to an attorney with the necessary credentials for practice. Other tasks that do not involve giving legal advice or representing clients in a court of law, the not-quite-professional tasks, such as recording the testimony of witnesses, formatting legal documents to conform to the requirements of courts and administrative agencies, registering documents, etc., fall to paralegals and legal secretaries or stenographers. In the early decades of this century, any bright young thing (male or female—no gender bias is intended) could become a legal paraprofessional. All it took was getting hired in a law office. The lawyers told you what you had to do and you did it. My mother, a legal stenographer during the 1920s, used to recount with great glee her forays into court in which she appeared before various judges to obtain court orders, writs, etc. Today, there are programs of study that aim to provide levels of knowledge appropriate to the tasks involved in each of those specialties. One can study for a year or less and become a certified paralegal, or specialize in legal stenography or secretarial work in a focused program, without learning how to be a lawyer. Some bright young things fresh out of college with baccalaureates still land jobs as paralegals, but it is becoming increasingly difficult for one important reason: By the time they are thoroughly trained and know how to operate independently, they go off to graduate school—usually law school.

The field of medicine is similar. Physicians and surgeons must have the proper academic degree as well as a period of apprenticeship or residency, during which they work under the supervision of senior practitioners, as well as state board certification in their area of expertise before they can begin independent practice. Physicians and surgeons are supported by many other health professionals who are not allowed to practice medicine (i.e., prescribe drugs or other medical therapies, or cut us open to fix our innards), such as nurses, nutritionists, physical therapists, and midwives. Those practitioners work on our physical well-being in other ways, and their training involves learning the theories, systems, and programs of their specialty. All of them perform important services, but they aren't doctors and they aren't expected to earn an M.D. They are expected to have the credentials appropriate to their work.

One critical fact to keep in mind is that people don't expect attorneys to do the work of legal secretaries, nor do they suppose physicians will give their hospitalized patients sponge baths or change their bedpans. In fact, in many busy hospitals, nurses don't do it, either. Those tasks fall to orderlies or nursing assistants, who might be whizzes at turning a patient gently without disturbing an incision or a wound but who are not trained to recognize when to call the doctor because the patient's behavior is awry.

LIBRARY PARAPROFESSIONALISM

In the library field, on the other hand, two different and disturbing steps have been taken. First of all, in a good many institutions the job descriptions of professional librarians are being trivialized by including a full-time allotment of tasks that people without a master's degree could do perfectly well. These job descriptions fail to distinguish between tasks that require the kind of knowledge imparted to degreed catalogers in programs of professional education and those that are quite rightly delegated to people with less education and lower-level skills. Second, and perhaps even worse, particularly for those institutions that do delegate tasks previously reserved for professionals to staff without the master's degree, the library community is not taking any responsibility for the proper training of the paraprofessionals. They are being let loose with whatever training each employer thinks is enough. Certainly, some employers give paraprofessionals a good measure of relevant knowledge, but others simply point them at a terminal and give them the password.

The work to which I am referring here is copy cataloging, although I suspect there are parallels in other areas of librarianship. In some libraries, practitioners holding M.L.S. degrees sit for thirty-six to forty hours a week at terminals matching records on their screens with books in hand and editing existing catalog records. In other libraries, untrained or insufficiently trained paraprofessional or nonprofessional staff are shown how to search the bibliographic source of choice, given a list of fields to be edited, and told to get to work. If they can't find an existing record, they just input a new record by emulating what they see in the source database.

These twin problems have twin solutions. Professionally degreed catalogers should not be expected to spend time doing copy cataloging, period, except as (1) part of an initial training period, employed to ease them into the "real world" from the laboratory environment of library school or into the unfamiliar environment of a new library or department or (2) to test their grasp of cataloging principles and practices. After a reasonable period of time (say, six weeks to three months), they should move on to professional work, such as original cataloging, evaluation of copy cataloging done by others, staff training, database design and planning, bibliography, and collection development. By the same token, paraprofessional staff should not be permitted anywhere near a terminal until they have acquired the requisite knowledge of descriptive cataloging, indexing, and classification appropriate for making decisions that affect bibliographic control and access.

ASSUMPTIONS AND PRESUMPTIONS

Statements in the previous paragraph pre-suppose two things: all degreed librarians are properly prepared to be bibliographic control specialists, and paraprofessionals need relatively extensive bibliographic knowledge to do copy cataloging, which cannot be obtained from in-service training. Both assumptions may not be entirely correct or they could be wrong. They need further analysis.

As for the first assumption, it is wrong at least some of the time. Some M.L.S. degrees are awarded to people who have not had so much as a single course in cataloging, and many more are awarded to people who have had only one. Cataloging now is sufficiently complicated that one course cannot cover everything needed for the specialty. A cataloging specialist should have at least three or four courses: two on the basic principles of bibliographic control and classification theory and one or two covering applications of cataloging, indexing, and classification systems for all types of materials. Also, there is no substitute for the addition of some practical experience in handling the myriad variations in materials that demand the most exquisite bibliographic decision making.

Regarding the second assumption, it is not quite fair to say that every paraprofessional needs extensive bibliographic knowledge, nor is it fair to believe it is impossible for them to get that knowledge on the job. In libraries where bibliographic sources furnish 100 percent of the data needed for the local catalog and where no changes need to be made to the records, the only knowledge a paraprofessional needs is how to select records from the database and process them into the local catalog. One could be taught fairly easily to input unique identifiers, such as ISBNs or LCCNs, and to match authors, titles, editions, publishers, or dates from the records thus retrieved with items in hand. This would work if all desired library materials came with ISBNs or LCCNs and if every item assigned such numbers was attached to an acceptable bibliographic record. (One way a library can minimize its original cataloging is to avoid purchasing items without LCCNs.) If a library such as this purchased an item for which an existing bibliographic record was not available, there would be several choices to solve the problem: (1) catalog the item locally in any way that suited the library but don't upload the record to the bibliographic source; (2) don't catalog the item at all, but place it in an uncataloged collection; (3) contract with a cataloging vendor to provide a record good enough to be uploaded to the cataloging source; or (4) return the item to its acquisition source.

Far from being far-fetched, these may become options that small general libraries dealing solely in mainstream materials can consider.

There also are some libraries in which the training afforded to entering catalogers (whether or not they have master's degrees in library and information science) is nearly equal if not superior to the formal course work offered in library schools. At Harvard College Library, catalogers have a lengthy, carefully controlled introduction to each part of the cataloging process, supervised all the way by senior professionals.[2] In a paper delivered at the 1989 Simmons College Symposium on Recruiting, Educating, and Training Cataloging Librarians, Michael Fitzgerald describes a learning process of which any library school might be proud. Such training goes beyond the first few weeks or months of employment and may be part of a program of continuing development implemented to meet continuous changes in bibliographic rules, tools, and systems.[3]

Given that some libraries do not need bibliographic specialists because they don't do any cataloging and that some libraries give good training to their cataloging staffs (i.e., degreed and paraprofessional staff alike, as appropriate), a reasonable hypothesis is that the rest, probably a majority of the nation's libraries, are failing in two of their important responsibilities: to do a good job of providing bibliographic control and access to materials for their patrons and to make their unique contributions to the combined national database.

SOLUTIONS AND CONCLUSIONS

Solving the problem begins by recognizing that it exists. Then, all it requires is assessing one's local needs for original and copy cataloging and providing the requisite training for each level of staff employed. It must be done by means of an appropriate mix of library school course work and in-service training, not one or the other.

Both the original cataloger and the copy cataloger require bibliographic knowledge. The copy cataloger might be very well prepared to do his or her work with the knowledge learned in the library school's cataloging curriculum plus enough on-the-job training to integrate him or her into the library's local practices. But the original cataloger needs more training, since he or she will have professional responsibilities that include creation of new catalog records and more. In addition to being able to create records "from scratch," the professional cataloger also needs to be able to make policy decisions (e.g., "we will not edit Library of Congress records," or, "we will trace all series in which any of the individual titles are likely to be classified in Q, R, S, T, U, V, or Z," etc.); to train copy catalogers; to perform other planning and supervisory tasks; and, perhaps, to perform public service tasks. All of these duties require preparation outside of the cataloging curriculum. The full M.L.S. (and probably more) is needed by this librarian, and the curriculum should include, in addition to cataloging course work, course work in general reference, special types of literatures or materials, general management, management of bibliographic systems and services, type-of-library administration, collection development, instruction, emerging technologies, and more.

It's time that librarians woke up to the fact that they trivialize their field if they are satisfied with doing jobs that should belong to well-trained paraprofessionals, and that insisting that those jobs be done only by persons with proper training will free them to do more challenging, interesting, and important work. However, building the field takes more than just saying what one won't do; it also takes saying what one will do. Catalogers with M.L.S. degrees must do more than say they won't do copy cataloging any more. They must be ready and anxious, not just grudgingly willing, to move from just plain cataloging into bibliographic management, and they must be ready to demand that the paraprofessionals they supervise be properly educated and trained. Finally, catalogers must prove that the paraprofessionals' training is worth the library's investment.

One way to control the quality of cataloging by paraprofessionals is to require testing, certification, or some other kind of evidence that proves they know what they are doing before they are hired. A system of certification also could raise their status, insure their ability to excel in a critical role, and point the way toward better pay scales. Librarians owe it to themselves to work toward that goal on behalf of their paraprofessional assistants. Unless one thinks it is perfect now, one knows that the field of library and information science must continue developing along paths similar to those taken by other professions.

NOTES

[1]Sheila S. Intner, "Rejecting the Standard Catalog Record: Implications for the Education of Cataloging Librarians," *Cataloging Heresy: Challenging the Standard Bibliographic Product: Proceedings of the Congress for Librarians, February 18, 1991*, St. John's University, Jamaica, New York, Bella Hass Weinberg, ed. (Medford, N.J.: Learned Publications, 1992), 119-130.

[2]Michael Fitzgerald, "Training the Cataloger: A Harvard Experience," in *Recruiting, Educating, and Training Cataloging Librarians: Solving the Problems*, Sheila S. Intner and Janet Swan Hill, eds. (Westport, Conn.: Greenwood, 1989), 341-353.

[3]An ongoing staff development process for copy catalogers that is in place at the University of California at Irvine is mentioned briefly by D. Kathryn Weintraub in "Using Management Tools for Cataloging Discussions," in *Recruiting, Educating, and Training Cataloging Librarians*, p. 375-389.

Bibliographic Policies

In the cataloging and classification fundamentals course I teach, I finish the semester with a lecture and discussion on bibliographic policies. One reason I do it is that I believe every library cataloging department ought to have a written document that covers all the basic policy issues governing its bibliographic products and services. Such decisions include the rules for and level of descriptive cataloging to be followed, how series will be handled, which classification system and subject heading list will be employed, and what rules for filing will be used. A second, less important, reason is that it serves to summarize the many topics covered in rapid succession during the course. Here are some of the elements practitioners might consider putting in their library's Bibliographic Services Policy.

DESCRIPTIVE CATALOGING

AACR2R, as the only standard for descriptive cataloging, should be followed by all libraries hoping to produce standard library cataloging. AACR2R is mandated by all the bibliographic utilities (OCLC, RLIN, Utlas, and WLN), the Library of Congress, and the national libraries of Canada and the United Kingdom, making it the most widely applied standard among generators of original cataloging for English-language materials. Special libraries and school library media centers, which often think they are exempt from library practices by virtue of their generally small size and unique settings, have much to gain from adopting the AACR2R standard even though they are the least likely to follow it.

There are three reasons why they should adopt AACR2R. First, it is the only standard; all bibliographic products that conform to standards employ AACR2R. Thus, using AACR2R gives the library the flexibility to use any standard product or service. Second, using AACR2R makes the library's bibliographic products and services interchangeable with the products and services of other libraries that use AACR2R. This enables the library to share data (or sell it, if the library owns it) with other users of standard products and services. Third, members of the public who have learned to use standard library data elsewhere will recognize the format and be able to transfer their knowledge to the use of local products and services; conversely, they can apply what they learn about local data to standard data in other libraries.

Making Use of AACR2R's Flexibility

AACR2R has two kinds of built-in flexibility, and bibliographic policies should address both. The first is the choice of level of description. Libraries with small general collections and unsophisticated clients should opt for the simplest cataloging, Level 1; others will probably be satisfied with Level 2 or Level 2 with added enrichment as necessary. Level 3, which mandates the use of all applicable rules, is probably beyond the needs of most libraries unless they are very large and have very complex materials. Even LC uses Level 2 for the most part (and, for serials, Level 1 with enrichments).

The second kind of flexibility is inherent in the many options written into the rules. The bibliographic utilities and many large academic libraries (whether members of utilities or not) have chosen to follow LC's practices. LC obliges by publishing its rule interpretations (LCRIs) in *Cataloging Service Bulletin*, a publication no library that does original cataloging of any kind should be without. Since LC provides this service at a small cost to anyone who is interested, it saves the individual library from going through every one of the rules and deciding on each individual option; LC's decisions are intelligently made, so, if there is no compelling reason to depart from them, there is every reason to follow them.

Nevertheless, following LC blindly in all instances may have less useful results, locally, than establishing customized rule interpretations. A local library should consider such departures as seem useful to their patrons, e.g., using all GMDs and not just those the Library of Congress chooses to use (a consideration especially important for libraries whose main holdings are not in book form) or assigning main and added entries to librettos differently than for their associated music (certainly an advantage of sorts for music libraries with extensive collections of both music and librettos that do not have to be collocated). Unless one's network affiliation or other contractual obligations mandate that no departures be made from LCRIs, catalogers should be free to follow whichever options produce the most useful products and services for their clients.

Series, Special Media, and Kits

Beyond AACR2R are decisions about how to treat series. Should all series titles be traced routinely or only some of them? How will traceable and non-traceable series titles be distinguished? Should members of the series be classified together or separately? Should the series constitute the bibliographic unit, i.e., catalog at the series level only, with a contents note and perhaps an added entry for the individual volumes? Like series, serials warrant policy decisions about their cataloging, classification, and indexing treatment. Should holdings information appear in the main catalog record or only in a special serials file? Should some issues of some journals be cataloged as monographic separates? Many libraries do not classify or index serials, avoiding the many decisions involved with multisubject titles. Some works appear to be hybrids—part series, part serials—requiring case-by-case decisions on appropriate handling.

The proper choice of the bibliographic unit for cataloging purposes is a difficult issue and it will become more difficult if newer, denser storage media, such as microforms and CD-ROMs, become more popular. Should one catalog the whole CD-ROM disk or the whole microform set as a unit, or should each individual work on the disk or set be cataloged analytically? Most libraries opt to do the former, but many are beginning to change their policies as more and more of their holdings are converted into formats that take up less room, last longer, and utilize the latest in computer-based systems for dissemination.

What about notes? Almost all descriptive notes are optional, although a few are mandated by the application of certain rules for title, responsibility, edition, or other areas of description. However, local libraries can choose to mandate certain notes if they wish to do so, e.g., publishers' (or plate) numbers for music and sound recordings, contents for multiwork items, and summaries and equipment requirements for nonbook materials that require hardware for use. As catalogs are computerized librarians are finding that the lack of this sort of enrichment in entries limits the flexibility and search potential of the records and prevents exploitation of fancy new system capabilities. Even if particular notes are not mandated, policies can indicate when they should be included, e.g., system requirements notes for computer software, content and summary notes for anthologies and items with titles that do not reflect their true contents.

One choice most people don't think much about is how to catalog multipart items that comprise more than one physical format. The cataloger has to decide whether such an item is a kit — defined as a multipart item in which the intellectual or artistic content can only be had by using all parts simultaneously — or a filmstrip, a sound recording, a book, or whatever, with the other parts being considered accompanying material. LC often chooses to make the latter choice, not because of the intellectual content but because their collecting policy does not include kits. Calling such an item a kit would prevent LC from acquiring and cataloging it. If, however, they call it a filmstrip with accompanying sound recording or vice versa, they can acquire and catalog it.

Emulating LC's cataloging for films and videos can create problems. Most of these titles were cataloged from data sheets supplied by producers or distributors before the program was discontinued in 1991. If the error rate in the data sheets was even half that of the publishers' materials on which CIP is based, it would have been too sizable a figure to be ignored. For these items librarians would do well to rely on the data in hand, not on the LC records.

General Issues

Establishing sound bibliographic policies for materials other than books and printed serials is important if these items are to be fully used. Policies can encourage good cataloging by mandating that hardware be made available for cataloging purposes when necessary and that nonbook entries be given at least the same level of treatment as books. Mainstreaming nonbook materials with books in the cataloging process is a good way to make their use as easy as possible for patrons and allows the same expertise to be used in providing access to nonbook items.

Policies on descriptive cataloging should include decisions about authority control. Will the library keep its own authority file? Will it rely on another library's? If authority work is done by the local library, who will see to it that documentation is done properly and conforms to appropriate specifications? These questions should be answered by bibliographic policy statements.

INDEXING

The most important indexing policy decision is which list of subject headings to use: *Sears List of Subject Headings*, *Library of Congress Subject Headings*, or another. For special libraries, thesauri intended for a particular subject area might be more appropriate to the collection, e.g., the National Library of Medicine's *Medical Subject Headings* (MeSH). One indexing vocabulary may not be enough, however. A small library might find Sears adequate for its general collection, but for some particularly large and varied subject or special collection, e.g., local history, it might need something more detailed — LCSH or another specialized list. The application of various subject authorities should be clearly defined.

The number of headings applied by LC and network sources, if not sufficient to provide the level of access desired by the library, can be enriched by additional headings according to one's policy. Hennepin County Library has, for years, augmented LC entries with their own list of subject headings. Indeed, they do not use some of LCSH's outdated, sexist, or otherwise unappealing headings at all, substituting their own choices. While this puts the burden of documenting and controlling the headings on the library that creates them, there is no doubt that it offers a method of increasing user access (and, therefore, user satisfaction).

One application of subject headings rarely controlled by the catalog or technical service department is the list used for the vertical file. These headings are usually assigned (and often made up) by reference librarians. Wouldn't it be better for library clients if the vertical file was arranged by the same or very similar headings as the catalog? Reference librarians may also make up subject headings for government documents or, worse, they may not index them at all, relying instead on the names of the agencies.

CLASSIFICATION AND SHELVING

Decisions similar to those made about indexing must be made for classification, including which standard classification scheme to use and what supplements or special applications need to be made for the local situation. Most general libraries follow either the Dewey Decimal (DDC) or the Library of Congress (LCC) classification. Special libraries may find and prefer using a classification that exists for one or more of the subject areas it emphasizes, e.g., the National Library of Medicine publishes a far more detailed classification for medical materials than the schedule found in LCC. However, specialized classifications may not cover unrelated subject areas, so they must be combined with a second scheme with more general coverage. The National Library of Medicine, for example, uses LCC for everything except medical materials.

After the classification is chosen, methods of applying it must be decided, and options for treatment of certain types of materials must be made. Users of the DDC know that there are several options for treating musical materials and for handling biographies. For libraries located outside of the United States, DDC offers options for highlighting a literature other than U.S. literature in English and in a language other than English. LCC offers fewer alternatives, but some can be found within its schedules. Wherever a local preference is to be followed in place of the recommendations in the printed schedules — whether the library uses DDC, LCC, or another specialized classification — the local library should document the changes carefully.

Classification numbers are the primary element in call numbers, but shelf addresses usually include other numbers, symbols, and locational devices as well. Cutter numbers may be formulated in several different ways, by following a printed table of numbers, such as the Cutter-Sanborn tables, or by applying LC's rules for building cutter numbers. Collection designations, such as *R* for Reference, *F* for Fiction, *J* for Juvenile/Children's or *FL* for foreign language, identify specific areas in the library as the place to find a particular item. Dates may be added to the call number to distinguish subsequent editions from the first. Volume numbers may be added to identify individual volumes in multivolume works. And copy numbers may become part of the call number when the library holds multiple copies of a title.

The complexity of call numbers stems from a more basic policy decision to assign unique call numbers to each item in the collection. If there is no desire to assign unique call numbers (and many libraries don't mind if a dozen or more books, films, or recordings have the same call number), a simpler combination of classification numbers and cutters may do. In the public library where I worked, only a few shelf marks were added to classification: a cutter letter, a collection designation, and, for encyclopedias and other multivolume works, volume numbers. No effort was made to distinguish between two general cookbooks written by different authors whose names both began with J. Both would have been assigned "641.5/J." But if one was part of the reference collection, it would have been designated "R/641.5/J". All the books assigned "641.5/J" were intershelved, although pages were trained to subarrange them by author's surname when there was time to do so.

OTHER ISSUES

The scope of one's bibliographic policy is critical. It should cover all library materials, regardless of their physical form or the audience for whom they are intended. If nonbook materials, children's materials, or some other type of materials are excluded, they will not be fully used. It is a shame to see money expended on good things that people cannot find.

The length of time materials can remain uncataloged in backlogs should be limited. Strategies for speeding up production (which may be included in a policy document) should not include pressuring people to work extra hours or complete more entries in a specified time but should rely on alternatives to current procedures if those procedures fail to accommodate the normal work flow. These strategies may include sorting materials into different batches for quicker processing, introducing minimal level cataloging for some or all materials, or hiring additional staff to handle certain materials.

Bibliographic Utilities

Joining a bibliographic utility requires making many local decisions that affect both the quality and speed of cataloging. To edit or not to edit is the primary question facing new utility participants. The tradeoff between having more perfect records and having cheaper records is a difficult one, since what we really want is cheap but perfect cataloging. If I were making a recommendation as a consultant, I would insist that, unless a majority of one's clients can be shown how to use a particular field that has been edited to take advantage of the local change (call numbers is a field most libraries use in individual ways), then the field should not be edited. I always opt for less editing and more imperfection, although, if editing can be justified as benefitting a majority of the public, I could be persuaded to mandate editing a field. Universities sometimes create bibliographic records suitable for their most sophisticated clients — post-doctoral researchers — even though these people comprise a decided minority of the public; at the same time, these universities accumulate great backlogs of uncataloged materials. I believe these institutions do their public a disservice and confound the purpose of acquiring materials in the first place. If they would devise cataloging policies that involve fewer editing and revising operations and expedite the process to eliminate the backlogs, they would furnish better service in the long run.

How many times should an item be searched in the database before original cataloging is done? In some libraries the search for data goes on for a year or more before the cataloger breaks down and puts the item into the original cataloging heap (possibly a backlog from which the item may never escape). I beg my students not to promulgate that sort of policy but to see to it that items are out on the shelves during their period of greatest usefulness — within the first year after publication.

The other side of the coin (at least in OCLC) is the policy that seems driven by FTU fever. How many search keys are tried and how carefully are existing entries scanned before an item is considered an FTU candidate? Often I see entries that appear to vary in their interpretation of data in minor fields (not edition, publication, distribution data, or another major element), yet they exist side by side in the database, cluttering up every inquiry for the title. Perhaps one can tolerate someone else's interpretation of data in order to minimize unnecessary duplications. Policies should insure that searching is thorough and that found entries are used as long as input standards permit it.

Fullness of entries is another issue. I've seen records in OCLC tagged I-level that barely contained enough data to identify an item at all, let alone uniquely. Sometimes I wonder whether copy catalogers and original catalogers use the same rules. In a utility, not only do AACR2R's rules but also the bibliographic input standards have to be satisfied. The responsibility to do as full and accurate an entry as possible is part of networking. Bibliographic policies should underscore that.

Filing Rules

Utility member or not, every institution must decide which filing rules to follow in its local catalog. ALA 1968, ALA 1980, or LC filing rules are the popular choices, although some people would rather fight than switch from earlier editions or peculiar local practices.

ALA 1980 was designed for computer filing and may be the best selection to have programmed into your OPAC. It isn't a bad choice for manual files also, since its guiding principle is to file words as they appear. The guiding principle of ALA 1968 differs; it mandates that many words be filed differently than they appear. In ALA 1968, *Dr.* is filed as if it were *Doctor*; *Mrs.* is filed as if it were *Mistress* or *Missus*; *McEwen* is filed as if it were *MacEwen*; and *1* is filed as if it were the word *one*.

The LC filing rules also are designed for computer filing, but they organize multiword headings according to an order of precedence identified by punctuation, which can be confusing to patrons who have no idea punctuation is meaningful in this context. Whereas ALA 1980 will file AGRICULTURE— PSYCHOLOGICAL ASPECTS after AGRICULTURE, ANCIENT, since no attention is paid to the fact that PSYCHOLOGICAL ASPECTS is a subject subdivision while ANCIENT is an inverted modifier, LC 1980 requires just the reverse, filing all the subdivisions (set off by dashes) before all the inversions (where a comma identifies the inversion, not to be confused with commas used to mark serial lists such as HANDBOOKS, MANUALS, ETC.), and the inversions before the qualifiers (enclosed in parentheses), and the qualifiers before multiword phrases, such as AGRICULTURE IN ART. LC 1980 also recognizes different subdivision subfields, organizing all the topical headings, chronological headings, and geographic headings into groups. LC filing is considerably more complex than ALA 1980, although it can be programmed into OPACs in the same fashion.

CONCLUSION

The issues discussed in this chapter are basic to any library's bibliographic services, although they don't exhaust the list of decisions affecting catalogs and shelving arrangements. Committing policies to writing in a policy document or database means first that they must be made and, presumably, followed. Second, it means that people can examine them; anyone who cares (reference staff, bibliographic instructors, selectors, preservationists, patrons) can find out how things are done in the library. Policies that can be examined are open to criticism and challenge as well as support. This is one reason cataloging librarians may be loathe to break their traditional silence and publicize their policies.

The difficulty posed by not publicizing cataloging and classification policies is that it leaves cataloging departments virtually invisible to everyone else in the library—other staff, administrators, and patrons. And if cataloging departments are out of sight and out of mind, they might also be out of budget negotiations and out of staff and space allocations. If it isn't clear just what catalogers do, people may think they don't do anything at all! Isn't it time that people learned the truth—and cataloging departments took the consequences?

30
Bibliographic Triage

The term *triage* entered our vocabularies relatively recently. It describes the process by which medical teams categorize patients during a crisis into groups of those who are likely to benefit from medical aid and those who aren't. This avoids wasting precious time and severely limited supplies on patients who have no chance of recovery despite the effort and allows the medical team to concentrate on the patients who do have a chance of survival. Triage is supposed to minimize the toll in human life and maximize the benefit of the available time, expertise, and supplies. Of course, benefits of triage might not be appreciated by the dying who are shunted aside to make way for those deemed saveable. Nevertheless, it is hard to argue that patients who might be saved should be ignored in order to take care of the dying, just because the dying happened to get to the head of the line first.

One of triage's lessons that might be applied to many fields, our own included, is that we must plan carefully, if hastily, to maximize the ultimate benefits (or outputs) when inputs are severely limited. It also points out somewhat more indirectly that we must keep our eyes on a single goal in order to make triage work. If the goal of triage was to minimize pain, for example, the patients selected for treatment might be quite different and the ultimate result might lead to greater loss of life. More pain does not necessarily mean fewer lives are saved, and, indeed, might mean just the reverse.

My grisly title warns you that I am going to relate this human life-and-death decision making to bibliographic systems. It is really quite apt. When more materials are acquired in a particular time period than can be processed by a library's staff using its available systems, a backlog results. If this situation continues for a period of time — say, a year or longer — and there is no likelihood that changes in the amounts of materials, staff, systems, or time will begin to reverse the accumulations, a crisis develops. In his now-famous article, "The Crisis in Cataloging,"[1] Andrew Osborn showed how, half a century ago, overly complex cataloging systems caused enormous backlogs to build in large libraries while catalogers wrestled with the rules of the 1908 Anglo-American code or with rules devised by the American Library Association or the Library of Congress.

Osborn pleaded for a simpler cataloging code, one with a few generally applicable principles that any sensible person could apply. Instead, he got the ALA code in 1949 — a model of arcane complexity — followed by AACR1 in 1967 and, twelve years later, AACR2. While we may chuckle at the thought that the

AACRs minimize complexity, they do differ from other codes. While other cataloging codes attempted to enumerate every possible application of every rule, the AACRs are based upon the Paris Principles, which are a limited number of fundamental concepts endorsed by the United States and many other nations at an international conference in 1961.

We are now experiencing a crisis in cataloging backlog buildup that makes the situation of the 1940s look mild by comparison. And, while we may believe the AACRs are complex — and they are — that is not the problem. We can ask whether the AACR's complexity is solely to blame for current cataloging backlogs, as Osborn claimed in 1941. I think not. Current backlogs are a result of several forces, including the information explosion, especially the diversity and complexity of materials; the conversion to computerized bibliographic systems, with the complexity resulting from the switch in technology; the cataloging code now made more complicated to deal with the materials and systems in place; and, perhaps most important of all, a decade of shrinking processing budgets. Many librarians would list another cause of the current crisis in cataloging: the absence of enough competent catalogers to handle the current load.

The point is that the cataloging backlog crisis exists and, in some large libraries, is expected to continue indefinitely. A few years ago, a colleague who was head of original cataloging at a major research institution told me that newly acquired items requiring original cataloging but lacking high priority status will not be cataloged in our lifetimes. If the situation is out of control, can the principles of triage be applied to maximize the benefit that can be realized from the limited inputs of time, money, and expertise currently available? Perhaps they can, if a few simple rules are followed.

The first rule is to have only one goal. One of the hallmarks of cataloging is that it tries to achieve a balance among opposing ideals, e.g., serving the finding list function and the collocation function of the catalog; providing a subject heading vocabulary that reflects user needs and at the same time follows the demands of a standard, uniform subject heading list; arranging materials with a classification that protects the integrity of numbers but also has the flexibility to account for the growth of knowledge. One would believe that catalogers are experts in dealing with delicate balances. (Perhaps that is the exercise that trains catalogers to take extraordinary delight in debate.) But triage does not allow for the balance, delicate or otherwise, of opposing goals. Triage will not work if one tries to help some of the dying *and* save those who might live. So what will the goal of bibliographic triage be? Will it be to catalog the most materials? Will it be to catalog the important materials? Will it be to catalog the unique materials? Are there other goals?

The second rule is that one must stiffen the upper lip to ignore the worthy who cannot be tended. Weary catalogers may be ready to follow the necessary path, but I doubt that university administrators, school principals, municipal leaders, or corporate vice-presidents would take kindly to the notion of paying for things that may never be used — at least not during their lifetimes.

The third rule is that one must stick to the goal without faltering until the crisis is over. Librarians in general and catalogers in particular have never evidenced such an unyielding will. This might be the most difficult posture to achieve. But first, a closer look at the suggested goals themselves is warranted.

CATALOGING THE MOST MATERIALS

Many of the catalogers I know are dedicated to the goal of cataloging as many materials as they can given the limits of staff time, computer time, and so forth. I can't blame them, since most are evaluated by their superiors according the quantity of work they produce. Few library directors are impressed with the quality of cataloging. Most are tuned in, primarily, to unit costs. If x dollars are spent on cataloging and y items are cataloged, the unit cost is easy to figure. More sophisticated administrators know that all items are not alike, and they may weigh different categories of material to account for it, coming up with a slightly more complicated equation: If x dollars are spent on cataloging and y monographs, z serials, and n nonprint items are cataloged, an average unit cost of t may be calculated. One must allow for a change in unit cost if the mix of y, z, and n changes.

In today's automated libraries the basic breakdown of materials may not be between monographs and serials or between print and nonprint materials but between copy cataloging and original cataloging. In fact, many institutions with fully developed online cataloging systems have few problems with copy cataloging. Their crisis is in original cataloging. It is difficult to make some administrators understand the discrepancy in cost between a complicated item cataloged using Library of Congress cataloging copy and another item of equal complexity cataloged originally in the institution. It is difficult to justify how so many university-trained, highly paid experts can produce so little output when just a few modestly paid, library-trained copy catalogers can produce so much. Some administrators appear to forget that some portion, however minor, of the materials they purchase will require original cataloging. These administrators phase out their MLS catalogers as quickly as possible — perhaps even before the replacement online bibliographic utility is in place. This contributes to the crisis.

The answer for these libraries may be to limit purchases of materials that require original cataloging and stick to publications for which cataloging is already online in a major utility. If that is not possible, the libraries should limit their purchases to items that are the easiest and cheapest to catalog: monographs with no attachments to series, no government documents, no nonbook materials, and no rare or unique materials. They should avoid buying any item that does not have an ISBN. They might limit cataloging to copy cataloged materials and allow any anomalous items that slip through the net to be shelved in a special section for uncataloged materials. This special section could be organized by simple principles, such as broad subject areas, alphabetical arrangement by title or author, or some combination of these. Access to this collection would be by browsing only. Some of these materials could be dispersed to departmental collections, whose staffs might be grateful to have the materials uncataloged rather than caught in an eternal backlog.

CATALOGING THE IMPORTANT ITEMS

Cataloging the important items requires first that catalogers be able to identify them. That may not be too difficult in academic libraries, where *important* can be defined narrowly, for example, as something requested by a faculty member. In public libraries it might involve items requested by any patron. But when a shipment of books or other materials arrive, someone must take the time to separate the important items from the rest, and the unimportant ones will have to be stored—perhaps forever—in some expandable facility.

What happens to unit costs if only the important items get cataloged? It is very likely they will rise, since important items may or may not have cataloging copy available. In addition, use of bibliographic utilities might fall and, insofar as greater use results in lower online unit costs, charges for using the databases would rise. No one said that triage was cheap, just that it would accomplish a single goal, in this case making the most important materials available to those who need them.

Although it costs more, this may well be the preferred method for research institutions that acquire as much as they can afford today for tomorrow's researchers. Perhaps there is no real need to make anything available until it is requested. True, the uncataloged backlog might be inconvenient to search before placing orders and, obviously, serendipitous finds will not be made there, but selection and processing of the most important materials must mean the cataloging department is serving its users most effectively.

CATALOGING THE UNIQUE ITEMS

A third goal is cataloging first those items likely to be owned first (or perhaps only) by one's own institution and contributing that data to a bibliographic network. This is not as easy as it sounds. First of all, it maximizes the amount of original cataloging to be done. For that reason, it is the most expensive goal. The cost cannot be justified by claiming to provide the most important materials to users. Why should any library choose this option?

The advantage of cataloging the unique items first is that this promotes the extension of bibliographic control to a larger universe of materials comprising a larger universe of information. Should another library obtain a copy of one of these items, it would be able to share the record. But more than altruism, the extension of the database to more materials makes the database itself more complete and valuable for a variety of other tasks as well, including scholarly research and the resulting exploitation of materials held in the collections.

In view of the value of this third and most costly goal, there might be some compensation to the library that undertakes to be a major contributor to the "national database," compensation that goes beyond the OCLC first-time use rebate or the limited satisfaction of knowing one's efforts are significant to one's colleagues. Shouldn't a library that opts for this goal be reimbursed? If there were an organized national database, such a reward might be forthcoming; but in the amorphous amalgam of bibliographic utilities, LC products, and local shared systems that constitute our national bibliographic resource, its realization is not very likely.

CONCLUSION

The only thing wrong with bibliographic triage is its implicit admission that there is no way to catalog both the backlog and all current acquisitions, even over time. Triage assumes there are patients who cannot be saved—books and other items that cannot be cataloged — and it forces us to identify them. With triage goes the assumption that the job can only be partly done, something librarians are loathe to admit. However, after taking a long, hard look at the rate of information production, the rate of library acquisitions, and the operational capabilities of catalog departments, it may be an admission whose time has come. Librarians only fool themselves if they fail to recognize the signs and keep hoping that the next budget cycle will restore the balance between acquisition and cataloging or that newer, faster computer systems will rectify the situation or that, somehow, somewhere, a grant will be given to catalog and process the whole ugly accumulation.

Alternatively, librarians might ask whether acquiring materials that cannot be accessed in the normal way is a sensible way to spend library money. If the materials cannot be accessed, should they be acquired at all? What other possibilities are there? Triage rejects can be given other treatments. Minimal level cataloging is one answer, an uncataloged browsing collection is another; or these materials can be eschewed altogether.

What is the cost of not acquiring the material? It may mean having to borrow it from another library if a member of the public requests it; that may result in a greater cost to that client. (The cost to the library may or may not be greater in the long run, considering the cost of storing the item and accessing it upon request.) Waiting for material — even material owned by the library but off the shelf for any one of a variety of reasons — never seems to bother librarians in large research institutions or in schools and it affects librarians in public libraries only mildly. Only special librarians appear to work up a real sweat over their inability to produce some requested item rapidly. Not buying some titles may mean not being able to provide that material — ever. In that instance, the library might lose its reputation for providing resources that serve its clients and the status of the institution in which it operates might decline as a result. However, everyone accepts that no individual library can own everything — so why must all requests be filled?

Where is the boundary between not buying things libraries can't afford and not buying things they can't make available for public use? This dilemma warrants more thought and analysis than currently is given to it. Bibliographic triage highlights the problem dramatically and begs the question: Should librarians attempt some answers or continue struggling to avoid it?

NOTES

[1]Andrew Osborn, "The Crisis in Cataloging," *Library Quarterly* 11 (October 1941):393-411.

31

Bibliographic Triage
Revisited

In chapter 30, I suggested there might be a valuable lesson for catalog managers in the practice of triage—a selection process used by medical personnel during crises in which there are many more patients than can be treated. Triage makes it possible to reduce the impossible case load to manageable proportions and maximize the ultimate benefits of their efforts by eliminating from immediate care those who cannot be saved—patients destined to die even if they receive every possible therapy that nurses, physicians, and surgeons can supply. The idea is not to treat patients first-come, first-served, as is done in doctor's offices and clinics, nor to treat the sickest first, as is done in hospital emergency rooms, but to attend first to those who are most likely to get well and relegate those who will die despite treatment to the back of the line.

I suggested that there might be an analogy to our field, namely, planning an appropriate response to the current crisis experienced by some catalog managers: accumulating backlogs that are reaching frightening proportions. For libraries facing that situation, bibliographic triage might help them to decide which items should be cataloged first in order to maximize the benefits derived from inputs of staff time and money.

Before describing the selection techniques, I asked that three basic rules be kept in mind.

1. Triage can achieve only one goal, not several.

2. Hearts must be hardened against the untreatable.

3. The goal cannot be abandoned in midstream but must be pursued until the crisis is over.

WHICH COMES FIRST?

I offered three ways to select the treatable, each having a different outcome that serves a different goal.

1. Choose materials that are easiest to catalog so that you can catalog the most materials.

2. Choose materials that are most important to the library's clients, in order to give the best local service.

3. Choose unique materials in order to supply the library's network with the greatest number of different titles and give the best service to the larger library community.

Easiest First

The first alternative is likely to be the most frequently used, because the performance of catalog departments usually is evaluated on the basis of numbers of items cataloged together with unit costs. The more items that can be cataloged with given inputs of staff time and money, the better those numbers look. Easily cataloged materials are those for which LC cataloging (the best copy requiring the least editing) is available online. Libraries pursuing this goal should limit their acquisitions to materials with LC card numbers or ISBNs, since those materials are most likely to be represented by authoritative entries in all the bibliographic utilities. This strategy will make the largest number of items available to the public in the traditional ways.

If collection developers in a library refuse to limit their acquisitions to easily cataloged materials, it seems to me that they have an obligation to enter the fray and help the catalog manager decide how to handle items that require costly, time-consuming editing or, still worse, original cataloging. The inevitable squeeze put on a catalog department to lower unit costs while simultaneously cataloging unusual and complicated materials simply cannot be borne alone. This is a classic management problem: the conflict between the goals of two groups, in this case collection developers versus collection organizers. One doesn't have to be a Solomon to recognize that ignoring the conflict will lead to more serious problems down the road.

Users First

The second alternative appears to serve a more important goal, since it puts better service to one's clients above merely producing better numbers. However, it requires a more sophisticated selection process, which is likely to cost more and result in fewer cataloged materials.

No catalog manager worth her or his salt can help but want to choose this goal, despite its higher cost. Librarians who develop priority systems for materials probably make this choice. If this option is chosen, it matters greatly who assigns the priorities. If clients determine the priorities, then the goal is well-served. If others make the choice, careful scrutiny of the criteria for assigning priorities must determine whether client needs are actually being served. For example, if books with LC card numbers or ISBNs get high priority, it is pretty much the same as choosing the first alternative.

Some librarians avoid making a complicated choice by separating their catalog operation into two divisions: copy cataloging and original cataloging. Budgets are allocated to each division and, one hopes, different standards are applied to evaluate the performance of each division. This arrangement makes a commitment to balance in cataloging, and the dollars allocated to each division reveal the way the balance is struck.

Unique Items First

The third alternative makes the greatest contribution to total library service, if there is such a thing, but it is the most costly process and produces the fewest cataloged materials. Despite its tug at our altruistic hearts, most catalog managers can say no to this option rather easily. With its high cost and small return that doesn't even have the grace to serve local users better, it seems to have no redeeming virtues.

Cataloging unique materials first offers one benefit that local catalog managers are unlikely either to welcome or to be rewarded for: Catalogers in other libraries will save money and time using entries that local staff supplied. Isn't this the idea behind cooperative cataloging in the first place? Perhaps this principle is only acceptable when the cost doesn't have an impact on the local budget. Many thousands of U.S. catalog managers seem entirely unperturbed when the costs affect LC's or another library's budget.

Unfortunately, the redeeming features of this option can be realized only over a very long term, and the benefits very likely will be felt not by catalogers but by reference librarians and users.

Catalogers measure the value of bibliographic databases according to how many entries they need can be found online and how much editing those entries require. Users and reference librarians judge bibliographic databases according to the number of queries they answer and how well they answer them. Naturally, if the database is more complete it has the potential to answer more queries. And, if the cataloging is accurate, complete, and easily accessed in a variety of ways, it should answer those queries best.

If unique or unusual materials are omitted routinely from bibliographic databases, what will happen? Would it hurt anyone? First, an increasing number of items would be invisible and a growing black hole would swallow ever-larger chunks of the universe of knowledge. Second, bibliographic databases would grow at a slower rate and the burden of growth would fall on fewer institutions. Third, costs would undoubtedly change in response to slower growth, and my expectation is that they would rise. One response to this situation might be the rise of smaller, more specialized networks for materials being omitted from the bibliographic utilities. This would fragment the national network still further and make it more difficult for information seekers—including those in the local library—to satisfy their needs. Another response might be the withering away of unique information resources as it becomes less likely that they can be identified and used (or purchased) by anyone outside the holding library.

So much for the alternatives.

Rx FOR DECISION MAKING

Five prescriptions that can make the decision-making process less traumatic for catalog managers who recognize that they must address the problems and issues outlined here.

Know Your Costs

Most important of all, catalog managers must know the costs (in total dollars and cents, in unit costs, and in the proportion of all library costs) of the various triage alternatives as well as the break points of various combinations of alternatives. My first basic rule is that triage can serve only one goal; that may be true in theory, but in practice librarians often try to do a balancing act, accomplishing a little bit of this and a little bit of that. Catalog managers who try the balancing act would do well to remember that such efforts detract from the achievement of each goal to a greater or lesser degree.

Knowing the costs of the cataloging operation is the first step in planning changes, regardless of the kind of changes the catalog manager intends to effect. Since triage is a management plan for the library's cataloging system, the techniques used in analyzing any system apply: determine where you are now and what is occurring. Even if the aim is to increase the department's output and lower unit costs by cataloging the easiest materials first, the catalog manager needs to know what the numbers are at the start in order to measure results. On the other hand, if a catalog manager intends to decrease the department's output and allow unit costs to rise in order to satisfy goals of better service for local clients or for the world, he or she had better know how much it will cost and be prepared to justify the expenditure.

Consider Long-range Effects

Each triage alternative has both short-term and long-term effects on the library, its bibliographic products and services, and its clients. Consider the most likely long-range effects, as well as the short-range effects, of each triage alternative. What do today's users need in the local catalog? The network catalog? How will each alternative affect the network in one year, in five years, and in ten years? How will this affect its potential value for both the local library and other libraries? What will happen to the triage victims?

Several commonly employed strategies for the untreatable are to give them some form of minimal level cataloging; to shelve them in separate ranges of stacks for uncataloged materials, where users can browse for desired items; or to keep them in inaccessible locations, such as back rooms or storage facilities. Each of these strategies warrants exploration. In the long run what is unforgivable is ignoring the untreatable completely.

Write Down the Plan

Write a series of proposals for short- and long-range plans, including cost projections. Putting alternatives on paper forces the manager to define them precisely and clearly. Once written, circulate the plans for consideration and response from others. Their input can furnish a more objective reading. No matter how objective one is, it is not possible for one person to see things from every possible point of view. Also, seeking input from others prevents the catalog manager from acting unilaterally as if the decisions have no bearing or impact on other sectors of the library.

Negotiate a Consensus

Manage by consensus with other sectors of the library, its parent body, and the user community, using written goals and objectives. Ask for input from representatives of the other sectors. Listen to what is said, particularly by reference librarians. Don't hesitate to be political and to promote the options you believe are best for the library, but remember that a catalog manager can't succeed alone—others must buy into the goals and objectives—and the catalog manager is the expert to whom others will turn for advice.

Go for the Possible

Be realistic. If at the end of negotiations things are still confused and blurry and no clear-cut solutions emerge, try to achieve a partial victory that minimizes the growth of the backlog.

CONCLUSION

Clearly, the choice is hard and the rewards strictly limited. For most librarians the choice of a single alternative will be the worst tasting medicine they have ever had to take and, I suspect, none will wish to take it. Nevertheless, it is clear that without outside support for the goals and objectives of bibliographic service units, all choices could prove to be wrong, no matter how inevitable they might appear to the catalog managers who make them.

For what it is worth, concerned catalog managers should know that the anxiety over both the problem and its solution is widely shared. Shortly after the first article on bibliographic triage (chapter 30) was published, I received a letter from someone at the Library of Congress who said LC is wrestling with exactly the problems I outlined. Of all institutions with obligations to outside groups, LC probably ranks highest, with the greatest number of obligations to the most people. If LC were just another library, its choice would be easier. But as the nation's de facto national library as well as Congress's library, it commits many dollars to cataloging things that will never be used by members of Congress or their staffs. Whenever librarians open their mouths to complain about something LC does wrong, they might think about that.

Nine Steps Toward Better Recruiting for Technical Service Librarians

My first professional act of the new year of 1991 was to lead a panel discussion at a state library conference; the subject was recruiting and educating technical service librarians. The panel included the dean of a library school (not my own), a public librarian working with a local network, and an academic librarian whose varied responsibilities included bibliographic instruction as well as cataloging and other technical service tasks. From the remarks of the panelists and the questions and comments from the audience, it seemed clear that despite all of the changes in technical service departments that accompanied automation, neither technical service work nor the need to attract good people to do it had disappeared or even diminished.

Two kinds of people were evident in the audience of about sixty: technical services department heads looking for staff and librarians looking for technical services jobs. Here was the ideal set-up for a free-for-all matchmaking session. Perhaps the panel didn't do as good a job as it might have in getting these two groups together. I say that because the audience behaved exactly like other audiences, listening politely and asking interesting questions, but audience members did not seem to initiate the steps to getting a new employee or a new job. There may have been more going on *sotto voce* than met my eye. I certainly hope so.

This chapter offers an amalgam of the suggestions and ideas expressed during the program. Some are mine, some came from my colleagues on the panel, and some came from members of the audience who spoke up during the session.

STEP 1:
DESIGN GOOD JOBS

Departments tend to lose staff members one by one. Department heads try to replace the person they have lost, even though it is very hard to clone the talents, skills, and experiences of any one librarian. But a staff member's leavetaking is a golden opportunity to make changes in the department, to assess and redesign work flow, and to recast not just the vacant job but several positions — or all of them. The changes can enhance everyone's work life. Although conventional wisdom says that people hate change, many heads in the audience nodded assent when the issue of boredom came up, and the idea that jobs could change for the better, with higher salaries to sweeten the deal, seemed more than acceptable to this crowd.

Members of the panel and audience alike spoke highly of the value of dual-role assignments — assignments that include both technical and public service work. All who spoke saw this as a step toward professionalizing the librarian's work and in reinforcing the librarian's skills in both job areas. That is, what the librarian learned in the technical aspects of the job would help him or her do a better job with the public, and the interactions with the public would help him or her make better decisions in the technical service work.

STEP 2:
DON'T LOOK FOR MORE
THAN YOU NEED

The issue of boredom raised another point. Every job, no matter how important or advanced, includes some drudge work. Everyone from deans and directors to pages and desk clerks have to accept some drudgery in their lot. But good jobs minimize the drivel and maximize the tasks from which a staff member can derive stimulation and satisfaction. One problem with the way librarians are recruited for positions in technical services is that the hiring libraries do not hesitate to ask for more credentials than the jobs really require. For a person with the required credentials the actual job duties may include too many repetitive tasks that, once learned, become stultifying.

Don't recruit a librarian to do a clerk's job, even if it means losing some of the professional lines that give the department its status. Don't ask for more languages, more education, more skills, or more anything than a position really requires.

A prime example of how technical service departments hire beyond the needs of the job is the hiring of multilingual, degreed librarians to do copy cataloging. Copy catalogers would be well-served by one, two, or more cataloging courses, but they don't need the whole MLS. On the other hand, it is cruel and unusual punishment to assign full-time copy cataloging to a professional who wants to be a cataloging specialist. Libraries that recruit degreed librarians to do such work exclusively can't offer enough challenge to make the job interesting and won't pay enough to make it palatable. The degreed copy cataloger will either move to another position with more challenge and better pay or grow progressively embittered because his or her career seems to have come to a dead end.

Wouldn't it be more appropriate to keep the salary where it is and hire bright baccalaureates, send them to library school for a couple of cataloging courses, and have them feel stimulated and well-paid? It is much easier to get better production from this kind of staff. And if there isn't enough cataloging work to fill the time, assign other tasks that bring this good paraprofessional into contact with members of the public and professional staff, such as conducting library tours, assisting with selection and weeding, or supervising shelf reading. Perhaps he or she will be tempted to investigate a career in professional practice.

STEP 3:
BUILD A RECRUITING NETWORK

When technical service department heads begin to recruit for a vacant position, to whom can they turn? It would be nice to be able to call on a network of people involved one way or another in the training and employment processes, such as student counselors, educators, or job placement officers. It takes effort to maintain contacts with nearby library school, college or university, or high school faculty and administrators, but it is worthwhile. Since you and they have common interests in the young people they teach and advise, you may not only develop a good source of recommendations but pleasant personal associations as well. Before I met him, my husband found the best secretaries he ever employed through a high school stenography teacher he was dating.

In some large libraries, a personnel office handles the whole affair from start to finish. Such offices usually are run by professionals skilled in recruiting, evaluating, and hiring. This has its advantages: the technical service department head doesn't have to do anything except say "We need someone to do...." The disadvantage of this arrangement is that it may exclude the people directly involved with the job from the recruitment process. Instead of having the supervisor review candidates' credentials and select the finalists, the personnel officer might do it. The supervisor and departmental colleagues may have only a brief interview with candidates, while others with no direct interest in the candidates' personalities, skills, education, ideas, and so forth spend much longer with them. Sometimes the supervisor is not allowed to select the successful candidate or veto someone selected by a person outside the department.

Personnel offices can help a great deal but not if they take over the whole process and exclude those directly involved with a new hire. Nor are personal contacts with employment agents, guidance counselors, library school professors, etc., a substitute for a personnel office. None of these people can take all the work out of finding a new staff member, but they can make one's efforts more productive by acting as important sources of both information and candidates for the job.

STEP 4:
LOOK BEYOND HOME BASE

When a library director is being recruited, chances are good that candidates will be sought from beyond the immediate locale of the library. The same may be true of department heads. As one moves down the organizational ladder to the ordinary librarians, clerks, and pages, it becomes less and less likely a search will go very far beyond the neighborhood. In general this pattern of action is not unjustified, since the more responsibilities a job involves, the more impact it has on the library as a whole and the more carefully and cautiously it should be filled. But care and caution are not the same as near and far. Good people to fill staff positions in various technical service areas might be waiting next door or on the next block, but it isn't logical to assume that an equally good pool of recruits can be developed solely from the local area as could be developed from statewide, regional, or national efforts.

Searches should encompass as large a territory as possible. While public library technical service directors cannot be expected to do national searches for high school pages, they can recruit not only from the nearest high school but from all the high schools in town and from contiguous towns as well, depending on the distances and opportunities for transportation. Judging from the size of high school parking lots, it is reasonable to assume that most high school students can drive or be driven to work in the event they don't drive themselves. Clerical and paraprofessional staff should be recruited from larger areas and librarians from statewide searches, if not national searches. Looking beyond one's own turf may attract candidates from diverse backgrounds, which is in itself a desirable goal.

Will the cost be greater? Yes. The cost of recruiting good lower level staff members should be perceived as a long-run investment in future higher level staff members and administrators, not solely as a short-run "fill this job only" procedure. According to recent studies, many librarians were attracted to the field through nonprofessional library experience.[1] Many libraries try to fill higher level jobs from the ranks before or even as they recruit outside the institution.

STEP 5: IDENTIFY CATEGORIES OF PEOPLE TO RECRUIT

Technical service recruiters complain that they have trouble building candidate pools large enough to give libraries a choice. At the 1989 Simmons College Symposium on Recruiting, Educating, and Training Cataloging Librarians, one library administrator from a large academic library said she had empty pools for several cataloging jobs and a pool of five ended unsuccessfully after eliminating the people without the necessary credentials and losing the rest to other job offers.[2] A good pool should have more than five people in it but not more than fifteen or twenty. Some candidates won't have all the desired skills, but flexible job design might make it possible to consider people with most of the requisite skills and other positive attributes.

One way to create larger pools is to identify categories of people rather than envisioning the ideal person. For example, the pool for an original cataloging position might include copy catalogers who are at least enrolled in an MLS program; the pool for a cataloging department head position might include heads of copy cataloging departments or original catalogers with three years experience who can pass a test in demonstrating how to search OCLC for a corporate main entry. This virtually insures that the pool won't be empty, unless there are other difficulties with the position, and recognizes that each individual will have a unique combination of talents and experiences.

STEP 6:
OFFER GOOD SALARIES

There were lots of smirks when I put forward this proposition, but there is no substitute for a living wage. Instead of trying to get away with something less than the going rate, libraries should offer the best salary they can afford. In many instances they will get only what they pay for.

No degreed librarian should have to work in a professional position without making enough money after taxes to pay a reasonable rent (or mortgage); buy enough food for three meals a day, clothing, medical necessities, and modest entertainment; and have a little left over for savings or for an occasional splurge. The minimum recommended salaries for entry-level librarians is as low as $21,000 in some states, although everyone agrees that isn't enough to support even a very modest lifestyle. It is about time the jobs that aren't worth more than $21,000 a year went to clerks and librarians were given jobs that pay salaries more in line with what other young professionals earn. Few better-paid positions are more enticing than many ill-paid ones, and the better-paid jobs will be more interesting (read: more difficult) and intellectually rewarding (read: powerful).

Publications devoted to the library profession ought to exert pressure on their advertisers to keep salaries up by refusing to run job advertisements that offer less than the minimums. Librarians ought to put pressure on their state organizations to raise those minimums. And no librarian should accept a job that pays less than a living wage. (Actually, no person should work full time at any job for less than a living wage, but that issue is beyond the scope of this book. Having spent the time, money, and effort to obtain a master's degree in library and information science, a new librarian shouldn't have to work two jobs to avoid being one of the working poor.)

STEP 7:
PROVIDE ATTRACTIVE STAFF SERVICES

A great selling point for new recruits is the prospect of working in a congenial organization where institutional programs give evidence that the employer cares about its employees. Thoughtfully prepared support services, staff development opportunities, and good training programs for staff members should be exploited for all they are worth. Library supervisors shouldn't forget how daunting a new job can be and should supply a system of support to integrate a new hire pleasantly into the workplace. If librarians have moved from another city or town, they should be introduced to the community and its activities by supervisors and colleagues. The new person should be invited to lunch, to local cultural events, or to parties where their presence would be enjoyed. While some people might think it an imposition, most are delighted to be asked to go to a movie or a concert, to play tennis or ski, or to do whatever it is that their colleagues like to do after hours. In large libraries, just learning where things are can be intimidating and having a colleague offer to help goes a long way toward making it less so. It isn't enough to leave such things to chance, nor is it enough to provide psychological counseling if trouble emerges, though the latter should be available.

Good training and staff development opportunities must be part of every professional career, or the career degenerates into a job that must be suffered. Career progress is neither solely the employee's responsibility nor solely the employer's, but the employer has some obligations to fulfill. First, good training is the employer's duty and, from what my former students tell me, many libraries shirk it. Yet every penny that goes toward good training will come back to the organization in the form of better work and good will. It is useless for libraries to expect library schools to make their graduates instant successes without additional training. Every library school graduate is aware of how much is crammed into the brief academic program, and each job requires a certain amount of localized training. Library directors must shoulder part of the training no matter how excellent the academic program.

Second, the library as an employer should make some contribution to staff development, although all costs need not be borne by the library and librarians should not expect endless release time, speakers, and workshops. In libraries where faculty status requires research and publication, the library must provide release time and research support services, such as computer facilities, access to databases, etc., in order to make it possible for librarians to conduct research projects. In libraries where being visible in the community is valued, librarians should receive recognition for taking on offices or heading committees. New hires could be integrated into this type of environment by being recommended for committee service or by being supplied with administrative support. Instead, what librarians may encounter is suspicion and close scrutiny to make sure no library time is devoted to anything but library tasks and no library-owned piece of paper is given over to any extracurricular activity.

Libraries, like people, can't have their cake and eat it, too. If a library wants staff members who are eager to take a professional's interest in their work and give more than the minimum needed to do their jobs, then the library must give more than the minimum it takes to keep staff members in place—it must give evidence that the professional well-being of staff members counts.

STEP 8:
EVALUATE JOB CANDIDATES OBJECTIVELY

When it comes to evaluating job candidates, objectivity is enormously important. Although there is a time and place for subjective reactions to looks, personality, and style, these should not be the primary or the sole criteria on which a person is judged for a job. Judging prospective staff members on these criteria might result in an attractive staff (at least in the eyes of the decision maker), but it won't supply needed knowledge, skills, and expertise. It also is patently unfair to the candidates.

The evaluation process should compare apples with apples and oranges with oranges. Measures of merit should be agreed upon in advance and formulated in measurable terms. It should be possible to rate candidates in terms of points, perhaps weighted to reflect the library's priorities. The interviewer should request or the candidate should offer evidence that shows the candidate has the requisite skills and that the skill levels measure up to expectations. There is nothing wrong with testing prospective catalogers (perhaps by having them perform several complicated searches on OCLC or provide original cataloging for a couple of government documents) or measuring the speed of inputters' word processing. Based on the experiences of my former students, I often wonder how interviewers judge communication and writing skills or knowledge of OCLC, AACR, LCSH, MARC, and LCC. What is "demonstrated evidence" of supervisory skills? Does it mean "We don't want to hire someone to supervise people for the first time" or "We don't care how well you did at your last job as long as it included supervising people"? I would be more interested in knowing how the person would handle tough situations involving interpersonal relationships, such as telling someone who is out sick too much without a valid reason that his or her job is in jeopardy, giving a bad job evaluation to someone known to be belligerent, or some of those other ticklish problems supervisors ought to know how to handle. It seems to me that anyone can supervise well-behaved, highly motivated, docile librarians.

STEP 9:
BE OPEN AND HONEST
WITH EVERYONE

Too often in my experience, the recruitment and hiring process is a secret one, known only to a select few and conducted behind closed doors. Sometimes the rejected candidates are not even given the courtesy of being informed that the decision was to select someone else and who the successful candidate was. Such callousness should create a bad reputation for the institution that suffers it.

Some libraries allow their departments little input into the hiring of a new department head; the departments are simply "provided" with a new head whom no one in the department has ever seen or spoken with. Staff members' apprehensions and hopes may have been ignored and their powerlessness highlighted. Ill-will and disgruntlement are likely to accompany that kind of process. The new department head, no matter how wonderful, is two strikes down before he or she begins.

The smaller the library, the more it is likely that any new staff member will have to interact frequently and closely with every other staff member. An open search with all the evaluative criteria laid on the table would make for better understanding of the selection process, even if a candidate were not the unanimous choice of the whole staff. At least staff members would know why the successful candidate was chosen and what special advantages he or she was thought to have.

The larger the library, the more important it is that staff members believe all personnel are treated fairly. An open search with both the criteria for selection and the candidates' qualifications clearly laid out is less likely to engender private grievances or feed petty rumors that someone's favorite was selected over better-qualified people. Such information need not be posted on a bulletin board in banner headlines or bandied about flippantly or carelessly but can be disseminated in a tactful, respectful manner appropriate to the gravity of the subject. Sooner or later, everyone knows who was selected. It is better if the decision makers are thought to be up front, objective, fair, and straight with everyone. In the long run, I would want to work for such folks, and I don't know anyone who would prefer the secretive, behind-closed-doors kind of boss instead.

CONCLUSION

Librarians should spend time thinking about how to attract the best and the brightest to do the essential work of gathering and organizing library materials for use. All the thoughts in the world won't make a difference, however, unless they are translated into actions. Computing didn't cause the demise of technical services, as was predicted back in the 1970s; instead it elevated technical service work to a more interesting and important plane. What could kill technical services is lack of good staff, which the failures in recent recruitment efforts appear to indicate is a far more likely reality.

NOTES

[1]William E. Moen, "Library and Information Science Student Attitudes, Demographics, and Aspirations Survey: Who We Are and Why We Are Here," in *Librarians for the New Millennium*, William E. Moen and Kathleen M. Heim, eds. (Chicago: American Library Association, 1988), 91-109.

[2]Marion T. Reid, "Recruiting Catalogers at the Louisiana State Libraries," in *Recruiting, Educating, and Training Cataloging Librarians: Solving the Problems*, Sheila S. Intner and Janet Swan Hill, eds. (Westport, Conn.: Greenwood Press, 1989), 133-150.

33

Theory into Practice: Making the Transition

What happens to people when they leave library school and move on to their first jobs? It must be traumatic for so many librarians to look back on their student days with rancor, as they seem to do, rather than with fond nostalgia. As with any new undertaking, the first job is scary, a big unknown into which many an unsuspecting beginner is thrust without much preparation or support. If the first job also involves a move away from home and familiar surroundings, family and friends, and replaces this comfortable environment with the burdens of wrestling alone with the dragons of life—grumpy landlords, tight finances, and loneliness, to name just a few—it can be dreadful indeed. And if the new librarian is anxious to make the best possible first impression, knowing that every detail will be closely scrutinized and compared with the work of veteran staff members, the fear of not measuring up could be so strong as to be fairly palpable.

Two things could help a great deal with the transition: good preparation and adequate support systems. The preparatory process should be the province of the library school, while support systems quite clearly lie within the purview of the employing library. What do I mean by preparation and support? Allow me to explain further.

PREPARATION FOR ONE'S FIRST JOB
Theory Plus

The first part of the preparatory process is the provision of a good grounding in what we usually term theory, which means the historical background, underlying principles, concepts, assumptions, and structures that form a foundation on which practice is built. Equally important, I believe, are clear expositions that relate the theories to specific elements in contemporary practice. It isn't fair to expect that everyone can make those connections without first having assistance in identifying them, similar to puzzle books in which the first answer is given to show the user how the solutions should be found.

Although some library educators and practitioners might disagree, I believe there is consensus among all groups within the profession that library school courses are the appropriate places to learn library and information theories and that learning such theories has value later on in practice. I am less convinced that either of the groups — educators or practitioners — realize how important it is that student-librarians be helped to apply what they learn to a variety of situations while they are still in school. Rather, I believe many of my colleagues are inclined to think that once the theory is explained, students would have to be stupid not to make connections with practical operations at once, alone, and without further explanation. This has not been the case for any but a few of the most sophisticated students I've encountered in library education, nor is it, I suspect, common among most people in the field. Once on the job, the theoretical concepts one was taught in library school recede from memory and, for the most part, there is no particular reason to bring them forward again.

So the first element in sound preparation for the first job should include discussions and exercises that link theory with its practical applications and clarify the relationships.

One effective means to relate theory and practice is the teaching library, explored by Robert M. Hayes in his oral presentation at the Simmons College Symposium on Recruiting, Educating, and Training Cataloging Librarians held in March 1989.[1] Schools of library and information science do not exist in a vacuum; many are located in the libraries of their colleges or universities. Informal channels already exist for training if the library takes advantage of its access to library students and hires them as student-workers. But in these unstructured situations, no specific efforts are made to relate what is going on in the classroom with what is going on at the desks and terminals or in the offices of the library. Neither the professor nor the library supervisors are bound to explain, "Here is the principle that this practice embodies" or "It is because of these assumptions and theories that we do this operation." The principles tend to be taught and the operations practiced side by side, but there is no obligation on anyone's part to relate them directly to one another.

The difference between holding a library job while one goes through library school (which is a good thing) and being taught in a teaching library is that the latter requires that the relationships between theory and practice be made explicit, analyzed, and understood as part of the curriculum. It takes time to do this — time that practitioners must be willing to invest in the process — as well as broad knowledge of theory. It also takes effort on the part of the professors, who must design and monitor the practice/curriculum and act as liaison to both students and librarians.

Unless the practitioners have a stake in the educational process that is approved and supported by their institutional administrations, such a program would be purely altruistic. Some risks would be involved for the library if production statistics fell off as a result of implementing the teaching component. (This is true for reference as well as cataloging departments.) The library school faculty would have to share some of their control over curriculum with the practitioner-partners, and the costs and benefits would have to be adequately assessed and fairly apportioned. In addition, the library school faculty might want assurance that the school's accreditation status would not be adversely affected by the experimental programs as well as assurance that they would not be expected to meet unreachable goals.

In the same category, but falling somewhat short of the extent of the teaching library concept, are practicums and internships. Practicums and internships are sometimes added to regular coursework and other times substituted for a specified number of credit-hours. They accomplish objectives similar to those of a teaching library program if they are sufficiently well-organized, monitored, and evaluated. The differences are in the scale of the program and its curricular goals, with practicums and internships usually term-long, nonrepeatable experiences that might or might not involve a specific kind of theory-practice exploration.

A useful addition to coursework and its alternatives is the student colloquium, in which guest lecturers are invited to discuss topics not usually taught in the curriculum. If representatives of different types of libraries with different types of responsibilities were asked to talk about what they want and expect from new staff and how they evaluate them, the process of becoming the newest staff member in that library might lose much of its mystery and the accompanying fear of the unknown. The best of these lectures would include illustrative case studies, show sample evaluation forms, and have topics that are as specific as possible. For example, the technical service librarian from an academic library might talk about supervising and evaluating new catalogers, while a media specialist from a school that purchases cataloging from a commercial supplier might talk about how new acquisition librarians or new reference librarians are supervised. All of them should explain their evaluation procedures in detail and provide documentation whenever possible. Colloquia should always include time for questions from the audience and give students opportunities to interact with the speakers.

One more suggestion to library schools for providing adequate preparation to students about to enter the world of practice, is conducting exit evaluations immediately before graduation that offer students an even-handed opportunity to rate their strengths and weaknesses. Such exit evaluations would not be "done to" students or result in grades or other measures of their status as compared to other students. Instead, they should help students conduct objective self-evaluations for the twin purposes of career planning and anticipating the types of postgraduate educational activities that appear to hold promise. Perhaps a spinoff benefit would be the introduction of new professionals to the idea of continuing education for practitioners — not just for those few people who decide to go for a doctorate or who are given money and time off for educational activities.

SUPPORT SYSTEMS FOR
NEW HIRES

Institutions that hire librarians, particularly the larger institutions, have much to gain from building a system of introductory support services for their employees. Employees of organizations that put such programs in place are likely to become more productive in less time and have lower rates of absenteeism and turnover than organizations that force new employees to cope with whatever problems they encounter entirely on their own. Not all of the suggestions are applicable to small libraries, although if a small library were part of a larger administrative unit its employees could participate at the larger unit level, e.g., school districts, county or regional networks, or corporate structures. The first suggestion is simple: Provide a professional version of the "welcome wagon" newcomer kit containing the names of realtors who specialize in relocations; coupons for discounts at local cafeterias and restaurants, bookstores, computer centers, etc.; a handbook of institutional information; checklists of bases to be touched with relevant information (e.g., filling out insurance forms with the name/address/phone of the person who handles them, registering to vote with name/address/telephone number of the office); and samples from each relevant production unit of the library (e.g., catalog entries, order entries, borrowing records, and interlibrary loan forms).

Second, I suggest that larger institutions provide a professionally directed support group to furnish psychological counseling and structured interactions with all new staff, not just those who develop problems requiring psychotherapy. These groups could last for a limited time and might include one or more optional social or quasi-social activities, such as going to local ball games, attending concerts, or having picnics, not just sitting around a conference room and talking about people's problems. Trained observers might be expected to recognize and address potentially serious problems before they become crises that have a negative impact on work flow, colleagues, and the personal career of the librarians involved.

The need for formal staff training must be acknowledged. According to what I have heard from former students and colleagues in the field, some institutions do a splendid job of training staff members while others only pay it lip service. At the Simmons College Symposium mentioned above, D. Whitney Coe of Princeton University described Firestone Library's training program as an advertised job perquisite that attracted applicants to a previously unfilled vacancy.[2]

Staff training should be handled by people who have been trained in how to train. It isn't very costly over the long run to invest a little time, money, and effort into preparing the trainers, since they will use the skills over and over.

Staff training should be aimed at two levels. The first general level should cover ways of functioning in the institution itself; the second level should be more specific, covering how one should fulfill particular job responsibilities. This dual-level training course might last a short time, a term or less, but it would ease newcomers into the ethos of the environment as well as into their niche within that environment.

New staff should be assigned extracurricular duties, such as serving on committees outside the scope of their immediate jobs, to bring them into contact with veteran colleagues outside their departments as well as to integrate them into the larger institution. Sometimes such activities are considered the exclusive province of senior staff members, but they also are a good way to plumb the fresh ideas and tap the enthusiasm of new people.

Some of my ideas require new staff members to commit time and put forth efforts that go beyond merely doing their stated jobs. Candidates who are made aware of these obligations and who don't wish to devote that much time and energy to integrating themselves into the library could eliminate themselves from consideration before they are hired. If this is truly the first step in a lifetime professional career, and not just a first job, some extra effort on the part of the person who will receive the training, attention, and recognition of the employing institution seems both appropriate and essential.

My last suggestion is that personnel evaluation processes be open and aboveboard, so the new librarian knows what's happening and where he or she stands with the immediate supervisor, department head, or other higher-level administrators. There should be no surprises in evaluation at the start of a new job unless the library and the new employee turn out to be a total mismatch.

THE BOTTOM LINE

Some of the suggestions I've made might be difficult for small or financially limited libraries to implement. Some might not be suitable for a particular environment or an individual library. But if the perspective of those responsible for supervising and training new staff members is to help new librarians integrate themselves into the profession, they will devise helping strategies that work in that direction. It's an investment in more than that one individual and it reflects how we, as the profession, perceive ourselves. Aren't we worth it?

NOTES

[1]Robert M. Hayes, "The Challenge of Excellence in Librarianship," in *Cataloging, The Professional Development Cycle*, Sheila S. Intner and Janet Swan Hill, eds. (Westport, Conn.: Greenwood Press, 1991), 3-11.

[2]D. Whitney Coe, "Recruitment, A Positive Process," in *Recruiting, Educating, and Training Cataloging Librarians: Solving the Problems*, Sheila S. Intner and Janet Swan Hill, eds. (Westport, Conn.: Greenwood Press, 1989), 53-72.

The Age of Access: Emulating the Real World

For more than thirty years, librarians have been adapting and adopting computer-based technologies developed originally for government, business, and industry to help them do their work. Efforts have been so successful that hardly a library remains that doesn't have at least one microcomputer system to track overdues; aid in cataloging or card printing; or help administrative staff with word processing, using spreadsheets, or other common office tasks. At the same time I remember a time not so long ago when successfully translating a bibliographic record into computerized form was considered a major breakthrough, because catalog records were long and full of complicated data that required variable fields, enormous amounts of storage space per entry, and other seemingly insurmountable obstacles to success.

Computing has changed library work in many ways. Computing made it possible for library catalogs to continue growing and developing without hogging all the library's floor space or requiring an exponential expansion of its filing battalions. Library computing revitalized flagging cooperative efforts—in particular, interlibrary loans—and gave new meaning to the term *union catalog*. Reference departments haven't been the same since the introduction of DIALOG, although some people still long for the good old days of quarterly supplements and quinquennial cumulations.

Next to online searching, circulation services have benefitted most visibly from the introduction of computing, making it possible for librarians to expose delinquent patrons in the act of borrowing more books; to answer the ultimate patron question, "Can I have [Title] right now?"; and to track the use of library materials in sophisticated ways that, among other things, provides management with information essential for planning and decision making.

Moreover, library computing has progressed to the point where it is changing our ideas about organization charts and job descriptions, about the kinds of services libraries should offer and how they should deliver them, and about the very materials and collections librarians should be gathering over the next five, ten, or twenty years.

Computing has also changed the world outside of libraries. These changes carry important implications for libraries. There are little things that don't seem to figure in plans discussed at conference programs or in research proposals and that are not announced in news columns in the library press. In this chapter, I want to draw your attention to three copycat services I believe libraries should consider offering to clients: a patron-run charging machine, the library version of the ATM; a library variation of the supermarket item locator, conveniently deployed throughout the library; and, library games of intellectual skill and chance to be played on Nintendo Gameboy.

THE LIBRARY ATM
A Patron Self-Charger

I think that libraries with computerized circulation control systems are missing the boat by failing to install self-run charging machines. Self-charging in the library could work exactly the way bank automatic teller machines (ATMs) do.

- First the user inserts his or her library card into the machine, along with a secret personal identifier, and waits to receive approval for transactions.

- Upon getting the go-ahead signal, the user types or scans in the barcodes of each item to be borrowed and waits for the transaction to be registered in the system.

- Each time a transaction is completed, a due-date slip that is generated automatically by the system pops out, just as cash pops out of an ATM. The person inserts that due-date slip in the appropriate item. Then the machine asks for the next item. The person hits a "Next" key and repeats the process or hits a "Quit" key to leave the system. At the conclusion of all transactions, the patron's identification number is cleared from the machine and the library card is released.

- If the library card is delinquent, the machine swallows it and refuses to give it back. If a book, recording, or film being charged is on reserve or is otherwise excluded from normal loan channels, the machine flashes a message that instructs the person go to the circulation desk or to place the item in a drawer that opens for that purpose so circulation staff can attend to it (much like the sliding drawers people use to give their passbooks to the tellers at bank drive-up windows). Meanwhile the machine holds onto the person's library card until the unchargeable item is placed in the drawer and its bar code is scanned into the system. The patron may then go on to another item or quit. In either case, the person must leave the machine without charging the unborrowable item and library policies are observed.

Various strategies can be devised to simplify self-charging machines or make them more sophisticated, e.g., they might be geared to handle only one type of material and loan period, for example, only stack books eligible for four-week loans, or they might be programmed to accept any type of borrowable item, reading the correct borrowing period from a field in the item record and translating it into an appropriate due date (ignoring days not counted in loan periods, such as Sundays and holidays).

Self-charging machines also could be programmed to renew materials automatically if no request for the items was pending.

Library users could be alerted to check the status of their library cards and the loan eligibility of their materials on any public access terminal before going to use a self-charging machine. A field in the catalog record could be highlighted if an item is ineligible for self-charging. Similarly, the person could check easily to see whether or not he or she was delinquent by inserting his or her library card into the terminal and entering the secret user identification number. There is no doubt in my mind that libraries with self-charging machines will thrive and their circulation will outstrip libraries that do not have them. My own college provides a good example. People at Simmons College, whether students, faculty, or administrative staff, have the option of getting cash on demand from an automatic teller machine in the basement of the library building. If you started a job or a program of study at Simmons, which bank would you use? Sure, that's easy. BayBank. Supposing the sponsor of the ATM changed to another bank. Would you switch banks? I certainly would, since using any other bank would mean having to cash personal checks in the Treasurer's Office, which is twice as far from my office as the ATM and often requires a wait lasting anywhere from a few minutes to a quarter of an hour while people do business related to their paychecks.

A few libraries have tried allowing library users to enter their own holds (i.e., requests for titles) directly into public access terminals as well as to charge out materials at specially designated terminals, and I am not aware of any dissatisfaction with those experimental services. But how heavily have they touted these services as client conveniences? As someone who would particularly like to have access to a self-charging machine when my library is closed (for renewals, placing holds, or leaving search requests for librarians), I think the library ATM would be a great improvement over the systems in current use at my libraries, which nearly always require some sort of waiting time. And I also suggest putting a local bank's ATM into every local library building — just in case someone runs out of cash to pay their fines.

THE LIBRARY MATERIALS LOCATOR

I'll never forget the first time I used a computerized item locator to find a jar of mayonnaise in a supermarket. It was in one of those ultra-splendid, glitzy Super Stop-and-Shops in Rhode Island, and I was en route to meet a friend for dinner. I was a bit early for the appointment, so I thought I'd stop in and buy a jar of mayonnaise for the next day's lunch. I went inside, rolled out a basket, and looked around. I must have stood there as though I'd been struck by lightning. It was the galaxy's largest supermarket. It was so big I couldn't see from one end of the store to the other, and the aisles were so wide that three super-sized baskets could pass without anybody feeling crowded. In addition to an enormous selection of groceries, frozen foods, meats, dairy products, produce, bakery goods, and specialties, it had a video store, a book store, a huge flower shop with fresh and dried flowers, a small clothing department, and more greeting cards and gift wrap than a Hallmark store. Believe me when I say I didn't want to find the mayonnaise by going up and down each of the aisles until I bumped into it.

As I pondered my next move, I saw a sign that said "Information" with an arrow pointing toward the end of the first aisle. I headed straight for it and discovered a little computer terminal on a pedestal that brought the screen up to a comfortable level for use. The computer had a brightly colored, touch-sensitive screen offering to guide me right to the mayonnaise. A few touches later I knew I had to go to aisle 13A, about halfway down the aisle, and look at the shelves on my right. A couple of minutes later I was heading for the checkout counter clutching my pint jar of mayonnaise and silently blessing the handy little information system that saved me from spending at least half an hour wandering around that store (and probably $50 or more worth of groceries I could do without and didn't want to lug home after dinner).

Why don't we have similar locators in libraries that will tell users exactly where to find the 1965 volume of *Library Literature*—which, in my library, isn't kept on the same tables that house the last ten years of volumes—or the nearby shelves that house the previous ten years' worth? Locators are especially important to have in convenient, well-marked places on every floor of multifloor libraries and in every building of multibuilding libraries, in library systems and multiagency cooperatives, and in all institutions large enough to require blocks of walking (along with climbing rickety stairs and riding creaky stack elevators) or miles of driving between stops with inconvenient parking at each destination.

And shouldn't library locators have bright, multicolored screens that tell users where they are, show them where the things they request are located in relation to where they are, and give directions for getting there? I don't care so much about the touch-sensitive terminals, though. Unless they are cheaper and more reliable than ordinary terminals it might be more practical to have keyboards for aficionados and mice for everyone else.

LIBRARY NINTENDO
The Next Generation

Finally, I think libraries need to take a lesson from "Jeopardy" and "Wheel of Fortune" and get with some programs to develop rapport with the next generation of potential clients (who also happen to be the up-and-coming generation of taxpayers, tuition payers, and every other kind of payers). "Jeopardy" and "Wheel" have counterparts played using Atari's Nintendo Gameboy—the toy of choice among nearly every group of kids in American society.

In my opinion, kids who play these games on Nintendo today will be the television shows' audiences of tomorrow. In this way the television program may bridge the generations one more time, if such a thing can be done. (If I'm not mistaken, today's "Jeopardy" is a reincarnation of the "Who? What? or Where? Show" of the 1950s and 1960s, so it has already bridged one generation.)

I suggest we jump on the bandwagon and develop library computer games and then tempt, cajole, beg, or shame Atari—or compatible game manufacturers—into enabling them to be used on the Gameboy. In this way librarians can bridge the gap between the generations as well as between what's fun and what's good for people, intellectually speaking.

Hand-held library computer games have the potential to be powerful bibliographic instruction tools. The games can take many forms. Why not a "Library Dungeons and Dragons" in which the Adventurer starts out in the murky Gift and Exchange Room in the basement of the Library, fights to gain control over the Serials Budget on the next level as a prerequisite to battling upward past hurdles of Accessioning, Shelflisting, Cataloging, and Classification to earn, eventually, a leading role in the war over the Control Room, where a many-headed dragon threatens to cut the cables of all online systems, plunging Earthling Society into a second Dark Age. Well, that's a bit too melodramatic, but it demonstrates the point.

Librarians tend to underestimate the power of games. It's time to rethink the intellectual uses of games and their hold on people of all ages. Librarians could find countless uses for computer games and get large numbers of kids hooked on libraries in the process.

CONCLUSION

Perhaps the ultimate lesson to be learned from all this is that libraries don't have to wait for people in business or industry or researchers funded by the government to decide that it's time for innovative equipment to be used for library functions (and then complain because they don't meet all the library's specifications). Librarians have the capacity to think up these or better uses of new technologies to provide faster, more effective, and more convenient services to the people who use libraries.

If librarians don't spend a little time thinking about these things and just continue to do business in traditional ways, the people who use libraries might find it is less trouble to do without library information than to get it — an outcome that could plunge society into an unhappy new era, indeed.

35

A Funny Thing Happened on the Way to the Future

In the 1940s Vannevar Bush wrote a prophetic article entitled "As We May Think,"[1] in which he drew a startlingly accurate picture of the revolutions that were to come in information production, distribution, and use, based on electronic text processing and communication. In the introduction to the article, the editor said Bush called for "a new relationship between thinking man and the sum of our knowledge."[2]

Later, especially in the late 1960s and early 1970s, others took up Bush's scenario and extended it, proclaiming that we would soon experience a paperless society in which the production of books and paperbound journals would be replaced by electronic equivalents. After all, they pointed out, printing of books and journals was being converted from the production of typeset text to electronically produced pages. It was just a short step to transmit the electronic images directly, eliminating the costly, time-consuming, and vastly less efficient procedures of putting the images on paper, collating the pages, binding them, and distributing them.

Some librarians spoke about the coming revolution of the paperless society, but most of their arguments were rebutted by other colleagues — the majority of librarians — who pointed out (perhaps somewhat erroneously, we might think, today) that newspapers had not been replaced by radio and television and that books had not been replaced by any of these media or by other kinds of aural or visual media. Even the great Marshall McLuhan — who demonstrated in his brilliant little picture book *The Medium Is the Massage* [sic][3] that new media would affect not only the physical manifestations in which messages were communicated but would alter the very message being communicated — admitted that new technologies do not replace the older ones entirely. Look at the alternatives, our colleagues scoffed. Books and journals were handy, mobile, inexpensive, and durable. Why would anyone trade their books or magazines for clunky machines that cost tens of thousands or hundreds of thousands of dollars, that required the knowledge of a Ph.D. to operate, and that could black out and destroy weeks or months of painstaking work whenever a fuse blew?

Nearly three-quarters of the way through the twentieth century, librarians were satisfied that the paperless society was a figment of a few people's imaginations. They had nothing to fear from the doomsayers who warned that books and journals were in jeopardy. Libraries had more pressing problems at the moment in rising costs. Staff salaries rose through the roof but couldn't keep up with a cost of living that rose even higher; heating and cooling charges assumed monstrous proportions as a result of world energy problems; purchasing dollars shrank with rising inflation and disastrous foreign exchange rates. Librarians now had to retrench and refocus their efforts. In examining budget allocations, forays into new services, such as online searching, and new media, such as video-recordings, stood out as being especially costly. It didn't seem to matter that they were popular with patrons, that each video circulated fifteen, twenty, or more times a year or that demand for online search services was so high librarians had to think of ways to discourage their use. A good many librarians chose to follow the advice of pundits who claimed the solution was to stick to basics and spend their precious dollars primarily, if not solely, on what we knew best — namely, books and reading.

In the libraries that decided to go back to basics, tentative efforts to establish online search services were rolled back, and experimental collections of video-tapes and musical compact discs were abandoned. Before long, even journal subscriptions began to come under scrutiny as titles proliferated and prices soared. The same librarians who once shouted "Freeze the book budget and protect our journals," now began to roar "Damn those greedy publishers! Not only are they starting new journals and raising prices, those reckless, feckless bums have the colossal nerve to charge libraries more than individuals! Let's give 'em the axe, and show 'em who's boss!" Collection developers entered a new era in which they selected titles they would not purchase. Articles in the professional literature explained how libraries chose titles to stop buying and how they got faculty to participate in sacking titles. Librarian-activists formed new committees to investigate ways to make war on the publishers or at least to obtain some revenge, and they started a couple of new journals in the process.

The result? Librarians turned inward and limited their vision to what had worked in the past. Most ironically, they realized that they were simultaneously facing a pressing need to spend a great deal of time, energy, and money just to preserve past purchases of books and paper-based journals, which, having been subjected to the twin stresses of poor storage environments and rough handling, were crumbling on library shelves and turning into dust.

THE FUTURE ARRIVES

Librarians have been standing around, telling each other that the paperless society is just a big joke, but the rest of the world has been moving along, taking up bits and pieces of the global electronic information revolution and incorporating them into products and services and into their daily lives. Students and faculty alike queue up in front of the ATM in the lower level of our library. My colleagues and I sit at home at our personal computers and call up the catalogs of a half-dozen local colleges and universities, OCLC, DIALOG. Pretty soon anything available in any online or optical full-text system will be accessible in our comfortable home offices.

In 1990 readers of *The New York Times Magazine*[4] found a feature article describing how Australian newspaper czar Rupert Murdoch was turning away from print media to mass marketing of satellite receivers to build a new video communications network. Mr. Murdoch bet his considerable assets on a new message in a new medium. Instead of leaving it to the ordinary consumer to go out and buy a satellite broadcast receiving dish, Mr. Murdoch marketed the hardware as well as the broadcasts — a strategy librarians know worked very nicely for library automation vendors. And in the English working-class neighborhoods where his experiment was launched, Mr. Murdoch did very well, indeed. A follow-up article a few months later reported Mr. Murdoch won a key lawsuit that prevented his primary British competitors from foiling his eventual success.

Each new issue of *Library Journal*, replete with hundreds of book reviews, also brings new advertisements for full-text online and optical products — all sorts of new computer-based materials and services. The options are impressive. Get OCLC on DIALOG. Get ERIC on OCLC. Buy UMI's new monster CD-ROM product, and get indexes and full texts of everything it covers. The list of bibliographic databases that now offer the full text of articles, encyclopedias, and so forth grows by leaps and bounds. Buy books on tape, tapes on disc, discs online, and get them all with full indexing and searchability by author, title, series, subject, keyword, Boolean operators, LCCN, ISBN, and virtually any other access point one might want.

How much longer will it be, do you think, before people carry their combination personal computer-satellite receivers in the form of hand-held devices the size of a calculator? Perhaps people will wear the gizmos on their wrists like Dick Tracy and change the color of the band to match whatever outfits they put on each day. How much longer will it be before apartment buildings and private homes are fitted out with built-in satellite dishes and wall-sized screens over which to receive Mr. Murdoch's or Ted Turner's or anyone else's broadcasts? And as surely as I sit here word processing this chapter on my IBM-PC, Ken Burns's marvelous textbook-on-video of the Civil War (a PBS broadcast) proved beyond a shadow of a doubt that video can teach as well as, or perhaps better than, books. Will it even take a whole generation from now for readers of books to sink into the minority and viewers of screens to inherit the world?

It took longer than the prophets predicted to get enough of the hardware, software, and networks in place so that the revolution could happen, but the future has finally arrived out there in the real world. It may take a while longer to trickle down into libraries, but it is just a matter of time until it does. Then librarians will have a choice: evolve quickly and keep up with the rest of the world or resist, hold the line, and be relegated to society's lowest priorities. (Some pessimists might say that wouldn't involve much of a drop, but society now makes believe it isn't so. Most universities still call their libraries the "heart of the institution" or some such grandiose title, even though they don't fund them very well, and most towns point with pride to their support of a public library, even if they starve it in the budget department.)

ARE WE IN IT?

Another development occurring simultaneously with the advent of the paperless society revolution is the reorganization of the Library of Congress to increase its efficiency and responsiveness to its primary constituency, the U.S. Congress. Not only is LC trying to charge more for its products and services, but it is abandoning some of the services that were valuable mostly to libraries and other constituencies outside of Congress. For example, in 1991 the demise of the data sheet program through which films and videos were cataloged was announced, along with the disbanding of the section responsible for most audiovisual cataloging. And everyone must remember the hue and cry that arose over the attempt to charge for third party use of the MARC database—a battle spearheaded successfully by the bibliographic utility that only a few years before had copyrighted its database to prevent its "free" distribution to third parties. And how about the false rumors that LC would not provide subject headings on its catalog records anymore? Or the true reports that LC will do copy cataloging using other people's original cataloging, and that a priority goal at LC is working off their backlog of uncataloged material? Librarians won't be able to turn to LC and say, "What shall we do?" and expect the response to be, "Don't worry, we'll take care of it."

Librarians will have to be their own saviors for a change, and it won't be easy. The universe turns upside down just thinking of LC looking to the library community for help in carrying the load! Just when the burden may be slipping and new problems are being heaped on top of it, will the library world accept that LC shows signs of wearying of its role as everybody's trailbreakers?

What will it all mean in the Brave New World of the twenty-first century? It probably will mean libraries creating their own bibliographic control policies and making their own decisions, instead of waiting to see what LC decides. It might mean making their own cataloging rules, subject descriptors, cutter numbers, classification schedules, MARC programs, and the like. Libraries already do most of their own original cataloging, but it will mean doing more of it. It might mean taking the lead in deciding how to handle interactive multimedia materials, remote-access microcomputer software, and all the fancy, new-fangled media coming down the pike. It might mean giving LC some of the expertise developed in working with these media. It might mean bearing the full cost of MARC development for classification or other things librarians want that won't have big payoffs for Congressional research (which could become LC's top priority). Critics won't have LC to kick around any more.

CONCLUSION

Some libraries are ready for the future. Their librarians forged ahead with newly established systems, services, and collections of new media despite the costs, the need for recruiting and training staff, and the difficulties of balancing the old objectives with the new ones and creating a new kind of organization. When decisions got tough, these librarians refused to give up their most forward-looking programs. They suffered and sacrificed, but they hung in there. They are the best prepared to handle the new present. They have the equipment, the networks, the systems, the procedures, and the cadre of trained staff members, both librarians and paraprofessionals. They sent their staff to workshops and institutes, brought in experts and trainers, bought supporting materials. They learned how to use the new tools, the new materials, the new systems. They were the ones who seemed to keep slipping as new processes were put in place and it took longer to do everything, but who believed that the payoff would come. Well, it's here now. Come and see.

The future is here, and everyone can see why it is too bad that more libraries didn't take up the future before it arrived. Librarians might have influenced it and shaped it more to their liking had they embraced the future back in the 1940s, '50s, '60s, or '70s. Or even in the '80s, when they had retrenchment problems. But now the future is here. Shall librarians take it up and go forward? Shall they hurry along and make up for lost time?

NOTES

[1]Vannevar Bush, "As We May Think," *The Atlantic Monthly* 176 (July 1945):101-108.

[2]Ibid., 101.

[3]Marshall McLuhan, *The Medium Is the Massage* [sic] (New York: McGraw-Hill, 1962).

[4]*The New York Times Magazine* 78 (Oct. 28, 1990).

36

Revenge Theory
and the Library

On rare occasions I glance through my husband's college alumni magazine, the *Princeton Alumni Weekly*. Generally, this weekly communique holds little of interest to nonalumni. But one cold, rainy Sunday afternoon, I picked up a copy and found the splendid article by alumnus Edward Tenner that is the subject of this chapter. The article was titled "Revenge Theory, or, Why New Highways Develop Gridlock, Labor-Saving Appliances Create More Housework, Simplified Tax Regulations Are Harder to Follow, Paperback Books Cost What Clothbound Books Used To, and Why Murphy Was an Optimist." (Edward Tenner graduated from Princeton University in the class of 1965 and is the author of *Tech Speak*, a Guggenheim fellow, and a visiting scholar at the Institute for Advanced Study. The same article appeared also in *Harvard Magazine*.)

The thesis of revenge theory is simple. It is that the solutions devised to alleviate human problems and aid the people affected have unintended and unforeseen negative results that eventually visit problems of even greater magnitude on the very folks who were supposed to be helped in the first place.

Tenner considers five kinds of revenge effects he calls "tendencies:" repeating, recomplicating, recongesting, regenerating, and rearranging. He offers both serious and amusing examples of each tendency, some of which have special zing for librarians, for example, the business in the title about paperback books costing more than hardcovers. The thought of interpreting recent library history in light of Tenner's five revenge tendencies was appealing—a challenging way to while away the afternoon hours. What follows here is the result.

REPEATING

Tenner illustrates the repeating effect with a scenario librarians will find all too familiar. After talking a bit about how home appliances like washing machines caused repeating, he turns to computing and says, at first discussing general business computing,

Much computing is information housekeeping. The billions of dollars of microcomputers installed in the 1980s replaced batch processing and mainframes, just as home appliances had defeated the laundries. If this unprecedented power had performed as advertised, productivity in services should have soared. Instead, it increased by only 1.3 percent a year between 1982 and 1986. In 1989-90, it grew by only 0.5 percent. The average growth rate during the largely precomputer postwar period has been fully 2.3 percent....[1]

Computers also force repeating because often at least some essential data aren't on line. Patrons at libraries with electronic catalogues, for example, usually have to check the old printed catalogues, too, probably increasing their total search time. *And they may discover that precious data are almost inaccessible because the tape formats are obsolete.*[2]

Some libraries have not just two but three or more catalogs to search, depending on the type of material a patron wants and the time period in which it was acquired and cataloged. Some computerized catalogs don't include cross-references or guide-card analogs, and limited numbers of public catalog terminals may increase both the waiting time to search and the stress level during the search, especially during peak hours.

A similar library problem resulted from the decision to improve classification operations and shelving by switching to the Library of Congress Classification from Dewey or some earlier shelving scheme. Since reclassification and reshelving is costly and hard to justify to funding bodies (can't you hear them saying, "We paid for a fancy classifier with a master's degree to deal with that stuff already, and now you want to do it all over again?"), most librarians simply leave the old stuff the way it was, even though browsers now must search two sets of shelves and never can find all the materials on a topic in one place.

Tenner adds that the Bureau of Labor Statistics reports an unpleasantly large proportion of hand injuries caused by the repetitive motions of data inputting at computer terminals.

RECOMPLICATING

All one needs to exemplify this effect is to think about AACR2 and the MARC format. Where, oh, where is Andrew Osborn now? Osborn's eloquent 1941 article, "The Crisis in Cataloging,"[3] was intended to promote simplification in cataloging rules. Get rid of the legalistic, one case equals one rule burden of the then-current cataloging code, he said, and develop instead a few simple principles that librarians can apply using their knowledge and good sense. What was the response to the outcry among library directors and catalogers? Incredibly more complicated cataloging rules that can't even be understood and used without the benefit of rule interpretations supplied by LC, internationally mandated punctuation that makes a mockery of grammar and syntax, and, for the icing on the cake, the overlay of MARC format computer encoding that makes the whole mess tortuously convoluted, difficult to teach and learn, and nearly impossible to do correctly. Catalog records now are so long that it is hard to see how anyone can process them without making at least one mistake. All one can do is pray that the mistakes don't affect access points and the filing and retrieval of the records.

RECONGESTING

Anyone who takes out books in an automated library and stands in line at the circulation desk is living proof of the recongesting effect. Congestion at the circulation control terminals is much worse in many of these libraries than it used to be when patrons had to write their names laboriously on slips and circulation desk clerks had to inspect the signatures or take pictures of them or stamp them with less complicated machines.

When libraries implemented automated circulation systems they discovered that they needed fewer people to write overdue notices. Not only did the computers print the overdue notices automatically, requiring only that someone burst the continuous feed forms and get them ready for mailing, but the library might not even have to send out any notices at all! The computer was happy to flag delinquent patron records automatically and beep the desk clerk whenever one of these people tried to use his or her library card. Circulation staff no longer had to wait for contrite patrons to return library materials and pay the fines on their own. Those nefarious people could be spotted anytime they showed up and the librarians could refuse to give them more service until they brought back the goods and paid their debts. Ultimately, libraries expected to give better circulation services to good patrons, since bad ones could be weeded out, as it were.

What actually developed? First of all, there were fewer desk clerks. Libraries that once were able to pull two or three typists from the back room (where they were working on overdues) to speed up checkout work at the front desk during peak hours no longer had any back room typists. And they had a limited number of terminals, so even if extra staff were available to work at the circulation desk, there weren't any added terminals for them to use to speed up borrowing and cut down on patrons' waiting time.

REGENERATING

Tenner uses several biological examples to illustrate regenerating, including the appearance of bigger and better bacteria to infect us and bigger and better pests to eat our crops or wreak havoc on the environment. I had recently read a research study that showed how the introduction of farm-raised trout into a lake for the purpose of increasing the fish population actually resulted, after a few years, in a drop in the total number of trout in the lake. There were not just fewer of the original group of wild fish or the added group of farm-raised fish, but of *all* trout regardless of origin. The researchers explained that the farm-raised fish tended to ignore the "rules of the lake." They crashed around causing trouble and snatching food away from the wild fish, who died off in larger numbers than usual. Pretty soon the farm-raised bullies were left to fend for themselves, which, of course, they were unprepared to do, so they died off, too, leaving fewer trout than before.

The library analog for the regenerating effect involves the longer term effects of the circulation control system, mentioned above. The circulation control system computer was generating lots of overdue notices automatically. Stamping and mailing them created an enormous postage bill. To contain costs, libraries began sending fewer notices. In recent years libraries began telling patrons that sending notices to remind them about their overdue books was a courtesy, not an obligation, and that they had better shape up and take responsibility for their loans. As a result more patrons than ever forget what they borrow and when it is due, creating even more overdues. Needless to say, this doesn't make for better services or fewer bad patrons. What it does is regenerate the problem.

REARRANGING

The rearranging effect simply moves the problem to another venue in time or space without eliminating it or alleviating the distress of the people involved. Tenner talked about hot subway cars. When air conditioning was introduced into hot subway cars to relieve the sweating commuters, stations and tunnels became much hotter—so hot, in fact, that this external heat caused the air conditioning units to break down, and.... Well, you get the picture.

How about the rearranging effect brought about by libraries' success in building bigger and better bibliographic databases? Local librarians used to complain because they couldn't find material on a good many topics in which patrons were interested. Now there are mammoth union catalogs that contain the holdings of thousands of libraries as well as gigantic computerized periodical indexes combining data from thousands of sources. These improvements allow library patrons to find materials published on nearly any topic they search, even though they haven't done much to change local collections. Nowadays, I may find the perfect article on pulverized carburetor gaskets listed in a fancy new CD-ROM index, but my library doesn't own the journal it's in—call it *International Automotive Quarterly*; or, although they used to own *IAQ*, it was so expensive the subscription was dropped before the issue I want came out; or, although the issue is supposed to be on the shelf, the copy is missing. But the database can tell me who does own the issue of *IAQ*. All I have to do is fill out an ILL request resembling the old IRS 1040 long form, submit it to the ILL office, and wait a week or two for the material. Where does my frustration go? It's been rearranged. Instead of venting my wrath on the reference desk staff or the serials librarian, I've shoveled it all over the ILL office.

CONCLUSION

And so it goes in this imperfect world of ours. Revenge theory. Don't forget those words. The next time an improvement in technology is being considered, watch out. In the 1940s, when revenge effects struck, folks said the gremlins were getting even. In the '80s, it was hunting bugs in the hardware and software and being careful to avoid becoming any vendor's alpha site. Who knows what dangers lurk in the '90s version of technological revenge?

NOTES

[1]Edward Tenner, "Revenge Theory, or, Why New Highways Develop Gridlock, Labor-Saving Appliances Create More Housework, Simplified Tax Regulations Are Harder to Follow, Paperback Books Cost What Clothbound Books Used To, and Why Murphy Was an Optimist," *Princeton Alumni Weekly* (October 23, 1991):10-13.

[2]Ibid., 11.

[3]Andrew Osborn, "The Crisis in Cataloging," *Library Quarterly* 11 (Oct. 1941):393-411.

Rights of Access:
Improving Interlibrary Loans

Interlibrary loan services in libraries are like the weather: Everybody complains about them but nobody does much to improve them. In an era when interlibrary loans have become part of a complex of important and, presumably, highly visible services called *document delivery*, and it is generally accepted that access to documents beyond those owned by one's own institution is not just a remote possibility but is supposed to be routinely provided to the public, it is amazing to find that the conduct of interlibrary loan service has changed so little.

In libraries I have used since college days, ILL departments (as they are usually acronymed) have been all but invisible, sometimes run as a back-room operation of the reference department without signs or separate offices to distinguish one from the other. ILL departments are perceived as a mixed blessing by librarians; they are described in great detail in college library handbooks but always with the cautions that ILL takes time, may cost special fees, and provides no guarantees.

In public libraries, ILL may be restricted to residents only, adults only, or people with notes from their doctors, lawyers, employers, professors, or mothers describing their desperate need for the item to be interloaned. Believe me, I am not kidding. According to a student survey of ILL services, the staff manual of a county library system in the Southeast that served a community with three colleges and universities stated that no one could request an interlibrary loan unless he or she proved to the head librarian's satisfaction that the need was overwhelming and no other route was available; holders of children's cards were categorically denied ILL.

This chapter explores questions that plague me about *modern* ILL. ("Modern" refers to the post-bibliographic utility era in which it is relatively easy to find out who owns what.) These include the following: Why isn't ILL *more* visible — in fact, why isn't it most visible? Why isn't ILL free? Why aren't ILL departments larger? Where do ILL departments belong administratively? Why don't library ILL departments employ technology more effectively? Why doesn't ILL seem to be taken more seriously as an alternative to owning materials?

VISIBILITY

Walk into a library and what do you see? It doesn't matter whether it is a public library or a library in a college, university, elementary or secondary school, or even a special library, chances are the circulation desk and the public catalog will be in full view.[1] These two staples of library service — finding and borrowing — are the most visible of all offerings to the public. One of the benefits a large library can realize from automating its card catalog(s) is freeing up the valuable space previously occupied by its gigantic card files, usually replaced by a relatively tiny bank of terminals. (If library managers are smart, they will deploy catalog terminals throughout the building — in the reading areas, the stacks, and elsewhere — and keep only a small number of terminals in their entrance areas.)

What will rarely be seen anywhere is the interlibrary loan department, office, or desk.[2] Articles in the library literature might talk about access replacing ownership of materials, but the plain fact is that people are made aware of where to go to deal with owned items, with a book in hand that one has retrieved from the shelf, but not where to go for materials to which the library only has access.

Only ambitious and determined clients exercise the rights of access, partly because only these few diehards have the staying power to find out where and how to do it. It is a miracle that post-bibliographic utility ILL counts are as high as they are, because none of the libraries I visit have ILL services one can find without asking for directions (and, in the larger buildings, getting lost once or twice on the way). Even when one arrives at the proper place, the office may not be staffed (there rarely are any backup staff for the ILL librarian) and the forms one must fill out are so daunting it is easier to do without the desired item (remember Mooer's law?).

I don't understand why the ILL librarian isn't part of the circulation desk. No one would have to ask for directions to consult the ILL librarian, and others working behind the desk could pinch hit when he or she was on break, at lunch, out sick, or on vacation. If libraries really intend to make access function effectively to make up for the library's inability to own everything its clients need or want, shouldn't ILL desks be put where they can be seen?

CHARGES AND FEES

I believe that ILL should be free or at least the charges should be minimized to reflect something roughly equivalent to an owned item. Not only does "free" ILL benefit patrons, it saves libraries the costs of cataloging and maintaining the materials as well as the administrative costs of keeping track of who owes what to whom, whether they paid, and if not, what penalties have to be levied, etc. In some institutions, it costs more to draw or deposit a check than to buy a book or subscribe to a popular magazine. If this is the situation, free ILL is much better than anything the library might recover from a fee-based system unless it bypassed the library's regular bookkeeping procedures.

Deciding how to subsidize free ILL is easy: just allocate dollars for it from the materials budget (perhaps from the cataloging and shelf maintenance budgets, too). Add a fifth line to the traditional four: books, periodicals, microforms, audiovisuals, and access. Then divide the total dollars available among the five according to some equitable formula. One way is to look at the circulation patterns of owned items and allocate the same proportions among the five categories according to their use. However, this method assumes periodicals and AV circulate, which might not be the case at some libraries. Another way is to look at the lists of previous ILL requests and allocate access dollars according to the proportions of media categories requested. A third way is to allocate access dollars exactly the way purchase dollars are apportioned, by subject or department, by medium, and by audience level.

If libraries can't support the entire access budget, then some pattern of subsidies can be arranged, e.g., books are subsidized by 25 percent, periodical articles by half, AV items by 75 percent; or, faculty pay five dollars per book, three dollars per periodical issue, and two dollars per video while students pay two dollars an item, regardless of the type of material (or vice versa); or everyone can have one hundred dollars worth of ILL free based on some schedule of fees, then they pay cost recovery or partly subsidized fees depending on their age, academic levels, or residence status.

Another option is to stop providing owned items free, charging the same fees for items whether they are part of the library's collection or borrowed from another source.

DEPARTMENT SIZE

Interlibrary loan departments, even in large libraries, often consist of one or two persons, sometimes working only part-time. These beleaguered staff members have to bear the brunt of the entire ILL operation, which has been growing in all libraries by leaps and bounds, from pre-order verification, if it is done, to each item's safe return to its home collection. The amount of work and numbers of staff to do it make ILL backlogs a common reality.

One question libraries might ask is whether their ILL desks are covered 100 percent of the time the library is open to the public. If the answer is "no," the next question ought to be "why not?" Unless other commonly provided public services are shut down during some open hours—services such as reference and circulation—there is no reason ILL should be closed while the library is open. The trouble is that some librarians fail to realize that ILL is a common patron service—they think of it as a special privilege bestowed out of unusual kindness. Some people think of ILL as a technical service so removed from interactions with members of the public that it doesn't have to operate before 9:00 a.m. or after 5:00 p.m. and never on weekends.

If ILL requests are increasing—and forecasts are that its growth will continue specifically because library budgets fail to provide patrons with all the materials they need—it is only logical and fair to increase the size of ILL staff. How large it should become ought to depend on how large a proportion of needed materials a library anticipates having to borrow from its ILL partners and how complex are the processes of doing so. Omitting bookkeeping from the list of ILL tasks seems likely to have a beneficial effect on staff size and productivity.

ADMINISTRATIVE NICHE

As mentioned above, ILL is one of those services that doesn't have the same administrative home in all libraries and information centers. In some places, ILL falls under the reference or public service umbrella; in others, it is under technical services or it may be part of circulation; in still others, it is part of a separate serials department or an autonomous automated systems department; or it may be completely independent of all of these. Does its administrative home really matter?

Two considerations affecting ILL department activities are linked to administrative placement: morale and visibility. Perceptions of the unit's status within its organization can have direct effects on how ILL staff view themselves and their work as well as on the image of ILL in the eyes of its peer units. The tangible effects are less direct. Holding positive views of the importance of one's work can result in higher productivity and greater satisfaction among the staff, better evaluations and, possibly, better funding. Poor self-image might result in lower productivity and greater dissatisfaction; its effects may be felt beyond the department in the form of decreasing budgets and less use.

Who are ILL's peers? Is it at a higher level than book or serial acquisition units, at the same level, or lower in the pecking order? Is it affiliated with a well-funded, high-status department, such as computer systems, or with a department in the process of being downsized, such as some serials departments? Is ILL's organizational distance from the library's main decision makers so large as to make it invisible to them? Is its staff perceived as a well-paid, highly skilled group of people or as the equivalent of mail room clerks in a large corporation? The answers to these questions will set a context for good or bad perceptions, both within and outside of the unit and both within and outside of the library.

USE OF TECHNOLOGY

Interlibrary loan has been transformed into an effective method of access by the twin developments of large computerized bibliographic databases and electronic communications systems. Together, these technological advances have given ILL departments an enormous boost in finding out which libraries own what items and subsequently requesting and receiving them. They also mean ILL departments functioning without computers, modems, fax machines, scanners, dedicated telephone lines or fiber optic networks, LANs, WANs, and other state-of-the-art systems are crippled in comparison with those that have them.

Imagine two ILL departments in two OCLC libraries, one equipped with the latest devices, the other operating manually except for its OCLC terminal. Library A can receive a request and fill it within hours for a similarly equipped partner. Library A gets the same speedy service from that partner in return. Library B might receive a request just as quickly, but a week or more might elapse before someone can act on it, after which several additional days will be needed for the document to be delivered to the borrower via the postal service. When Library B requests something, it can't obtain it by fax or file transfer; it must wait to receive hard copy through the mail as well.

In spite of peer pressure, network pressure, and other pressures to improve ILL turnaround times, libraries can only do what they can do. If they operate without the assistance of computer-based technologies, they are unprepared to join better endowed institutions. Eventually their ILL operations will suffer because their lack of technical capability makes them poor partners.

THE ILL ALTERNATIVE

If access is so important, how come the ILL alternative isn't routinely easy and quick? How come ILL isn't more highly publicized, funded, and staffed? Even at the library I currently use, which is one of the most patron-centered I've encountered, it takes anywhere from several days to several weeks to obtain an ILL request. With a few notable exceptions, by the time most of my ILL requests arrive, I've forgotten why I asked for them.

Perhaps the answer to my questions is that ILL suffers from tradition just like other library services. It's difficult to change things and stop doing whatever librarians were accustomed to doing. For example, it is difficult to get people to consider changing from library-to-library ILL to other forms of document delivery. It is difficult to get people to change from the postal service to courier service, fax, or file transfer. It is difficult to get people to think of ILL as a high priority service, not the last thing in line after everything else is funded. And it may be that it is difficult to get ILL librarians to think of two or three days as slow and get them to set shorter and shorter turnaround targets.

CONCLUSION

To recapitulate quickly, this chapter offers several suggestions for improving ILL service.

1. Put the ILL librarian out on the floor in the public eye, in the best space—maybe as part of the circulation desk. If ILL services outgrow local circulation, as they well might if local libraries avail themselves of coordinated collection development, let the ILL desk replace circulation as the central service and put local circulation in with it.

2. Make ILL free or at least minimize the charges to reflect something equivalent to owned items.

3. Staff ILL desks 100 percent of the time the library is open to the public, and increase staff proportionally as ILL becomes a larger part of all items provided to patrons.

4. Place ILL prominently in the organizational chart with other access or document delivery services.

5. Provide ILL librarians with adequate equipment, software, and needed expertise to make the library a desirable partner.

6. Streamline ILL procedures to the point that patrons can genuinely believe the library treats access to materials that aren't in the collection as efficiently and effectively as access to materials that are.

NOTES

[1]I have observed some exceptions to this rule, e.g., at Columbia University's Butler Library one enters on ground level but circulation, reference, and the public catalog are on the floor above. All one sees inside the main entrance are two large, curving stairways leading up. My recollections of the New York Public Library's 42nd Street building is that it, too, does not have circulation and public catalogs in plain view of the front entrance, but I might be incorrect about this.

[2]Interestingly, Butler Library's ILL office was just a few steps down a gloomy hallway leading off the main entrance foyer, but it was not clearly marked and when no attendant was available, which seemed to happen often, it was closed.

38

Our Electronic Heritage

In the last few years, several library writers have posed serious questions about the bibliographic control of electronic publications—cataloging records that will furnish to inquirers of the future clear evidence of what came out, by whom, in which version, from where, and, perhaps most important of all, when it appeared. The most eloquent plea for attention to the matter came in the late 1980s from Robert M. Hayes, speaking at an American Library Association Annual Conference preconference on collection development in the electronic age.[1] Although Hayes was keynoting a collection development conference, the challenge he presented was for bibliographic control. In particular, he was concerned about how to get and keep a bibliographic handle on intellectual material being produced and distributed when an item might metamorphose every time it is "read" or "used."

THIS ISN'T THE FIRST TIME

As one might expect, there are analogies in the precomputer environment from which to draw enlightenment. Some rather disquieting similarities can be found in the processes by which sound recordings, films, and videos are made. Far from being the result of a single recording, filming, or taping effort, nearly all of today's commercially marketed sound recordings, films, and videos are compilations of multiple "takes:" excerpts of numerous recordings made at different times, neatly spliced, edited, mixed, and matched, until the results are as perfect as recording engineers can make them. A nice living is being made by traffickers in funny failures edited out of professionally made films and videos, whether they are set-ups, as they are for televisions shows like "Candid Camera" or completely unintentional, as in the "bloopers" shows. The notable exceptions are real-life, one-time-only events recorded live, such as concert performances, sports events, Academy Awards ceremonies, etc.; but even these happenings are being altered by the availability of electronic records as, for example, when changes are made in football penalties after game officials look at the video instant replays.

Maria Callas, the brilliant soprano, was said to be unwilling to permit the release of any recording of her voice if it wasn't doctored to perfection. In fact, nasty rumors spread among opera lovers that Callas hadn't sung for years, but highly-paid sound engineers with sophisticated equipment made it seem as though she had.

Certainly no 1970s TV viewer of "Mission Impossible" can be unaware of the potential impact of modern technology on the accuracy of contemporary historical records. Week after week the "Mission Impossible" team confounded our nation's enemies' sound, film, and video-based security systems and won psychological battles with faked news broadcasts, interviews, appearances, etc. These patriotic agents specialized in fooling eyewitnesses as well as all of us who relied merely on recorded evidence.

Personally, I've always marveled at jazz buffs who were so knowledgeable and had such sensitive ears they could detect the differences between several recording sessions for a particular number by a favorite musician (identifiable, if you know where to look, by their matrix numbers), much as oenophiles can tell the vintage as well as the name of a wine with their first taste. Somehow, they knew when a performer had done three or four repetitions of an album program (that's the kind of thing jazz buffs talk about), and they recognized individual album releases by the group of songs each contained.

WHAT'S THE PROBLEM NOW?

The main difference for bibliographic control between these examples of earlier "doctored" products and current computer-based electronic materials are the following: With the former, once the sound engineers, film and tape editors, dubbers, and other technical experts get through with their work and proclaim a "wrap," consumers can expect every copy of that particular title to be identical in every way to the master recording and to every other copy made from it. With the latter, however, there are no guarantees that the copy someone calls up on his or her computer screen hasn't been altered by someone—authorized or not—who accessed the document before they did.

The problem is pinning Jello to the wall. How shall original "editions" or "versions" of electronic documents be identified and distinguished from subsequent editions or versions when any version can be altered at will by each of its readers? Even the most diligent cataloger would not expect a title to have as many bibliographic records as it has readers.

How many versions must an electronic document go through before catalogers give up? The Rule of Three might help: After three versions, stop making new catalog records. Or only count as new versions those documents containing more than three revisions. Or only count as a new version those documents containing revisions to three or more of the following elements: author, title, sponsoring body or bodies, material-specific details, physical description, series, or standard number(s).

How significant must alterations be to cause a document to be recognized as a new version? Descriptive cataloging rules already put this decision-making burden on catalogers of computer files, stating plainly, "Do not treat an issue of a file that incorporates minor changes as a new edition" and identifying five kinds of changes to ignore: spelling corrections, rearrangement of the same contents, different output formats, display media, or physical characteristics.[2]

Another example of differences now routinely incorporated into a single catalog record are novels or adventure games that allow readers or players to select their own endings. Each game or story gets one bibliographic record for all its endings. The potential variations are described somewhere in the record — usually toward the end of the description in the notes — and then forgotten. No one has come forward to demand a separate bibliographic record for each possible ending. Is it useful or necessary to identify editions or versions in an environment in which alterations to documents can't be controlled? And if there isn't enough energy or money to tackle the job, how will today's decisions affect future historians when they begin seeking the research record for our time?

THE PATH OF LEAST RESISTANCE

It would be easy to say that this isn't a library's bibliographic control problem at all. It's a problem for computer center managers, database vendors, network operators, etc., but not for the librarians in the institutions that access the documents. This argument already enables librarians to avoid cataloging each of the poems, plays, stories, or songs in the anthologies they buy, or the articles that appear in the journals they buy, or the individual monographs issued together in the microfilm sets they buy — all of these are considered too large a number of works contained in one physical manifestation to be recognized and cataloged individually by the library. Instead, librarians rely on publishers and database vendors to provide these individual analytic bibliographic records and gladly pay them for their products.

Frankly, I don't understand it, but librarians reason it is less costly to buy indexes that don't contain data for some of the things the library acquires and do contain data for other things the library doesn't acquire than to catalog themselves all the things — and only those things — that the library adds to its collections. This cost-benefit relationship is universally accepted despite the fact that searchers lose access entirely to acquisitions that aren't commercially indexed and that the library must supplement the indexes with enormous inputs of reference assistance for patrons who have to be taught or can't figure out how to use them. If it really is better to buy commercially published indexes than to do your own cataloging and indexing, why don't libraries buy *Public Library Catalog* or *Books for College Libraries* and *Fiction Catalog* and use them in place of the public catalog? Think of the money that could be saved by really eliminating all cataloging!

It would be easy to say that it's all right to ignore differences of many kinds in documents as long as a generic catalog record of some sort is made for all the intellectual contributions sharing a particular author and title. This is an extension of the idea behind the kind of multiple versions records the Library of Congress used to make for audiovisual titles bearing the same content but issued in several physical forms. It would just be too bad if, for example, the version of "Elements of Superiority in Private Liberal Arts College Financial Management Schemes" the library provided to my terminal didn't contain the postscripted comments by Utopia University's Provost I. Graften Waste that give great stock tips for educational investors — the part of the document that I was after. The library's circulation department could still claim it as a successfully filled request because I accessed a copy of a document bearing the number of the right generic catalog record.

The difficulty with these measures lies in their inability to permit a researcher to retrace the steps it took to develop a work or recreate the processes by which an idea emerged, advanced and flourished, or declined and died, if, indeed, a researcher ever wanted to do so.

THE CONTINUUM OF CONTROL

If a range of alternative solutions falling at various points on a continuum is considered, the extremes would go from no access, in which librarians and other bibliographic providers ignore electronic materials entirely, to total access, in which librarians or other bibliographic providers create catalog records for every variant version of every electronic "work." Total access, however, is likely to furnish so large a file of records with so many duplicate and near-duplicate headings that it could turn out to be as useless as no access at all. Viable, practical bibliographic control must consist of a compromise of some sort in which some content variations are recognized while others are ignored.

Moving now to decision-prompting value judgments, if one accepts the premise that total access is neither attainable nor desirable and that no access is an unconscionable abrogation of librarians' cataloging responsibilities, then the solution to the problem of bibliographic control for electronic publications becomes one of determining which variations ought to be recognized and which may safely be ignored.

CRITICAL VARIATIONS

What is needed is a list of significant variations. One way to negotiate the perfect bibliographic compromise is to list all the potential variations that could occur in an electronic document and decide, one by one, whether each is sufficiently significant to prompt making a new catalog record. This is the most thorough and objective way to accomplish the task. Another way is to compile a list of significant variations by including those usually considered critical to searchers or those for which a satisfactory justification can be made.

These two approaches — list all possibilities and weigh them one at a time or build a selected list of elements based on experience and anticipated use — might be called the "tear 'em down" and "build 'em up" methods of listing significant bibliographic variations. (The former begins with a large list from which elements are eliminated when they fail to meet the tests of significance, hence "tear 'em down," while the latter begins with nothing and adds only those elements someone thinks merit inclusion, or "build 'em up.") Does it matter how one goes about the task? One imagines the final list of significant variations will be the same regardless of the method used, but there aren't any guarantees. Failure to list all possibilities may mean some escape notice entirely and aren't ever considered. The missing elements won't surface unless their absence causes major searching problems later on. The difference in the two approaches also is one of economy, with the build 'em up method taking less time and, therefore, costing less.

For the moment, let's try the build 'em up method. It shouldn't be hard to obtain agreement that variations in an electronic publication's title(s) or author(s) is significant enough to warrant making a new catalog record. Continuing down the list of descriptive areas, changes in the name of an edition (also known as version, release, etc.), which are almost always considered significant for other forms of material, might or might not be important for electronic publications. Clearly, the four types of variations already designated by the cataloging rules as "minor" would not count. What others ought to be ignored? One good candidate for the "forget it" list is grammatical or stylistic corrections that go beyond spelling and punctuation, e.g., changes in tenses of verbs, singular and plurals, "which" to "that," "who" to "whom," etc. These go only a tiny bit further than spelling corrections and probably don't constitute significant variations.

Another candidate for the "forget it" list might be uninvited reader or user comments appended to the original document. Comments specifically invited by authors or publishers, on the other hand, might comprise an enhanced version of the document that warrants creation of a new catalog record. To minimize the proliferation of duplicates, however, only one catalog record would be needed to describe the enhanced document, with a contents note naming all invitees, whether or not they contribute anything. Or, the record for the original document could contain a "plus invited commentaries" note, and one record might describe both the original and enhanced versions.

Changes to material-specific details might be significant or not depending on the type of material (serial, map, computer file, music) and the type of detail (numbering, projection, file characteristics, presentation). Similarly, changes in the places and names of publishers and distributors might not matter as much for electronic documents as they do for books, and issue dates (except perhaps for the date when a document first appeared on a particular system) would be much less meaningful. Physical descriptions would be omitted, since the assumption is that electronic documents have no physical manifestations. Series statements could create problems if electronic purveyors put the same document into different series or multiple series, but this is not unique to electronic publishing. ISBNs and ISSNs, which don't always indicate changed contents, may not be assigned to electronic publications and therefore will not become an issue.

At the same time, other descriptive elements not now included in catalog records might be added, e.g., the number of times and dates an electronic document was accessed might be tracked automatically by the system providing it and a running tally included in the catalog record. This information would tell the person consulting the catalog record something about the document's popularity and indicate the likelihood that many or few alterations occurred since it entered the system.

PRELIMINARY CONCLUSIONS

This analysis seems to show that only a few of the many possible variations in electronic documents require the creation of multiple catalog records, although those that do present tricky issues that defy simple solutions. I didn't try to be comprehensive in listing the possibilities. I've only skimmed the surface of a problem that might turn out to be an iceberg with many unseen ramifications.

One solution I didn't explore is having authors and publishers of electronic documents fill out descriptive cataloging forms in addition to recommending index terms that cover their products' subject content. (The latter already is *de rigueur*.) Who should know better than an item's own creators and issuers whether it is a new work needing a new catalog record? Networks distributing electronic documents could have a built-in algorithm to match all incoming catalog records with those in the database and to merge duplicates that are inadvertently entered by ignorant or careless authors and publishers.

If the scholarly world embraces electronic media as it appears it will in the foreseeable future, prompted by the growth of the INTERNET, NREN, and the computer industry's continuing efforts to make them accessible, affordable, simple to use, and more powerful, the priority for solving bibliographic control problems for electronic publications should rise swiftly. Otherwise, librarians will be caught with their bibliographic pants down and great gobs of humanity's electronic heritage will be lost to posterity. This kind of loss goes against the grain of human nature—against catalogers' instincts—and against the fundamental tenets of library and information service. Let's not wait for the crisis but start solving the problem now.

NOTES

[1]Robert M. Hayes, "A Summary of the Institute on Collection Development for the Electronic Library," *Library Acquisitions: Practice & Theory* 14 (1990):359-370.

[2]Michael Gorman and Paul W. Winkler, eds., *Anglo-American Cataloguing Rules*, 2d ed., 1988 Revision (Chicago: American Library Association, 1988), 227.

39

Implications of
Cataloging Interactive Media

Microcomputer software no longer is the new kid on the block. That dubious honor has been usurped by interactive media, also known in its various forms as multimedia, hypermedia, and full-motion video. The introduction of interactive media materials into library collections and the problems being raised in connection with its bibliographic control suggest that while AACR's existing chapters could be used to describe titles in this group of media, librarians would be considerably more comfortable if rules in the code addressed them specifically; and newer media appear certain to have more complicated architecture than previous formats. As a result, this might be a good time to consider more than the problems of this particular type of material. It might be the right moment to think about the implications for the future and the value of broader solutions that would encompass a greater variety of formats.

A WORD OR TWO OF BACKGROUND

Initially, descriptive cataloging rules, subject heading lists, and classifications had to treat only books. Today, even though all of these tools are routinely applied to maps, music, sound recordings, computer files, etc., titles in the nonbook media remain anomalies that have to be fitted somehow into the book image while developers of the tools still tend to operate as if they were dealing solely with books. Library of Congress classification numbers and subject headings are difficult to use with nonbook materials. Dewey Decimal classification and Sears subject headings are a shade more flexible. Dewey offers the ability to add AV or computer-related facets from auxiliary table 1 to numbers from its main schedules, and the new faceted music schedule with its designation for recorded music give it an edge; while the open-ended, permissive nature of *Sears List of Subject Headings* makes it possible to add needed headings without having to wait for anyone's permission.

For nonbook materials, the best of the lot of standard tools is the descriptive cataloging code, which was expanded in 1978 to accommodate all sorts of unusual things, such as videos and computer files (then called machine-readable data files), and whose ability to describe them all in parallel fashion has continued to improve and sharpen with each passing year. (Credit should be given to codemakers that they did not flinch when faced with pet rocks or abstract paintings, nor did they take the easy way out by saying that descriptive cataloging rules only applied to items intended for communicating *information*. They stepped right up and devised rules for the most commonly encountered types of unintended informational communications, wisely assuming that if a library tried to catalog them they were entitled to a fair chance at success.)

Interactive media exhibit some of the old, familiar nonbook problems as well as entirely new ones. But in thinking about both the problems and potential solutions, one thing became crystal clear: The rapid evolution in information storage is going to continue and libraries are going to have to keep up with it—even though they may wish it would politely go away. Finding solutions one at a time as a new medium appears adds a few patches to the crazy quilt of bibliographic control but never addresses the core problem: how to deal with a dynamic information storage environment. It's like devising medications that alleviate one or another symptom of a disease without treating the disease itself. The assistance provided by the medication is better than no help at all, but it never gets down to the nitty gritty cause of the symptoms.

PROBLEMS OF INTERACTIVE MEDIA

Interactive media, defined imprecisely as combinations of video- and computer-based materials, although they can and do include other formats, present four kinds of problems, as follows:

- each item often, though not always, involves more than one physical piece of material to be cataloged,

- the pieces comprise more than one type of storage medium,

- using the material requires more than one piece *and* one type of equipment, and

- the content of each item contains a large number of potential "presentation parts" to be individualized by each person who uses it.

The first and second problems are not new. They are solved by AACR's rule for multi-part items, rule 1.10.[1] This rule forces two difficult decisions on the poor cataloger. First, the cataloger must determine whether there is a predominant item among the pieces and, if so, the rule directs the cataloger to select that part as the catalogable entity, making everything else accompanying material. Second, if there is no predominant piece, the cataloger must select one of three ways of describing the physical makeup of the item.

By making these decisions for the description, the subject heading and classification problems are solved, too. If there is one predominant piece, subject headings and classification will be assigned solely with that piece in mind, ignoring the rest of the pieces. If not, subject headings and classifications general enough to encompass the whole are assigned.

The third problem, that using the item requires several pieces of different types of equipment, also has been encountered before. Kits consisting of a sound recording and a filmstrip employ different pieces of equipment in concert, and this information can be accommodated easily in the Note area of the catalog record. It makes for a long record, which causes catalogers to grumble since their production statistics go down as record length increases, but there is no question that it can be done.

The fourth problem is unique to this medium, although educational kits offer a prototype if they are analyzed carefully. Some of the best educational kits contain many kinds of materials designed in modular form and intended to be used creatively in different ways by individual teachers. Catalogers, however, don't have to think about the different ways the materials can be combined. They only have to list "various pieces," "for grade 2," "games that teach addition, subtraction, multiplication, and division," etc., and assign umbrella headings and classification numbers to the whole kit, provided they classify them at all. With traditional kits, the fourth problem can safely be ignored provided important contents are listed in the description and represented in subject headings and class numbers. (Importance is determined by the cataloger.)

Why not do the same with interactive media? Ignore the details of the contents and tread the path of least resistance.

The answer is simple: Librarians don't want to catalog interactive media materials as kits.

WHY NOT A KIT?

Kits are the ugly ducklings of cataloging, destined never to emerge into swanhood. In order to appreciate how much catalogers loathe kit cataloging, one must see catalogers' faces when the suggestion is made that interactive media should be cataloged as kits. An instinctive, ingrained reflex makes them withdraw physically from the speaker as their faces contort into expressions of disgust. And it doesn't only happen when you speak to book catalogers from university research libraries. It happens even when you speak to nonbook catalogers from small college and public libraries. Of all the anomalies in the nonbook formats, kits are the least attractive and least understood.

In trying to imagine the reason for the negative aura surrounding kits, I wondered if they weren't inextricably bound up with visions of clumsy boxes of elementary school materials aimed at classroom teachers, not librarians. Those seemed like a great new idea in the 1940s, but soon lost favor even with their target audience. Among the drawbacks was the fact that great sounding new kits sometimes turned out to be old kits with new titles and new packages. Even when a kit wasn't identical to an older title, it might contain pieces from backlisted titles that the producer was trying to recycle. Another drawback was that it took no little amount of effort on the teacher's part to figure out how to use the pieces together effectively—sometimes so much effort that the kit just sat on the shelf gathering dust. A third drawback was that the associated hardware often did not perform easily or reliably, leaving an exasperated teacher or embarrassed librarian holding the bag (no pun intended).

Asking university research librarians to catalog sophisticated high-tech interactive media as kits is about as appealing and appropriate as inviting them to lunch at a four-star French restaurant and serving them a meal of Pablum mixed with condensed milk. But isn't a videodisc plus a microcomputer floppy disk or two — with or without some CD-ROMs and a pack of microfiche — exactly analogous to a set of filmstrips plus sound cassettes — with or without some posters, photographs, flash cards, and a diorama or two? Except for the differences in the specific formats involved and their anticipated uses, how do interactive media differ from yesteryear's kits? Don't they both involve multiple pieces in multiple formats? Aren't the different types of pieces played on different kinds of equipment used in combination?

Why couldn't the same options offered for kit cataloging be applied effectively to interactive media materials?

A COMPROMISE TO CONSIDER

One way out of the unhappy dilemma for U.S. catalogers is to eliminate the word kit and adopt the British term for these materials: *multimedia*. This would veil the fact that the same general material designation also was being applied to any old-fashioned, elementary school boxes filled with filmstrips and sound cassettes, etc. And U.S. librarians could hop on the industry bandwagon, which appears to be using multimedia as an umbrella term for video-plus-computer titles. In fact, the industry uses the term for other things as well, including plain old CD-ROMs and plain old videocassettes without any special interactivity beyond the usual machine-user interface.

To make the compromise palatable, AACR might be altered to make the multimedia rules more acceptable. One way to accomplish this is to take them out of chapter 1 and create a new chapter — chapter 14, called "Multimedia" — for multipart items. Rule 1.10 could be eliminated except as a reference to chapter 14. There, each element of description, from sources for the bibliographic data to standard numbers could be reiterated for multipart items, with many examples of all kinds. It seems appropriate to follow analysis (chapter 13) with multimedia.

Another suggestion is to revise chapters 2-11 by deleting every reference in them to chapter 1 and changing them into a larger number of very short expansions (a page or two) that solely treat material-specific details, physical descriptions, and unique elements affecting individual formats (e.g., sound discs, computer cartridges, or videocassettes, *not* sound recordings, computer files, or videorecordings). Although there would have to be a great many format-specific expansions, the overall result would be a considerable diminution of AACR, since the endless repetitions of the instruction to consult chapter 1 could be eliminated.

Other benefits of this major overhaul to AACR would include an enhancement of inter-medium consistency, since rules that perpetuate unnecessary, unintended, or unwanted variations could be eliminated. Two examples that come to mind are putting identifying terms for film and video credits *before* the names but for musical credits *after* the names, and punctuating some constructed notes with ISBD-style punctuation but others with ordinary grammatical punctuation. In fact, all exceptions and minor variations now present in the code could be — and probably should be — reconsidered and eliminated if they cannot meet stringent tests of usefulness (what does this exception do?) and practicality (does the cost of doing it this way have a justifiable payoff in added service?).

If catalogers want rules for sound tape reels, they won't have to plow through pages of rules relating to sound cartridges, cassettes, disks, and films before sorting out the rule segments they seek. Chapters 8 and 10 in particular (graphics and three-dimensional materials) would be much easier to use if they were arranged this way. Examples in the supplements could illustrate complete physical descriptions and complete material-specific details for each type of medium that uses them, not merely segments here and there. And a GMD could be dropped from the North American list for a change, instead of added.

WHAT KIND OF ACCESS
WOULD RESULT?

Multimedia cataloging as it stands today, even without any other alterations, can produce excellent descriptions for inventories and catalogs. Take, for example, a package known as *Chemistry at Work* — a title selected at random from the "Multimedia" column of the *T.H.E. Magazine* (also known as *Technological Horizons in Education*). Based on what it said in the column and filling in the blanks with plausible though hypothetical data, the following catalog record could be made:

540 Chemistry at work [multimedia]. — Computer data and
pro-.C43 grams. — Seattle, WA : Videodiscovery, 1991.
1 videodisc : sd., col. ; 12 in.
2 computer disks : sd., col. ; 3 1/2
1 periodic chart ; 22 x 29 cm.
All in container, 33 x 47 x 5 cm.
+ 1 user's guide (47 p.). — (Science at work series ; no. 3)
System requirements: Macintosh; HyperCard version 2.0; hard
drive, and interface cable; and Laservision CAV system with
hi-resolution monitor.
Title from videodisc label.
Title on computer disk label: Chemistry.
"Contains 800 photos and 3D computer graphics to demonstrate
processes in human and natural environments, actual photos of
historical scientific figures and equipment, and chemical
materials." — Container.
Also issued for PS/2 and DOS; videodisc will run on Apple II
computers equipped with a player.
1. Chemistry. I. Videodiscovery, Inc. (Firm). II. Title:
Chemistry. III. Series.

There is no way of knowing if having a separate chapter with elaborate rules for the description of interactive media would do better than the record shown above. There is access to the title *Chemistry at Work*, to the variant title on the computer disk, *Chemistry*, to the content, the producer-distributor, and the series. The Dewey number indicates this is a general work on chemistry — it would be simple to provide an LC classification number instead. A collection designation such as "Interactive Video" above the call number immediately identifies the

228 Implications of Cataloging Interactive Media

nature of the material to the searcher as something other than a book, as does the GMD "multimedia."

CONCLUSION

It seems such a simple and logical thing to switch from "kit" to "multimedia" that I can't help but wonder why my nonbook cataloging colleagues and I spent hours at several meetings in order to suggest "interactive media" instead. It might be something of a defeat to admit that the British had a better idea about their list of GMDs than we North Americans, but I've envied them for years being able to use "graphic" and "object" in place of our long list of terms for chapter 8 and 10 materials that frequently seem distressingly off-the-mark and misleading. It would be a refreshing change for catalogers to adopt the same terminology that seems to have caught on in the world at large. A "Multimedia Exposition" took place in Washington, D.C. last June for producers/consumers of interactive media products, the column I referred to above is named "Multimedia," and the term is often used in newspaper and magazine articles. How unlike catalogers it would be to select a popular term in place of something arcane like "machine-readable data file," or "realia."

Here, also, is an opportunity to rethink the usefulness and practicality of the rules for description. They cry out for simplification. Lately, I've begun thinking about taking bets on how many revisions it will take for AACR to break 1,000 — pages, that is. A new chapter for multimedia materials would add at least a dozen more to the current 677.

Catalogers also ought to think about simplifying AACR's language. It might not be as elegant or precise to think of "main" titles and "other" titles as to have titles proper, parallel titles, alternative titles, uniform titles and other title information. It might not be as graceful to deal with "authors" and other "contributors" as to have creators and statements of responsibility. It is, however, more easily understood by the masses, many of whom, being catalogers or searchers, must process this information in order to store or retrieve the documents they represent. The future can contain a continued complication of bibliographic access — or it can be a genuine improvement based on the solid foundation provided by current tools and valid principles.

NOTES

[1]Michael Gorman and Paul W. Winkler, eds., *Anglo-American Cataloguing Rules*, 2nd ed., 1988 revision (Chicago: American Library Association, 1988), pp. 56-58.

Index